Microsoft® Office Excel 2003: Quick Course 1 of 3

Microsoft Office Excel 2003: Quick Course 1 of 3

JUDY MARDAR
Community College Workforce Alliance

RUSSEL STOLINS
Santa Fe Community College

LABYRINTH
PUBLICATIONS®

Microsoft Office Excel 2003: Quick Course 1
by Judy Mardar and Russel Stolins

Copyright © 2004 by Labyrinth Publications

LABYRINTH
PUBLICATIONS®

Labyrinth Publications
3314 Morningside Drive
El Sobrante, California 94803
800.522.9746
On the Web at labpub.com

President and Publisher:
Brian Favro

Series Editor:
Russel Stolins

Managing Editor:
Laura A. Lionello

Production Manager:
Rad Proctor

Editorial/Production Team:
Holly Hammond, Nancy Logan,
Nancy Roberts

Indexing: Joanne Sprott

Cover and Interior Design:
Seventeenth Street Studios

ISBN 1-59136-036-6

Manufactured in the United States of America.

10 9 8 7 6   R

Microsoft Office Specialist Program

⚠ NOTE!

To be fully prepared for the Microsoft Office Excel 2003 and Microsoft Office Excel 2003 Expert exams, complete all three Quick Courses: Microsoft Office Excel 2003: Quick Course 1, Microsoft Office Excel 2003: Quick Course 2, and Microsoft Office Excel 2003: Quick Course 3.

What Does This Logo Mean?

It means this courseware has been approved by the Microsoft® Office Specialist program to be among the finest available for learning Excel 2003. It also means that upon completion of this courseware, you may be prepared to become a Microsoft Office Specialist.

What Is a Microsoft Office Specialist?

A Microsoft Office Specialist is an individual who has certified skills in one or more Microsoft Office desktop applications such as Microsoft Word, Microsoft Excel, Microsoft Outlook®, Microsoft PowerPoint®, or Microsoft Project. The Microsoft Office Specialist program typically offers certification exams at different skill levels.* The Microsoft Office Specialist program is the only Microsoft-approved program in the world for certifying proficiency in Microsoft Office desktop applications and Microsoft Project. This certification can be a valuable asset in any job search or career advancement.

Which Exam(s) Will This Publication Prepare You to Take?

Microsoft Office Excel 2003: Quick Course 1, *Microsoft Office Excel 2003: Quick Course 2*, and *Microsoft Office Excel 2003: Quick Course 3*, used in combination, have been approved by Microsoft as courseware for the Microsoft Office Specialist program. After completing a three-course sequence, students will be prepared to take the Microsoft Office Excel 2003 and the Microsoft Office Excel 2003 Expert exams.

For more information:

- To learn more about becoming a Microsoft Office Specialist, visit www.microsoft.com/officespecialist/.

- To purchase a Microsoft Office Specialist certification exam, visit www.microsoft.com/officespecialist/.

- To learn about other Microsoft Office Specialist approved courseware from Labyrinth Publications, visit labpub.com/mos/.

---

* The availability of Microsoft Office Specialist certification exams varies by application, application version, and language. Visit www.microsoft.com/officespecialist/ for exam availability.

Microsoft, the Microsoft Office Specialist logo, PowerPoint, and Outlook are either registered trademarks or trademarks of Microsoft Corporation in the United States and/or other countries.

Labyrinth Publications is independent from Microsoft Corporation, and not affiliated with Microsoft in any manner. This publication may be used in assisting students to prepare for a Microsoft Office Specialist exam. Neither Microsoft, its designated review company, nor Labyrinth Publications warrants that use of this publication will ensure passing the relevant exam.

Microsoft Office Excel 2003 and Microsoft Office Excel 2003 Expert objectives covered in this book

Objective Number	Skill Sets and Skills	Concept Page References	Exercise Page References
XL03S-1-1	Enter and edit cell content	11–12, 15, 17–18, 40, 42, 138	12–13, 15–16, 18, 40–42, 138
XL03S-1-2	Navigate to specific cell content	6, 155–156	8, 156–158
XL03S-1-3	Locate, select, and insert supporting information	159	159–160
XL03S-2-3	Insert and modify formulas	67–68, 72–73	69–72, 74–78
XL03S-2-4	Use statistical, date and time, financial, and logical functions	64, 80–82, 140	64–67, 81, 83–85, 140–141
XL03S-2-5	Create, modify, and position diagrams and charts based on worksheet data	178–179, 182, 184–185, 198	179–193, 198–199
XL03S-3-1	Apply and modify cell formats	100–103, 106–108, 111, 113, 116, 145	101–102, 104–105, 107–109, 111–112, 114–117, 139–140, 146–147
XL03S-3-3	Modify row and column formats	105, 142, 145, 147–148, 151, 153–154	106, 142–145, 149–150, 152–155
XL03S-3-4	Format worksheets		177
XL03S-5-2	Insert, delete, and move cells	117–118, 120, 124, 151	118–119, 121–125
XL03S-5-4	Organize worksheets	176	177
XL03S-5-5	Preview data in other views	46	46
XL03S-5-7	Setup pages for printing	48	49
XL03S-5-8	Print data	46–47	47–48
XL03E-2-4	Format charts and diagrams	187–189, 192–194, 196, 199	188–190, 193–197, 199–200
XL03E-5-3	Modify Excel default settings	109	110

Contents in Brief

Contents

Index of Quick Reference Tables

List of Keyboard Shortcuts

Document Commands

`Ctrl`+`O` to open

`Ctrl`+`P` to display the Print box

`Ctrl`+`S` to save

Editing Commands

`Ctrl`+`Delete` to delete text to end of line

`Ctrl`+`Y` to redo

`Ctrl`+`Z` to undo

`Enter` to complete an entry and move the highlight down to the next cell

Find/Replace Commands

`Ctrl`+`F` for Find

`Ctrl`+`H` for Replace

Format Font Commands

`Ctrl`+`1` to display Format Cells dialog box

`Ctrl`+`B` for Bold

`Ctrl`+`I` for Italic

`Ctrl`+`U` for Underline

Format Style Commands

`Ctrl`+`~` to display or hide formulas

`Ctrl`+`Shift`+`!` for Comma Style

`Ctrl`+`Shift`+`$` for Currency Style

`Ctrl`+`Shift`+`~` for General Style

`Ctrl`+`Shift`+`%` for Percent Style

Fomula Commands

`Alt`+`=` for AutoSum

=TODAY() to insert the current date

Preface

Microsoft Office Excel 2003: Quick Course 1 enables students to master the fundamental skills required for effective use of Microsoft Excel 2003. When used as part of a three-book sequence with *Microsoft Office Excel 2003: Quick Course 2* and *Microsoft Office Excel 2003: Quick Course 3*, it also prepares students to pass either the Microsoft Office Excel 2003 exam or to master the more advanced skills required to pass the Microsoft Office Excel 2003 Expert exam.

The focus of *Microsoft Office Excel 2003: Quick Course 1* is basic skills. The text leverages Labyrinth's renowned ease-of-understanding expertise in introducing basic Excel skills through creative case studies. Topics covered include data entry, cell formatting, formulas, cell references, restructuring worksheets, and charting. This book assumes students understand how to use a mouse and drop-down menus, save files to some type of storage media, and other basic skills required to run Windows programs. Upon completion of this course students will be prepared for the subject matter and challenges found in the Level 2 and 3 Quick Courses.

Over the last 10 years of writing and publishing Microsoft Office courses, Labyrinth has developed a unique instructional design that makes learning faster and easier for students at all skill levels. Teachers have found that the Labyrinth model provides effective learning for students in both self-paced and instructor-led learning environments. The material is carefully written and built around compelling case studies that demonstrate the relevance of all subject matter. Mastery of subject matter is ensured through the use of multiple levels of carefully crafted exercises. The text includes Concepts Review questions and Hands-On, Skill Builder, Assessment, and Critical Thinking exercises.

The course is also supported on the Labyrinth Website with a comprehensive instructor support package that includes a printable solutions guide, detailed lecture notes, PowerPoint presentations, a course syllabus, extensive test banks, and more.

We are grateful to the many teachers who have used Labyrinth titles and suggested improvements to us during the 10 years we have been writing and publishing Office books.

About the Authors

Judy Mardar has been an independent computer trainer, technical writer, and consultant for many years. She teaches, writes, and consults at the Community College Workforce Alliance, as well as with private training companies, the state government, and small businesses. She is a certified Microsoft Office Expert and has trained thousands of people to use computers and business software over the last 10 years. Judy is coauthor of *Microsoft Office PowerPoint 2003: Essentials Course* and *Microsoft Office 2003: Essentials Course*.

Russel Stolins (MA, Educational Technology) teaches at Santa Fe Community College. He has been teaching adults about technology since 1982, including courses on desktop publishing, computer concepts, Microsoft Office applications, multimedia design, and the Internet. He is recognized nationwide as an expert in classroom teaching techniques and instructional technology, often being invited to present at education conferences throughout the U.S. In the fall of 2000, Russel developed his first Web-based course using the Blackboard Learning System in Georgia. The course has since been rolled out nationwide and new courses for the Blackboard Learning System and WebCT are currently under development. Russel's latest books, *Laying a Foundation with Windows XP* and *Welcome to the Internet,* were published by Labyrinth Publications in 2003. Russel is also a coauthor of *Microsoft Office 2003: Essentials Course.*

Introduction

Welcome to Labyrinth Publications, where you'll find your course to success. Our real world, project-based approach to education helps students grasp concepts, not just read about them, and prepares them for success in the workplace. Our straightforward, easy-to-follow language is ideal for both instructor-led classes and self-paced labs. At Labyrinth, we're dedicated to one purpose: delivering quality courseware that is comprehensive yet concise, effective, and affordable. It's no wonder that Labyrinth is a recognized leader in Microsoft Office and operating system courseware.

More than a million users have learned Office our way. At Labyrinth, we believe that successful teaching begins with exceptional courseware. That's why we've made it our goal to develop innovative texts that empower both teachers and students. We give educators the necessary resources to deliver clear, relevant instruction and students the power to take their new skills far beyond the classroom.

Labyrinth Series Give You More Choices

Labyrinth offers seven exceptionally priced series to meet your needs:

- Microsoft Office 2003 Series—These full-length, full-featured texts explore applications in the Office 2003 system. All application-specific books in this series are Microsoft Office Specialist approved for the Microsoft Office 2003 certification exams, and the Word and Excel books are also approved for the Microsoft Office 2003 Expert certification exams.

- Silver™ Series—Designed especially for adult learners, seniors, and non-native speakers, this series includes larger fonts and screens, our unmistakable straightforward design, and fun hands-on projects.

- ProStart Foundations™ Series—These full-length, full-featured texts for operating systems and applications include the new Microsoft Windows titles and are designed to lay a solid foundation for students.

- ProStart™ Series for Office XP—These full-length, full-featured texts walk students through the basic and advanced skills of the primary Office XP applications. Most are Microsoft Office Specialist approved. The Office XP Essentials and Comprehensive courses offer surveys of all the primary Office XP applications.

- Briefcase™ Series for Office XP—The popular and inexpensive choice for short classes, self-paced courses, and accelerated workshops (or mix and match for longer classes), these concise texts provide quick access to key concepts. Most are Microsoft Office Specialist approved.

- Off to Work™ Series for Office 2000—Full-length, full-featured texts set the standard for clarity and ease of use in this series. All books in this series are Microsoft Office Specialist approved.

- Briefcase Series for Office 2000—Designed for short classes, self-paced courses, and accelerated workshops, each lesson in this series is broken down into subtopics that provide quick access to key concepts. All books in this series are Microsoft Office Specialist approved.

Microsoft Office 2003 Series Teaching Resources

Instructor Support Material

To help you be more successful, Labyrinth provides a comprehensive instructor support package that includes the following:

Teaching Tools

- Detailed lecture notes, including a topic sequence and suggested classroom demonstrations

- PowerPoint presentations that give an overview of key concepts for each lesson (also available online for students)

- Answer keys for the Concepts Review questions in each lesson

- Comprehensive classroom setup instructions

- A customizable sample syllabus

- A teacher-customizable background knowledge survey to gather information on student needs and experience at the beginning of the course

Testing Tools

- Printer-friendly exercise solution guides and solution files for Hands-On, Skill Builder, Assessment, and Critical Thinking exercises

- Teacher-customizable, project-based Assessment exercises

- Teacher-customizable test banks of objective questions for each lesson and unit

- TestComposer™ test generator for editing test banks with Microsoft Word (and for creating new question banks and online tests)

These resources are available on our Website at labpub.com and on our instructor support CD, which you can obtain by calling our customer service staff at 800.522.9746.

Website

The Website labpub.com/learn/excel03/ features content designed to support the lessons and provide additional learning resources for this book. This main page contains links to individual lesson pages. Some of the items you will find at this site are described below.

PowerPoint Presentations The same presentations available to instructors are accessible online. They make excellent tools for review, particularly for students who miss a class session.

 Web-Based Simulations Some exercises contain topics that have Web-based simulations. These simulations can be accessed through the lesson pages.

Downloads Required course files can be downloaded on the lesson pages.

Student Exercise Files The student files needed to complete certain Hands-On, Skill Builder, Assessment, and Critical Thinking exercises are available for download at labpub.com/students/fdbc2003.asp.

Labyrinth's Successful Instructional Design

In conjunction with our straightforward writing style, Labyrinth books feature a proven instructional design. The following pages point out the carefully crafted design elements that build student confidence and ensure success.

Lesson introductions present clear learning objectives.

Case studies introduce a practical application that integrates topics presented in each lesson.

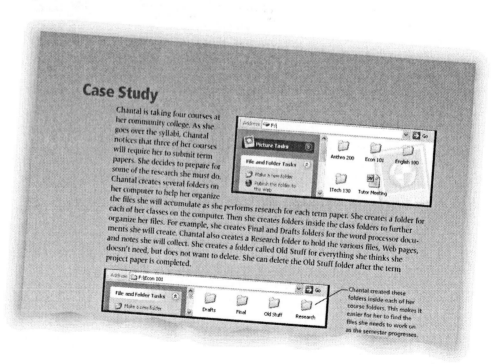

Concepts discussions are kept concise and use illustrations for added clarity and to help students understand the material introduced.

Quick Reference tables provide generic procedures for key tasks that work outside the context of the lesson.

Hands-On exercises are detailed tutorials that help students master the skills introduced in the concepts discussions. The illustrations provide clear instruction and allow unparalleled ease of use.

The Help Window Toolbar

You will encounter this toolbar when viewing Help topics in the Microsoft Word Help Window.

The Auto Tile button displays the Word window and the Help window tiled. If the window is already tiled, the button name changes to Untile. Clicking it causes the Help window to float over the Word window.

Move back one topic.
Move forward one topic.
Print the topic.

QR

QUICK REFERENCE: MOUSE MOTIONS		This motion is used...
Motion	**How to Do It**	
Click	Gently tap and immediately to release the left mouse button.	to "press" a button or select a menu option or object on the screen.
Double-click	Click twice in rapid succession.	as a shortcut for many types of common commands.
Drag	Press and hold down the left mouse button while sliding the mouse. Release the mouse button when you reach your destination.	to move an object, select several objects, draw lines, and select text.
Right-click	Gently tap and immediately release the right mouse button.	to display a context-sensitive menu for the object at which you are pointing.
Point	Slide the mouse without pressing a button until the pointer is in the desired location.	to position the pointer before using one of the four motions above, to select an object on the screen, or to get a menu to appear.

Hands-On 2.7 Move and Size the WordPad Window

In this exercise, you will move the WordPad window to a different location on the Desktop, then change the size of the window.

1. Follow these steps to move the WordPad window:

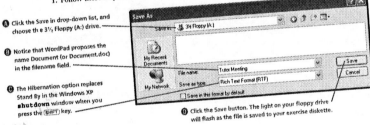

A Click the Save in drop-down list, and choose the 3½ Floppy (A:) drive.

B Notice that WordPad proposes the name Document (or Document.doc) in the filename field.

C The Hibernation option replaces Stand By in the Windows XP **shutdown** window when you press the (SHIFT) key.

D Click the Save button. The light on your floppy drive will flash as the file is saved to your exercise diskette.

122   Lesson 2: Working with Windows Programs

The Concepts Review section at the end of each lesson includes both true/false and multiple choice questions.

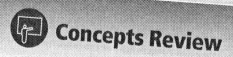

Concepts Review

True/False Questions

1. A Contents (or Home in Windows XP) search of online Help lets you locate Help topics by typing keywords.

2. A My Computer window lets you view the files and folders on the computer.   TRUE   FALSE

3. Windows organizes drives and folders in a hierarchy.   TRUE   FALSE

4. You can use the CTRL key to randomly select a group of files.   TRUE   FALSE

5. Folders can have subfolders within them.   TRUE   FALSE

6. You can use the Cut and Paste commands to move files.   TRUE   FALSE

7. Files are sent to the Recycle Bin when they are deleted from floppy disks.   TRUE   FALSE

8. The Properties command displays how much space is left on a floppy disk.   TRUE   FALSE

9. An Exploring window gives you a two-panel view of files and folder.   TRUE   FALSE

10. A quick way to open a file is to double-click on it in a My Computer windows.   TRUE   FALSE

Multiple Choice Questions

1. Which of the following methods would you use to view files and folders on the computer:

   a. Open a My Computer Window

3. Which command is used to create a new folder?

   a. File→Folder→Create

   b. File→New→Folder

Skill Builders, Assessments, and Critical Thinking exercises provide fun, hands-on projects with reduced levels of detailed instruction so students can develop and test their mastery of the material.

Skill Builders

Skill Builder 3.1   Work with Online Help

In this exercise, you will practice looking up various topics in Windows' online Help.

1. Click the [start] button and choose Help from the Start
   Window

Assessments

Assessment 3.1   Edit a Document

In this exercise, you will edit a document that is marked up for changes.

the Standard toolbar.

Critical Thinking

Critical Thinking 3.1   On Your Own

Compose a new letter to Donna Wilson using the AutoCorrect shortcut you just created. Request that Donna send you information on Citizen Bank's new Small Business Credit Line program. Let Donna know that because you are starting a new business venture (you choose the venture), you are interested in obtaining financing from the bank. Save the letter as **Wilson Letter 2** then close it.

How This Book Is Organized

The information in this book is presented so that you master the fundamental skills first, and then build on those skills as you work with the more comprehensive topics.

Visual Conventions

This book uses many visual and typographic cues to guide you through the lessons. This page provides examples and describes the function of each cue.

Type this text

Anything you should type at the keyboard is printed in this typeface.

Tips, Notes, and Warnings are used throughout the text to draw attention to certain topics.

Command→Command

This convention indicates multiple selections to be made from a menu bar. For example, File→Save means to select File then select Save.

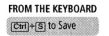

These margin notes indicate shortcut keys for executing a task described in the text.

Quick Reference tables provide generic instructions for key tasks. Only perform these tasks if you are instructed to in an exercise.

This icon indicates the availability of a Web-based simulation for an exercise. You may need to use a WebSim if your computer lab is not set up to support particular exercises.

Hands-On exercises are introduced immediately after concept discussions. They provide detailed, step-by-step tutorials so you can master the skills presented.

The Concepts Review section includes both true/false and multiple choice questions designed to gauge your understanding of concepts.

Skill Builder exercises provide additional hands-on practice with moderate assistance.

Assessment exercises test your skills by describing the correct results without providing specific instructions on how to achieve them.

Critical Thinking exercises are the most challenging. They provide general instructions, allowing you to use your skills and creativity to achieve the result you envision.

Microsoft Office Excel 2003: Quick Course 1

LESSON 1

Creating a Simple Worksheet

In this lesson, you will develop fundamental Excel 2003 skills. This lesson will provide you with a solid foundation of skills so you are prepared to master the advanced features introduced in later lessons. For example, you will learn basic skills, including navigating around a worksheet, entering various types of data, and selecting cells.

Microsoft Office Excel 2003 objectives covered in this lesson

Objective Number	Skill Sets and Skills	Concept Page References	Exercise Page References
XL03S-1-1	Enter and edit cell content	11–12, 15, 17–18	12–13, 15–16, 18
XL03S-1-2	Navigate to specific cell content	6	8

Additional learning resources are available at labpub.com/learn/excel03/

Case Study

Susan Lee is a student intern at Computer Depot, a discount computer and computer accessories retailer. Joel Williams, the buyer for Computer Depot, has asked Susan to maintain a list of PCs, notebook computers, printers, and monitors sold during a five-day period. Joel instructs Susan to report the data on a daily basis. After analyzing Joel's request, Susan decides that Excel 2003 is the right tool for the job and proceeds to organize the data in a worksheet. A portion of Susan's worksheet is shown below.

	A	B	C	D	E	F	G
1	Computer Depot Weekly Sales Data						
2							
3			Wednesda	Thursday	Friday	Saturday	Sunday
4	PCs						
5		Compaq	3	10	12	15	16
6		IBM	4	8	10	13	14
7		Acer	6	13	15	18	19
8		Total					
9	Laptops						
10		Apple	2	5	4	10	8
11		IBM	3	7	5	12	10
12		Empower	4	8	11	14	14
13		Toshiba	2	3	5	5	3
14		Total					
15	Printers						
16		IBM	3	5	5	6	8
17		HP	6	1	2	3	7
18		Canon	8	2	3	4	5

What Is Microsoft Excel?

Microsoft Excel is an electronic spreadsheet (or worksheet) program that takes the chore out of working with numbers. Excel can assist you in virtually every aspect of worksheet creation and analysis. Whether you're creating dynamic charts for a presentation or interactive worksheets for group collaboration, Excel has the right tool for the job. For these and many other reasons, Excel is the most widely used worksheet program in both homes and businesses.

Why Use Microsoft Excel?

Excel provides a number of important features and benefits:

1. GUI—Excel's graphical user interface (GUI) is so easy to use that even beginning computer users find it simple. The interface reduces the need to memorize commands, thus increasing your productivity.

2. Charting—Have you heard the expression, "One picture is worth a thousand words"? This is especially true with financial and numeric data. Excel's charting and formatting features let you display your data in a powerful and convincing graphic format.

3. Widely used—Excel is the most widely used spreadsheet software. Excel is the right choice if you are trying to develop marketable skills and find employment.

4. Integration with other Office programs—Excel 2003 is part of the Microsoft Office 2003 suite of programs that includes Word, Access, PowerPoint, Outlook, and others. The ability to exchange data with these programs is one of the most powerful and attractive features of Excel.

5. Web integration—Excel 2003 lets you easily publish your worksheets to Websites on the World Wide Web and your company's intranet.

It's Time to Learn Excel

You will be amazed at the power and simplicity of Excel and how easy it is to learn. The knowledge you are about to gain will help you become proficient in Excel.

Starting Excel

The method you use to start Excel depends in large part on whether you intend to create a new workbook or open an existing workbook. A workbook is a file containing one or more worksheets. To create a new workbook, use one of the following methods. Once the Excel program has started, you can begin working in the new workbook that appears.

- Click the **start** button and choose Microsoft Office Excel 2003 from the All Programs menu. (Depending on your installation of Microsoft Office, you may need to choose Microsoft Office from the All Programs menu, and then choose Microsoft Office Excel 2003.)

- Click the Microsoft Excel 2003 button on the Quick Launch toolbar located at the left edge of the taskbar. (This button may not appear on all computers.)

Use one of the following methods if you intend to open an existing Excel workbook. Once the Excel program has started, the desired workbook will open in an Excel window.

■ Navigate to the desired document using Windows Explorer or My Computer and double-click the workbook.

■ Click the button and point to My Recent Documents. You can choose the desired workbooks from the documents list, which displays the most-recently used documents.

 Hands-On 1.1 Start Excel

In this exercise, you will start the Excel program.

1. Start your computer and the Windows Desktop will appear.

2. Click the button and choose (All) Programs.

3. Choose Microsoft Office Excel 2003.

NOTE! *You may need to first choose Microsoft Office from the All Programs menu, and then choose Microsoft Office Excel 2003 from the submenu.*

The Excel program will load and the Excel window will appear. Don't be concerned if your window appears different from the following example.

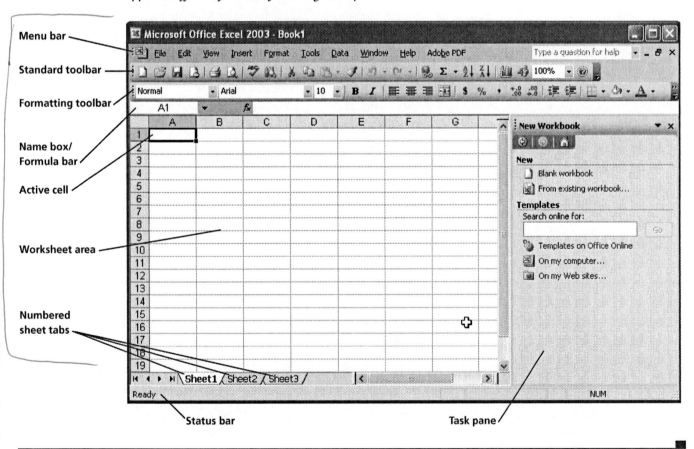

Using Worksheets and Workbooks

Excel displays a blank workbook the moment you start the program. A workbook is composed of worksheets. This is similar to a paper notebook with many sheets of paper. You enter text, numbers, formulas, charts, and other objects in worksheets. Excel displays three worksheets in a new workbook. The maximum number of worksheets you can insert is limited only to the amount of available memory on your computer.

A worksheet has a grid structure with horizontal rows and vertical columns. A new worksheet has 256 columns and 65,536 rows. However, at any given time only a small number of the rows and columns are visible in the worksheet window. The intersection of each row and column is a cell. Each cell is identified by a reference. The reference is the column letter followed by the row number. For example, A1 is the reference of the cell in the top-left corner of the worksheet. So, we refer to this as cell A1.

The Task Pane

In Excel 2003, the task pane appears on the right side of the worksheet area. You can use the task pane to open workbooks, create new workbooks, and perform other common activities. The task pane is context sensitive, displaying different options depending on the state of your worksheet. You can display or hide the task pane with the View→Task Pane command. You can also close the task pane by clicking the Close button at the top-right corner of the task pane window.

Navigating in a Worksheet

The thick line that surrounds the active cell is called the highlight. You move the highlight by clicking in a cell or by using the keyboard. Moving the highlight is important because data is entered into the active cell. The vertical and horizontal scroll bars let you navigate through a worksheet; however, scrolling does not move the highlight. You must position the highlight in the desired cell after scrolling. The following table lists important keystrokes that move the highlight.

QUICK REFERENCE: NAVIGATING A WORKSHEET	
Keystroke(s)	**How the Highlight Moves**
→ ← ↑ ↓	One cell right, left, up, or down
Home	Beginning of current row
Ctrl + →	End of current row
Ctrl + Home	Home cell, usually cell A1
Ctrl + End	Last cell in active part of worksheet
Page Down	Down one screen
Page Up	Up one screen
Alt + Page Down	One screen right
Alt + Page Up	One screen left
Ctrl + G	Displays Go To dialog box—enter cell reference and click OK

Hands-On 1.2 **Move the Highlight and Explore the Excel Window**

In this exercise, you will practice moving the highlight around a worksheet.

Close the Task Pane and Navigate with the Mouse

In the first part of this exercise, you will close the task pane. Later, you will redisplay it.

1. If the task pane is displayed on the right side of the worksheet area, choose View→Task Pane to hide it.

TIP! *You can also close the task pane using its Close ☒ button in the top-right corner of the pane.*

2. Slide the mouse, and the pointer will have a thick cross ✚ shape when it is in the worksheet area.

3. Click the pointer on any cell and notice that the highlight moves to that cell.

4. Move the highlight five times by clicking in various cells.

Navigate with the Keyboard

In the next few steps, you will navigate around the worksheet with the keyboard. You should use the keys on the center part of your keyboard, between the main part and the Numeric keypad on the far right.

5. Use the →, ←, ↑, and ↓ keys to position the highlight in cell F10.

6. Tap the ⟨Home⟩ key and see that the highlight moves to cell A10.
   The ⟨Home⟩ key always moves the highlight to column A in the active row.

7. Press ⟨Ctrl⟩+⟨Home⟩ to move the highlight to cell A1.

8. Tap the ⟨Page Down⟩ key two or three times.
   Notice that Excel displays the next 20 or so rows each time you tap ⟨Page Down⟩.

9. Press and hold down the ↑ key until the highlight is in cell A1.

Use the Scroll Bars

10. Click the Scroll Right ▶ button on the horizontal scroll bar until columns AA and AB are visible.
    Excel labels the first 26 columns A–Z and the next 26 columns AA–AZ. A similar labeling scheme is used for the remaining columns out to the final column IV.

11. Click the Scroll Down ▼ button on the vertical scroll bar until row 100 is visible.
    Notice that the highlight has not moved. To move the highlight, you must click in a cell.

12. Take a few minutes to practice scrolling and moving the highlight.

Use the Go To Command

As you learned in the preceding Quick Reference table, you can use Ctrl+G to display the Go To box, where you can go to a specific cell by entering the desired cell reference in the Reference box and clicking OK. You can use Ctrl+Home to select cell A1.

13. Press Ctrl+G to display the Go To dialog box.

14. Type **G250** in the Reference box and click OK.
    The highlight should move to cell G250.

15. Use the Go To command to move to two or three different cells.

16. Press Ctrl+Home to return to cell A1.

Explore the Excel Window

17. Follow these steps to explore the Excel window:

Ⓐ Notice the Name box on the Formula bar. Don't worry if your Formula bar is not displayed. You will learn to display and hide the Formula bar soon. The Name box displays the name of the active cell.

Ⓑ Click the Sheet2 tab and notice that blank worksheet appears. The number of worksheets you can have is limited to the amount of available memory in the computer.

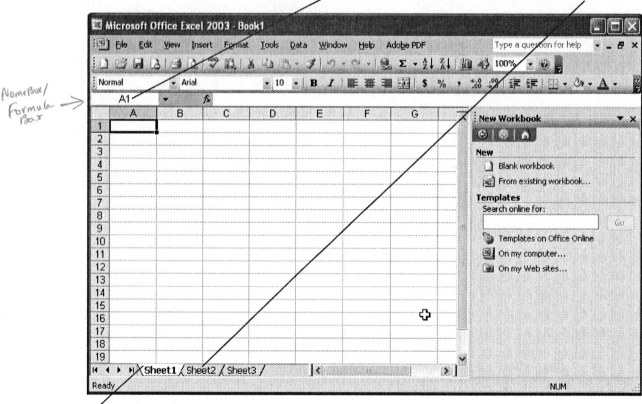

NameBox/ Formula Box →

Ⓒ Click the Sheet1 tab.

18. Press Ctrl+Home to move the highlight to cell A1, if necessary.

Managing Toolbars

Excel 2003 features more than 20 toolbars to assist you in creating and formatting worksheets. The Standard and Formatting toolbars contain the most frequently used buttons so they are located at the top of the Excel window just below the menu bar. When you hold the mouse over a toolbar button, a small pop-up message called a ScreenTip gives you the name of the button, as shown in the following illustration.

TIP! *All toolbar buttons require only one click.*

Displaying and Hiding Toolbars

You display and hide toolbars by first displaying the Toolbars list then choosing the desired toolbar(s) from the list. The Toolbars list is displayed using the View→Toolbars command or by right-clicking any displayed toolbar. A checkmark appears on the Toolbar list next to each toolbar that is currently displayed.

Moving Toolbars

You can move toolbars to any screen location. For example, many users like to position toolbars as floating pallets over the worksheet area. You move a toolbar by dragging the Move handle located on the left end of the toolbar.

 The Move pointer appears when you point to a Move handle. You can move a toolbar to any screen location by dragging the Move handle.

Displaying the Standard and Formatting Toolbars on Separate Rows

In Excel 2003, the Standard and Formatting toolbars are placed side by side on a single row just below the menu bar. This arrangement was introduced in Excel 2000. In earlier versions of Excel, the Standard and Formatting toolbars are displayed on separate rows. The following illustration describes the various toolbar options.

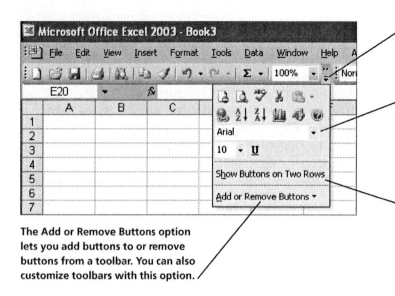

The Toolbar Options button appears on the right edge of all toolbars. Click here to display a menu with several options.

When the Standard and Formatting toolbars are on the same row, not all of the buttons fit. Buttons not visible on the toolbar are displayed on this list. You can choose a command by clicking a button on the list.

The Show Buttons on Two Rows option positions the Standard and Formatting toolbars on separate rows. When the toolbars are on separate rows this option becomes Show Buttons on One Row.

The Add or Remove Buttons option lets you add buttons to or remove buttons from a toolbar. You can also customize toolbars with this option.

 Hands-On 1.3 **Display the Formatting Toolbar on a Separate Row**

In this exercise, you will display the Standard and Formatting toolbars on separate rows.

1. Start Excel and follow these steps to display the Standard and Formatting toolbars on separate rows:

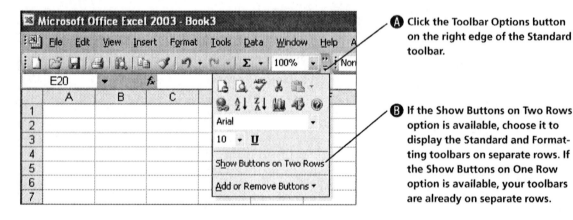

A Click the Toolbar Options button on the right edge of the Standard toolbar.

B If the Show Buttons on Two Rows option is available, choose it to display the Standard and Formatting toolbars on separate rows. If the Show Buttons on One Row option is available, your toolbars are already on separate rows.

 IMPORTANT! *From this point forward, the instructions in this text will assume that the Standard and Formatting toolbars are displayed on separate rows. This will make it easier for you to locate buttons when instructed to do so.*

Entering Data

You can begin entering data the moment Excel is started. Data is entered into the active cell (the cell with the highlight). Text and numbers are used for different purposes in a worksheet. Text is used for descriptive headings and entries that require alphabetic characters or a combination of alphabetic and numeric characters and spaces. Numbers can be calculated using formulas. Excel recognizes the data you enter and decides whether the entry is text, a number, or a formula. You will learn about entering formulas in Lesson 3, Introducing Formulas and Functions.

Data Types

Entries are defined as one of two main classifications: constant values and formulas. Constant values can be text or numeric, or a combination of both. The one thing that makes an entry constant is that the value does not change when other information changes. Conversely, formula entries display the results of calculations, and a result can change when a value in another cell changes.

Completing Cell Entries

Text and numbers are entered by positioning the highlight in the desired cell, typing the desired text or number, and completing the entry. You can use Enter, Tab, or any of the arrow (→ ← ↑ ↓) keys to complete an entry. When you complete an entry with Enter, the text or number is entered in the cell and the highlight moves down to the next cell. When you complete an entry with the Tab key, the text or number is entered in the cell and the highlight moves to the next cell to the right. When you complete an entry with an arrow key, the text or number is entered in the cell and the highlight moves to the next cell in the direction of the arrow key. If you are entering text or numbers and change your mind prior to completing the entry, you can press Esc to cancel the entry.

The Enter and Cancel Buttons

The Enter ✓ and Cancel ✗ buttons appear on the Formula bar whenever you enter or edit an entry. The Enter button completes the entry and keeps the highlight in the current cell. The Cancel button cancels the entry, as does the Esc key.

The Cancel and Enter buttons appear when an entry is being entered or edited.

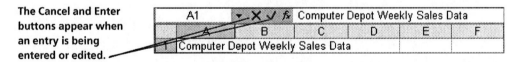

Deleting and Replacing Entries

You can delete an entire entry after it has been completed by clicking in the cell and tapping Delete. Likewise, you can replace an entry by clicking in the cell and typing a new entry. The new entry will replace the original entry. You will learn all about editing entries in Lesson 2, Expanding on the Basics.

Long Text Entries

Text entries often do not fit in a cell. These entries are known as long entries. Excel uses the following rules when deciding how to display long entries:

- If the cell to the right of the long entry is empty, then the long entry displays over the adjacent cell.

- If the cell to the right of the long entry contains an entry, then Excel shortens, or truncates, the display of the long entry.

Keep in mind that Excel does not actually change the long entry; it simply truncates the display of the entry. You can always widen a column to accommodate a long entry.

	A	B	C
1	Computer Depot Weekly	Sales Data	
2			
3			Wednesda
4	PCs		

The entry, Computer Depot Weekly Sales Data, is a long entry. The entire phrase is entered in cell A1 although it displays over cells A1–C1.

 ## Hands-On 1.4   Enter Text

In this exercise, you will enter text into the worksheet.

Type a Long Entry

1. Make cell A1 active by clicking the mouse pointer ✚ in it.

2. Type **Computer Depot Weekly Sales Data** and tap ⎵Enter⎵.
   The text is entered in the cell and the highlight moves down to cell A2. Excel moves the highlight down when you tap ⎵Enter⎵ because most people enter data column by column. Notice that the entry displays over cells B1 and C1. The long entry would not display over these cells if they contained data.

3. Click cell A1 and note the appearance of the Formula bar.

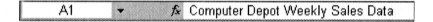
| A1 | ▼ | *fx* Computer Depot Weekly Sales Data |

Notice that the Formula bar displays the name of the active cell (A1) as well as its content. In this example, the cell's content is the title, Computer Depot Weekly Sales Data. The title is a long entry because it is wider than cell A1. Cells B1 and C1 are empty so the long entry is displayed over them. Keep in mind, however, that the entire entry belongs to cell A1. This concept will be demonstrated in the next few steps.

Verify that the Entry Belongs to Cell A1

4. Tap the → key to make cell B1 active.

5. Look at the Formula bar and notice that cell B1 is empty.
   The long entry belongs to cell A1 even though it is displayed over cells A1–C1.

Type Additional Text Entries

6. Use the → and ↓ keys to position the highlight in cell C3.

7. Type **Wednesday** and tap → once.

Notice that the entry is completed and the highlight moves to cell D3. You can always use the arrow keys to complete an entry and move the highlight in the desired direction.

8. Type **Thursday** in cell D3 and tap →.

Notice that the display of Wednesday is shortened, or truncated. However, the Wednesday entry is still contained in its entirety in cell C3. A long entry is always truncated when the cell to the right contains text or a number.

9. Enter the remaining text entries shown in the following illustration:

	A	B	C	D
1	Computer Depot Weekly Sales Data			
2				
3			Wednesda	Thursday
4	PCs			
5		Compaq		
6		IBM		
7		Acer		
8		Total		
9	Laptops			

 TIP! *If the Smart Tag feature is turned on, when you type IBM a maroon triangle will appear in the bottom-right corner of the cell. Excel recognizes IBM as a stock ticker symbol. If you click in the cell, you will see a smart tag that you can click to get a menu of choices. You can ignore the smart tag for now.*

You will continue to enhance your worksheet in the next exercise.

AutoComplete

The AutoComplete feature is useful when you want the same entry repeated more than once in a column. If the first few characters you type match another entry in the column, then AutoComplete will offer to complete the entry for you. You accept the offer by tapping Enter or reject the offer by typing the remainder of the entry yourself.

FROM THE KEYBOARD

Enter to complete an entry and move the highlight down to the next cell

Hands-On 1.5   Use AutoComplete

In this exercise, you will continue to enter more text entries in the worksheet.

1. Type the letter **A** in cell B10 and notice that AutoComplete displays the word Acer in the cell.
   You could accept this proposed text by completing the entry; however, you will continue to type in the next step, thus typing over the proposed entry.

2. Type **pple** (to make the entry Apple) and tap ⌷Enter⌷.
   AutoComplete always tries to assist you in completing text. You can either ignore AutoComplete and continue typing your entries or complete the entries that AutoComplete proposes.

3. Enter the following laptop brands into the next three cells, accepting AutoComplete suggestions for the IBM and Total entries by tapping ⌷Enter⌷ when Excel proposes the suggestions.

	B
11	IBM
12	Empower
13	Toshiba
14	Total

4. Enter the remaining text entries shown below using AutoComplete for all text entries in column B—except the entries in cells B17 and B18. You must type the complete entries in cells B17 and B18 since that text does not appear anywhere else in the column.

	A	B
1	Computer Depot Wee	
2		
3		
4	PCs	
5		Compaq
6		IBM
7		Acer
8		Total
9	Laptops	
10		Apple
11		IBM
12		Empower
13		Toshiba
14		Total
15	Printers	
16		IBM
17		HP
18		Canon
19		Total
20	Monitors	
21		IBM
22		HP
23		Compaq
24		Total

You will continue to enhance the worksheet throughout this lesson.

Using Number Entries

Numbers can only contain the digits 0–9 and a few other characters. Excel initially right aligns numbers in cells, although you can change this alignment. The following table lists characters Excel accepts as part of a number entry.

 TIP! *Entering numbers using the Numeric keypad is very quick. The keypad is designed like a calculator. It includes its own decimal point and an Enter key.*

Valid Characters in Number Entries
The digits 0–9
The following characters: + – ( ) , / $ % .

Number Formats

It isn't necessary to type commas, dollar signs, and other number formats when entering numbers. It's easier to simply enter the numbers and use Excel's formatting commands to add the desired number format(s). You will learn how to format numbers soon.

Decimals and Negative Numbers

You should always type a decimal point if the number you are entering requires one. Likewise, you should precede a negative number entry with a minus (–) sign or enclose it in parentheses ( ).

 Hands-On 1.6   Enter Numbers

In this exercise, you will practice entering numbers and canceling entries before completion.

Use the Enter Button

1. Position the highlight in cell C5.

2. Type **3** but don't complete the entry.

3. Look at the Formula bar and notice the Cancel ⊠ and Enter ✓ buttons.
   These buttons appear whenever you begin entering or editing data in a cell.

4. Click the Enter ✓ button to complete the entry.
   Notice that the highlight remains in cell C5. You can use the Enter button to complete entries, though it is more efficient to use the keyboard when building a worksheet. This is because the highlight automatically moves to the next cell. The Enter button is most useful when editing entries.

Use the Cancel Button and the Esc Key

5. Position the highlight in cell C6 and type **4**, but don't complete the entry.

6. Click the Cancel ⊠ button on the Formula bar to cancel the entry.

7. Type **4** again, but this time tap Esc on the keyboard.
   The Esc key has the same effect as the Cancel button.

8. Type **4** once again and this time tap ⬇.
Notice that Excel right aligns the number in the cell.

9. Enter the remaining numbers shown in the following illustration.

 TIP! *To use the Numeric keypad to enter numbers, the* Num Lock *light must be on. If it's not, press the* Num Lock *key on the keypad.*

	A	B	C	D	E	F	G
1	Computer Depot Weekly Sales Data						
2							
3			Wednesda	Thursday			
4	PCs						
5		Compaq	3	10	12	15	16
6		IBM	4	8	10	13	14
7		Acer	6	13	15	18	19
8		Total					
9	Laptops						
10		Apple	2	5	4	10	8
11		IBM	3	7	5	12	10
12		Empower	4	8	11	14	14
13		Toshiba	2	3	5	5	3
14		Total					
15	Printers						
16		IBM	3	5	5	6	8
17		HP	6	1	2	3	7
18		Canon	8	2	3	4	5
19		Total					
20	Monitors						
21		IBM	3	6	8	7	2
22		HP	5	3	2	2	1
23		Compaq	2	2	6	8	3
24		Total					

10. Take a moment to check the accuracy of your text and numbers.
Accuracy is very important when entering data in worksheets. Excel's formulas, charts, and other features are of little use unless your data is accurate. You will learn how to save the workbook later in this lesson.

Working with AutoFill

AutoFill allows you to quickly extend a series, copy data, or copy a formula into adjacent cells by selecting cells and dragging the fill handle. You will learn about using AutoFill to copy formulas in Lesson 3, Introducing Formulas and Functions. If the selected cell does not contain data that AutoFill recognizes as a series, the data will simply be copied into the adjacent cells. The fill handle is a small black square at the bottom-right corner of the active cell. A black cross appears when you position the mouse pointer on the fill handle. You can drag the fill handle to fill adjacent cells as described below:

- Copy an entry—If the entry in the active cell is a number, a formula, or a text entry, the fill handle copies the entry to adjacent cells.

- Expand a repeating series of numbers—If you select two or more cells containing numbers, Excel assumes you want to expand a repeating series. For example, if you select two cells containing the numbers 5 and 10 and drag the fill handle, Excel will fill the adjacent cells with the numbers 15, 20, 25, etc.

- AutoFill of date entries—If the active cell contains any type of date entry, Excel will increment the date value filling in the adjacent cells. For example, if the current cell contains the entry Q1 and you drag the fill handle, AutoFill will insert the entries Q2, Q3, and Q4 in the adjacent cells.

The following table and illustrations provide examples of series that AutoFill can extend.

Selected Cell(s)	Extended Series
Mon	Tue, Wed, Thu
Monday	Tuesday, Wednesday, Thursday
Jan	Feb, Mar, Apr
January	January, February, March
Jan, Apr	Jul, Oct, Jan
1, 2	3, 4, 5, 6
100, 125	150, 175, 200
1/10/04	1/11/04, 1/12/04, 1/13/04
1/15/04, 2/15/04	3/15/04, 4/15/04, 5/15/04
1st Qtr	2nd Qtr, 3rd Qtr, 4th Qtr

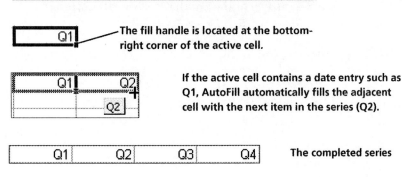

The fill handle is located at the bottom-right corner of the active cell.

If the active cell contains a date entry such as Q1, AutoFill automatically fills the adjacent cell with the next item in the series (Q2).

The completed series

AutoFill Options

The AutoFill Options button appears below your filled selection after you fill cells in a worksheet. A menu of fill options appears when you click the button.

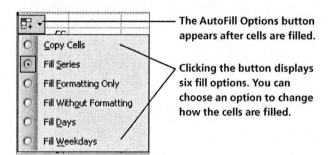

The AutoFill Options button appears after cells are filled.

Clicking the button displays six fill options. You can choose an option to change how the cells are filled.

Hands-On 1.7 Use AutoFill

In this exercise, you will extend the weekday series to include Friday, Saturday, and Sunday.

Use AutoFill to Expand the Weekday Series

1. Click cell D3.

   Notice that cell D3 contains the heading Thursday. Excel recognizes Thursday as the beginning of the series Friday, Saturday, Sunday, and so forth.

2. Follow these steps to fill the adjacent cells:

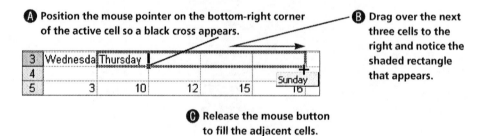

Ⓐ Position the mouse pointer on the bottom-right corner of the active cell so a black cross appears.

Ⓑ Drag over the next three cells to the right and notice the shaded rectangle that appears.

Ⓒ Release the mouse button to fill the adjacent cells.

Excel recognizes quarters (1st Qtr, Quarter 1, Q1, First Quarter), days of the week (Sunday), months (January), and other date values as the beginning of a series. You can expand any of these series with the fill handle.

3. Click the AutoFill Options button and note the various fill options.

   If desired, choose an option to change how the cells are filled.

4. For now, just tap [Esc] to dismiss the menu.

Zooming

The Zoom control lets you zoom in to get a close-up view of a worksheet and zoom out to see the full view. Zooming changes the size of the onscreen worksheet, but has no affect on the printed worksheet. You can zoom from 10% to 400%.

You can type a zoom percentage in the Zoom box and tap Enter **or . . .**

. . . click the drop-down button and choose an option from the list.

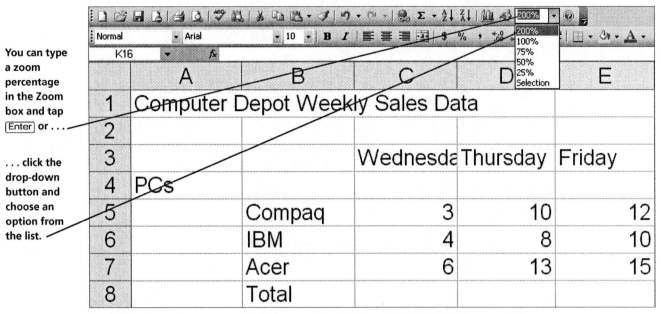

Notice how large the onscreen worksheet appears. However, it will print in the normal size.

 Hands-On 1.8   Use the Zoom Control

In this exercise, you will zoom in to get a close-up view of a range then zoom back to 100%.

1. Follow these steps to adjust the zoom percentage:

   A Click in the Zoom box, type **150**, and tap Enter.

   B Click the Zoom drop-down button and choose **200%**.

   C Zoom to 100%.

2. Click cell A3.

3. Zoom to 100% and continue with the next topic.

Selecting Cells

When you want to change something in a worksheet—for instance, move, copy, delete, format, or print specific data—you must first select the cell(s). The most efficient way to select cells is with the mouse, though you can also use the keyboard method. You can select one or many cells. A group of contiguous cells is called a range.

 TIP! *The background of the first cell in the range remains white as in the range B10:C13 in the following illustration.*

Earlier in this lesson, you learned that each cell has a reference. For example, A1 refers to the first cell in a worksheet. Likewise, a range reference specifies the cells included within a range. The range reference includes the first and last cells in the range separated by a colon (:). For example, the range C3:G3 includes all cells between C3 and G3. The following illustration highlights several ranges and their corresponding range references.

	A	B	C	D	E	F	G	
1	Computer Depot Weekly Sales Data							
2								
3			Wednesda	Thursday	Friday	Saturday	Sunday	Range C3:G3
4	PCs							
5		Compaq	3	10	12	15	16	Range B5:B8
6		IBM	4	8	10	13	14	
7		Acer	6	13	15	18	19	
8		Total						
9	Laptops							
10		Apple	2	5	4	10	8	Range B10:C13
11		IBM	3	7	5	12	10	
12		Empower	4	8	11	14	14	
13		Toshiba	2	3	5	5	3	

The following Quick Reference table describes selection techniques in Excel.

 QR

QUICK REFERENCE: SELECTING CELLS

Technique	How to Do It
Select a range	Drag the mouse pointer over the desired cells.
Select several ranges	Select a range then press Ctrl while selecting additional range(s).
Select an entire column	Click a column heading or press Ctrl+Spacebar.
Select an entire row	Click a row heading or press Shift+Spacebar.
Select multiple columns or rows	Drag the mouse pointer over the desired column or row headings.
Select an entire worksheet	Click the Select All button at the top-left corner of the worksheet or press Ctrl+A.
Select a range with Shift	Position the highlight in the first cell you wish to select, press Shift, and click the last cell in the range.
Extend a selection with Shift	Press Shift while tapping an arrow key.

Hands-On 1.9   Practice Selecting

In this exercise, you will practice selecting multiple ranges and entire rows and columns using the mouse. You will also use the [Shift] *and* [Ctrl] *keys to practice selecting cell ranges.*

1. Position the mouse pointer ✛ over cell C3.

2. Press and hold down the left mouse button while dragging the mouse to the right until the range C3:G3 is selected.

3. Deselect the cells by clicking anywhere in the worksheet.

Select Multiple Ranges

4. Select the range C3:G3 as you did in steps 1 and 2 above.

5. Press and hold down [Ctrl] while selecting the range B5:B8, as shown to the right.
Both the C3:G3 and B5:B8 ranges are selected now. The [Ctrl] *key lets you select more than one range at the same time.*

	A	B
5		Compaq
6		IBM
7		Acer
8		Total

6. Press and hold down [Ctrl] while you select another range.
You should now have three ranges selected.

7. Deselect the ranges by releasing [Ctrl] and clicking anywhere in the worksheet.

Select Entire Rows and Columns

8. Follow these steps to select various rows and columns:

Ⓐ Click the column A heading to select the entire column.

Ⓑ Position the mouse pointer on the column C heading and drag to the right until columns C, D, and E are selected. Column A will be deselected.

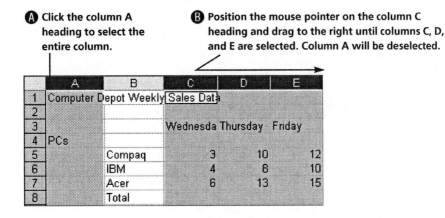

Ⓒ Click the Select All button to select the entire worksheet.

Ⓓ Click the row 1 heading to select the entire row.

Ⓔ Drag the mouse pointer down over the headings to rows 5–8 to select them.

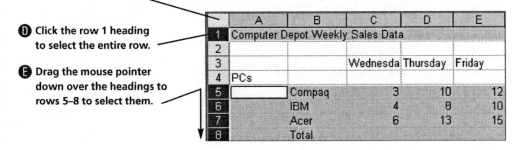

Use Keyboard Techniques

9. Click cell B5.

10. Press and hold down the [Shift] key and click cell G8 to select the range B5:G8.

11. Click cell B11.

12. Press and hold down [Shift] then tap [→] five times and [↓] four times.
The range B11:G15 is selected. Notice that the [Shift] key techniques give you precise control when selecting. You should use the [Shift] key techniques if you find selecting with the mouse difficult.

13. Take a moment to practice selection techniques.

Understanding Save Concepts

One important lesson to learn is to save your workbooks frequently! Power outages and careless accidents can result in lost data. The best protection is to save your workbooks every 10 or 15 minutes, or after making significant changes. Workbooks are saved to storage locations such as floppy disks, hard disks, shared network drives, and to Websites on the World Wide Web.

Storing Your Exercise Files

Throughout this book you will be referred to files in your "file storage location." You can store your exercise files on various media such as a floppy disk, a USB flash drive, the My Documents folder, or on a network drive at a school or company. While many figures in exercises may display files in the 3½ Floppy (A:) drive, it is assumed that you will substitute your own location for that shown in the figure. See the appendix for additional information on alternative file storage media.

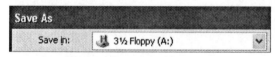

The Save In box as it appears in the book

The Save In box as it might appear if you are saving your files to a USB flash drive

The Save Command

FROM THE KEYBOARD
[Ctrl]+[S] to save

The Save ⊟ button on the Standard toolbar and the File→Save command initiate the Save command. If a document has been saved previously, Excel replaces the original version with the new, edited version. If a document has never been saved, Excel displays the Save As dialog box. The Save As dialog box lets you specify the name and storage location of the document. You can also use the Save As dialog box to make a copy of a document by saving it under a new name or to a different location. Your filenames can have up to 256 characters, including spaces, giving you the flexibility to create descriptive names for your workbooks. The following illustration outlines the Save As dialog box functions.

Locating Workbooks

Both the Save As and Open dialog boxes (discussed later in this lesson) let you locate workbooks on your local drives, network locations, and on the Web. The Places bar appears on the left side of the Save As and Open dialog boxes. You can use the Places bar or the Save In list to locate workbooks, as described in the following illustration.

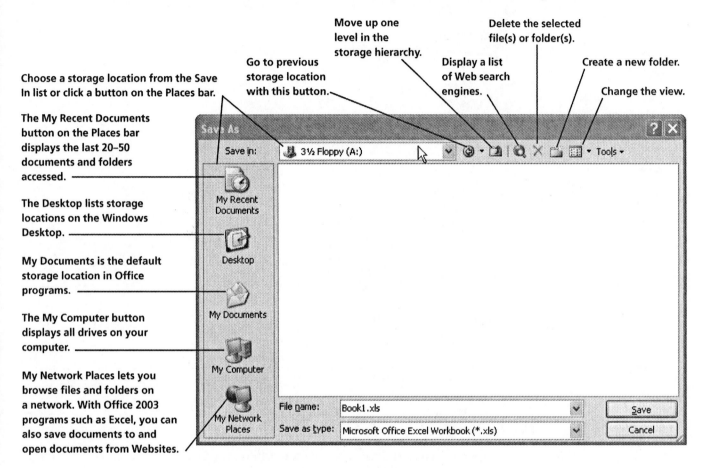

Move up one level in the storage hierarchy.

Go to previous storage location with this button.

Delete the selected file(s) or folder(s).

Display a list of Web search engines.

Create a new folder.

Change the view.

Choose a storage location from the Save In list or click a button on the Places bar.

The My Recent Documents button on the Places bar displays the last 20–50 documents and folders accessed.

The Desktop lists storage locations on the Windows Desktop.

My Documents is the default storage location in Office programs.

The My Computer button displays all drives on your computer.

My Network Places lets you browse files and folders on a network. With Office 2003 programs such as Excel, you can also save documents to and open documents from Websites.

 Hands-On 1.10 **Save the Workbook**

In this exercise, you will save the workbook created in the previous exercises to your file storage location.

Before You Begin: If you have not done so already, please turn to Downloading the Student Exercise Files section of the appendix (page 215) for instructions on how to retrieve the student exercise files for this book from the Labyrinth Website, and to copy the files to your file storage location for use in this and future lessons. See also pages 217–221 for additional details about using this book with a floppy disk, USB flash drive, the My Documents folder, and a folder on a network drive.

1. Click the Save 🖬 button.
   The Save As dialog box appears because this is the first time you are saving the workbook.

2. Follow these steps to save the workbook:
Keep in mind that your Save As dialog box will display files.

(A) Navigate to your file storage location. It is most likely 3½ Floppy (A:). ——

(B) Notice that Excel proposes the filename Book1 in the File Name box. ——

(C) Type the name **Weekly Sales** and it will replace the proposed name. (If you switched disk drives, you may need to click in the File Name box, delete the proposed name with `Delete` and/or `Backspace` then type the new name.)

(D) Click the Save button. ——

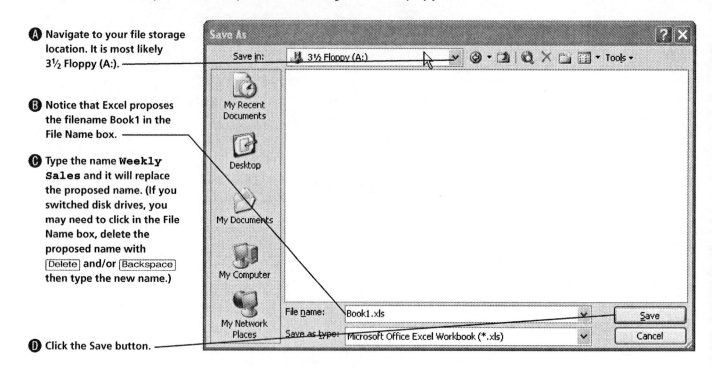

Notice that the workbook is saved and remains on the screen. You can continue to use this workbook or close it if you are finished working.

Closing Workbooks

The File→Close command is used to close an open workbook. When you close a workbook that has not been saved, Excel prompts you to save the changes. If you choose Yes at the prompt and the workbook has previously been saved, Excel simply saves the changes. If the workbook is new, Excel displays the Save As dialog box, allowing you to assign a name and storage location to the workbook.

 Hands-On 1.11   Close the Workbook

In this exercise, you will close the workbook that you saved in Hands-On 1.10.

1. Choose File→Close from the menu bar.

2. Click the Yes button if Excel asks you if you want to save the changes.
Notice that no workbook appears in the Excel window. The Excel window always has this appearance when all workbooks have been closed.

Opening Workbooks

The Open button on the Standard toolbar and the File→Open command display the Open dialog box. The Open dialog box lets you navigate to any storage location and open previously saved workbooks. Once a workbook is open, you can browse it, print it, and make editing changes. The organization and layout of the Open dialog box are similar to the Save As dialog box.

FROM THE KEYBOARD
[Ctrl]+[O] to open

 Hands-On 1.12   Open the Workbook

In this exercise, you will open the workbook you closed in Hands-On 1.11.

1. Click Open on the Standard toolbar.

2. Follow these steps to open the Weekly Sales workbook:
   Keep in mind that your Open dialog box will contain more files than shown here.

Ⓐ **Navigate to your file storage location. It is most likely 3½ Floppy (A:).**

Ⓑ **Choose the Weekly Sales.xls file.**

Ⓒ **Click the Open button.**

Open				? ☒
Look in:	3½ Floppy (A:)	⊙ · ☐ · ☒ · X · ☐ · ☒ · ▾ Tools ▾		
	Name ▲		Size	Type
	Weekly Sales.xls		14 KB	Microsoft Exc

File name:	▾ · Open ▾
Files of type:	All Microsoft Office Excel Files (*.xl*; *.xls; *.xlt; *.htm; *) ▾ · Cancel

Notice that the worksheet is exactly as it was before it was closed.

⚠ **TIP!** *You can also double-click a document on the list to open it.*

Exiting from Excel

The File→Exit command is used to close the Excel program. You should close Excel and other programs if you are certain you won't be using them for some time. This will free up memory for other programs. When you close Excel, you will be prompted to save any workbooks that have unsaved edits.

 Hands-On 1.13   Exit from Excel

In this exercise, you will exit from the Excel program.

1. Choose File→Exit from the menu bar.
   Excel will close without prompting you to save the workbook because you have not changed it since it was opened last.

Concepts Review

True/False Questions

1. Each workbook can have a maximum of one worksheet.   TRUE   FALSE

2. A worksheet is composed of horizontal rows and vertical columns.   TRUE   FALSE

3. Text entries can contain spaces.   TRUE   FALSE

4. Numbers can only contain the digits 0–9. No other characters are permitted.   TRUE   FALSE

5. A filename can contain spaces.   TRUE   FALSE

6. A colon (:) is used to separate the beginning and ending cells in a range reference.   TRUE   FALSE

7. You select an entire row by clicking the row header.   TRUE   FALSE

8. You can select multiple cell ranges.   TRUE   FALSE

9. The task pane can be used to create a new workbook.   TRUE   FALSE

10. You can store a file on a floppy disk, a hard drive, or a shared network drive.   TRUE   FALSE

Multiple Choice Questions

1. Which of the following keystrokes moves the highlight to cell A1?
   a. [End]
   b. [Ctrl]+[Tab]
   c. [Ctrl]+[Home]
   d. [Ctrl]+[Insert]

2. What happens if you select a range of cells and then click the mouse pointer anywhere in the worksheet?
   a. It adds the new cell you clicked into the selection.
   b. The selected cells are deselected.
   c. Nothing happens to the selection.
   d. The selection is deleted.

3. What happens when you insert an entry in the cell to the right of a long text entry?
   a. The display of the long entry is truncated.
   b. The long entry is replaced by the entry in the cell to the right.
   c. It has no effect on the long entry.
   d. None of the above

4. What happens when you insert an entry in the cell to the left of a long text entry?
   a. The display of the long entry is truncated.
   b. The long entry is permanently truncated.
   c. It has no effect on the long entry.
   d. None of the above

Skill Builders

Skill Builder 1.1   Create a Worksheet

In this exercise, you will create a worksheet. You will start Excel then enter text and numbers that contain two decimal places.

Start Excel and Enter Text

1. Start Excel by using (All) Programs from the Start menu.
   Notice that a blank workbook is displayed when you open Excel.

2. Enter text in rows 1 and 3 as shown in the following illustration.
   Try using the Tab *key to enter the data in row 3.*

	A	B	C	D	E	F	G	H
1	Order Tracking Sheet							
2								
3	Order #	Cust ID	Ord Stat	Item #	In Stock?		Ord Tot	Shipping Address

3. In cells A4:E8 and G4:G8, enter the data shown in the following illustration.
   Make sure to type the entire shipping address in column G.

	A	B	C	D	E	F	G	H	I	J	K
1	Order Tracking Sheet										
2											
3	Order #	Cust ID	Ord Stat	Item #	In Stock?		Ord Tot	Shipping Address			
4	1	341	S	A423	Y			1603 Catalina Avenue, Redondo Beach, CA 90277			
5	2	234	S	A321	Y			Will Pick Up			
6		567	I	S345	N			450 Terrace Drive, Santa Clara, CA 95050			
7		879	H	D567	N			No address at this point			
8		233	I	B444	Y			23 Maple Lane, Crawfordsville, IN 47933			

Enter Numbers with Decimals

4. Click cell F4.

5. Type **100.91** and tap Enter.
   You should always type a decimal point if the number requires one.

6. Type **45.87** and tap Enter.

7. Enter the numbers shown in the following illustration into cells F6, F7, and F8.

	A	B	C	D	E	F	G	H	I	J	K
1	Order Tracking Sheet										
2											
3	Order #	Cust ID	Ord Stat	Item #	In Stock?		Ord Tot	Shipping Address			
4	1	341	S	A423	Y		100.91	1603 Catalina Avenue, Redondo Beach, CA 90277			
5	2	234	S	A321	Y		45.87	Will Pick Up			
6		567	I	S345	N		43.23	450 Terrace Drive, Santa Clara, CA 95050			
7		879	H	D567	N		78.92	No address at this point			
8		233	I	B444	Y		23.45	23 Maple Lane, Crawfordsville, IN 47933			

Leave the worksheet open, as you will use it in the next exercise.

Skill Builder 1.2   Enter Data Using AutoComplete and AutoFill

In this exercise, you will enter repeated text entries using AutoComplete. You will also extend a series of numbers using AutoFill.

Use AutoComplete to Enter Repeated Text Entries

1. Click cell D9 and type **S**.
   Notice that AutoComplete displays the previous entry S345.

2. Tap ⌷Enter⌷ to accept the entry.

3. Enter the data in rows 9:11 as shown in the following illustration using AutoComplete where applicable.

	A	B	C	D	E	F	G	H	I	J	K
1	Order Tracking Sheet										
2											
3	Order #	Cust ID	Ord Stat	Item #	In Stock?	Ord Tot	Shipping Address				
4	1	341	S	A423	Y	100.91	1603 Catalina Avenue, Redondo Beach, CA 90277				
5	2	234	S	A321	Y	45.87	Will Pick Up				
6		567	I	S345	N	43.23	450 Terrace Drive, Santa Clara, CA 95050				
7		879	H	D567	N	78.92	No address at this point				
8		233	I	B444	Y	23.45	23 Maple Lane, Crawfordsville, IN 47933				
9		234	I	S345	N	43.23	Will Pick Up				
10		879	S	E123	Y	58.79	No address at this point				
11		341	H	D567	N	78.92	1603 Catalina Avenue, Redondo Beach, CA 90277				

Notice that you may have to type several characters until you see the AutoComplete suggestion. This happens when more than one entry in the column begins with the same character. Also, since Auto-Complete only works with text entries, you will not see the AutoComplete suggestion when entering addresses until you type the first letter of the street name.

Use AutoFill to Extend a Series of Numbers

4. Select cells A4:A5.
   Notice the small, square fill handle at the bottom-right corner of the selection.

5. Point to the fill handle and the mouse pointer will change to a small, black cross. Drag down column A until you have a list of numbers from 1–8.
   Leave the worksheet open, as you will continue to use it.

Skill Builder 1.3   Save, Close, Open, and Exit

In this exercise, you will save and close your new worksheet. You will also open a workbook, add new data to it, save the changes, and then exit from Excel.

1. Click the Save 🖫 button and save the workbook to your file storage location as **Order Tracking**.

2. Close the workbook after it has been saved using the Close Window ⊠ button.
   Be sure to use the bottom Close button; the top one closes Excel.

3. Click the Open 📂 button and double-click on the Weekly Sales file from your file storage location.

4. Click cell H1 and type today's date.

5. Close Weekly Sales without saving first.
   Notice that you get a message asking if you would like to save the changes you made.

6. Click Yes to save the changes to the workbook.

Assessments

Assessment 1.1   Create a New Worksheet

In this exercise, you will create a new worksheet, enter numbers using AutoFill, save the worksheet, and close the workbook.

1. Open a New 🗋 workbook.

2. Create the worksheet shown in the following illustration. Make sure the numbers match.

	A	B	C	D	E
1	Big City Diner Q1 Expenses				
2					
3	Item		January	February	March
4	Building	Rent	800	800	800
5		Utilities	340	400	250
6		Phone	250	200	300
7		Insurance	350	0	0
8		Total	1740	1400	1350
9					
10	Food Cost	Produce	2500	2320	1700
11		Meat	4000	3400	3700
12		Grains	1000	1200	890
13		Total	7500	6920	6290
14					
15	Salaries	Simmons	800	780	800
16		Swanson	750	650	870
17		Martinez	900	780	680
18		Richardson	1200	1000	990
19		Total	3650	3210	3340
20					
21	Other	Advertising	500	300	0
22		Uniforms	0	340	0
23		Janitorial	200	200	200
24		Misc	100	2000	0
25		Total	800	2840	200

Use AutoFill to extend the months in row 3.

3. Save the workbook as **Q1 Expenses**, and then close it.

Assessment 1.2   Edit a Workbook

In this exercise, you will expand on the workbook you created in the Skill Builder exercises for this lesson.

1. Open the workbook named Order Tracking.

2. Complete the worksheet as shown in the following illustration. Follow these guidelines when entering the data in rows 12–16:

   - Use AutoComplete whenever appropriate
   - Select cells A7:A8, and then use the fill handle to extend the series of order numbers.

	A	B	C	D	E	F	G	H	I	J	K
1	Order Tracking Sheet										
2											
3	Order #	Cust ID	Ord Stat	Item #	In Stock?	Ord Tot	Shipping Address				
4	1	341	S	A423	Y	100.91	1603 Catalina Avenue, Redondo Beach, CA 90277				
5	2	234	S	A321	Y	45.87	Will Pick Up				
6	3	567	I	S345	N	43.23	450 Terrace Drive, Santa Clara, CA 95050				
7	4	879	H	D567	N	78.92	No address at this point				
8	5	233	I	B444	Y	23.45	23 Maple Lane, Crawfordsville, IN 47933				
9	6	234	I	S345	N	43.23	Will Pick Up				
10	7	879	S	E123	Y	58.79	No address at this point				
11	8	341	H	D567	N	78.92	1603 Catalina Avenue, Redondo Beach, CA 90277				
12	9	555	S	E442	Y	50	3325 Carolina Avenue, Richmond, VA 93261				
13	10	234	I	S345	N	43.23	Will Pick Up				
14	11	567	S	D102	N	115	450 Terrace Drive, Santa Clara, CA 95050				
15	12	879	H	B444	Y	23.45	No address at this point				
16	13	341	S	B352	Y	27	1603 Catalina Avenue, Redondo Beach, CA 90277				

3. When finished, use File→Save As to save the workbook with the new name **Completed Order Tracking**.

Assessment 1.3   Enter Data in Various Ways

In this exercise, you will use your skills for entering data into a worksheet in different ways.

1. Open the workbook named Stamp Sales.
   Notice that column A is already widened for you. You will learn to widen columns yourself in Lesson 4, Formatting Cell Contents.

2. Use these guidelines to create the worksheet shown in the following illustration:

   - Use the keypad for numeric entries. Remember, the Num Lock light must be on to use the numeric keypad. If the light is not on, tap the Num Lock key.
   - Use AutoComplete to enter repeated text entries.
   - Use the fill handle to extend the data series in row 2.

	A	B	C	D	E	F	G
1	2004 Stamp						
2	Stamp Style	Jan	Feb	Mar	Apr	May	Jun
3							
4	Scenic	68	55	25	4	12	2
5	Rescue Guys	16	6	2	2		1
6	Order of the Eastern Star		1			25	1
7	Policemen Rule		5				1
8	Rescue Guys	31	20	3	7	2	7
9	Space Place		1		3	11	1
10	Marine Corps Guy		2		68	55	25
11	Scenic	3			16	6	2
12	Columbus Days		1			1	
13	Space Place	22	14	4		5	
14	Fireman Association	2	3		31	20	3
15	Rescue Guys	36	10	5		1	
16	Ducks in a Row	4	12	2		2	
17	Colonial Days	2		1	3		
18	State Seal of Approval		25	1		1	
19	Fireman Association			1	22	14	4
20	Policemen Rule	7	2	7	2	3	
21	Order of the Eastern Star	3	11	1	36	10	5
22	Ducks in a Row			1	4	12	2
23	Colonial Days		4	1	2		1
24	Dear Hunter		5			25	1
25	Scenic	2		1			1
26	Marine Corps Guy		1		7	2	7
27	Space Place		2		3	11	1

3. When finished, save and close the file.

Critical Thinking

Critical Thinking 1.1   On Your Own

Jeremy Diemer is a math teacher at Washington High School. Jeremy wants an Excel workbook that tracks students' test scores for his trigonometry class. Students receive a final letter grade for the course that is determined by the total number of points they accumulate throughout the course. Students are given four 1-hour tests, a midterm, a final, and four extra credit homework assignments. They can receive a maximum of 100 points for each of the four tests, 200 points for the midterm, 300 points for the final, and 25 points for each extra credit homework assignment. Thus, the total number of possible points for the course is 1,000. Letter grades are assigned as follows:

A   900 or more points

B   800–899 points

C   700–799 points

D   600–699 points

F   less than 600 points

You have been assigned the task of setting up a worksheet for Jeremy. The worksheet should list the points received by each student for the tests, midterm, final, and homework assignments. Include scores for the following four students: Jack Simmons, Samantha Torres, Elaine Wilkins, and Tonya Robertson. Assign points to the students, as you deem appropriate. Save your workbook as **Grades**.

Critical Thinking 1.2   On Your Own

Tanisha Jones is running for president of the Westmont Community College Student Association. Westmont College regulates student campaigns in various ways. In particular, the college imposes a maximum fundraising limit of $1,500 on each candidate running for office. In addition, there are strict reporting requirements for campaign contributions. Each contribution must be reported and include the date of the contribution, the individual or organization making the contribution, and the amount of the contribution. The reports are made available to the public in print and on the college's Website. You have been assigned the task of setting up a worksheet to track Tanisha's campaign contributions. List five contributions in your worksheet from the following individuals and organizations: Cindy Thomas, Richardson Vending Services, Campus Computer Equipment, Elaine Wilson, and Party Time Music and Video. You determine the contribution amounts and the dates. Save your workbook as **Campaign Contributions**.

Critical Thinking 1.3   On Your Own

Big Slice Pizza is a rapidly growing pizza chain that serves the best deep-dish pizza in town. An important part of Big Slice's growth strategy is the development of a franchise network using independent franchise owners. Recently, Big Slice launched the West Coast Advertising Campaign to attract new franchise owners. You have been assigned the task of collecting the franchise applications and creating a worksheet that summarizes the application information. Your worksheet should include each prospective franchise owner's name, city and state, investment amount, telephone number, and whether or not the prospect has previous franchise experience. Include information for the following prospects: Ben Barksdale, Sylvia Ramirez, Bill Chin, Wanda Stone, and Terry Collins. You determine the remaining information for each prospective owner. Save your workbook as **Pizza Franchises**.

Critical Thinking 1.4   Web Research

Alexia Williams is the Information Systems Manager for Bellmont Health Care, a rapidly growing health care company with more than one billion dollars in FY 2003 revenues. Alexia has mandated that, beginning in FY 2004, at least 50% of Bellmont's technology purchases will be made using online purchasing systems. Alexia believes this strategy will reduce costs and increase the efficiency of the procurement process. As an intern working under Alexia's direction, you have been assigned the task of locating five online vendors that sell personal computers and accessories. Alexia has asked you to construct a worksheet that includes the vendor's name, Website URL, and customer service telephone number. Use Internet Explorer and a search engine of your choice to conduct your research. Record your results in a worksheet saved as **Computer Buys Online**.

Critical Thinking 1.5   Web Research

George Miller is the Operations Manager for Speedy Package Delivery Service, a same-day package delivery service. Speedy is located in the heart of Silicon Valley. George needs to purchase six new minivans to be used for package delivery. He has assigned you the task of locating three Websites that have information on different minivans and where they can be purchased. Use Internet Explorer and a search engine of your choice to locate three Websites that specialize in vehicle sales. Set up a worksheet that lists the Website name and URL of three such Websites. For each Website, include the posted retail price range and the dealer invoice price for Ford Windstar, Chevrolet Astro, and Dodge Caravan minivans. Use a consistent vehicle configuration from each Website so the pricing comparisons are valid. Include any additional vehicle information that you think would be useful to George. Save your workbook as **Car Pricing**.

Critical Thinking 1.6   On Your Own

Set up a worksheet to record whether people have used Windows, Outlook, Word, Excel, Access, PowerPoint, and Internet Explorer in a business environment. Survey five of your friends, relatives, or coworkers and record the results of your survey in the worksheet. Use a 1 to indicate experience with a particular program and a 0 to indicate no experience. Examining the figures should give you some idea of how much each program is used in business. Save your workbook as **Survey**.

LESSON 2

Expanding on the Basics

In this lesson, you will expand on the basic skills you learned in Lesson 1. You will learn various methods of editing worksheets: replacing and deleting entries, using Undo and Redo, working with AutoCorrect, and more. You will also learn about printing Excel workbooks. When you have finished this lesson, you will have developed the skills necessary to produce carefully edited and proofed worksheets.

Microsoft Office Excel 2003 objectives covered in this lesson

Objective Number	Skill Sets and Skills	Concept Page References	Exercise Page References
XL03S-1-1	Enter and edit cell content	40, 42	40–42
XL03S-5-5	Preview data in other views	46	46
XL03S-5-7	Setup pages for printing	48	49
XL03S-5-8	Print data	46–47	47–48

Additional learning resources are available at labpub.com/learn/excel03/

Case Study

Donella Prusko is an entrepreneur and the founder of Donella's Deli. Donella recently resigned from her corporate position to pursue her dream and passion—a deli that serves delicious, healthy food at reasonable prices. Donella realizes that the health of her business is just as important as the health of her customers. For this reason, she wants to develop a detailed worksheet to track her income and expenses. To ensure the data she enters is correct, Donna uses Excel's powerful editing, error checking, and correcting tools to produce her worksheet. Microsoft Excel is an important tool for any entrepreneur in today's highly competitive business world.

	A	B	C	D	E
1	Donella's Deli				
2	Income and Expense Worksheet				
3		Quarterly Income			
4	Food Sales	Q1	Q2	Q3	Q4
5	Dine-in Sales	21000	23000	28000	42000
6	Takeout Sales	12000	16000	25000	56000
7	Subtotal				
8	Other Income				
9	Gratuities	2500	2700	3000	4500
10	Sublease	500	500	500	500
11	Subtotal				
12	Total Income				
13					
14		Quarterly Expenses			
15	Expenses	Q1	Q2	Q3	Q4
16	Rent	3000	3000	3000	3000
17	Utilities	400	310	290	380
18	Marketing	800	800	800	800
19	Salaries	12000	12000	14000	14000
20	Supplies	15000	15500	18000	24000
21	Equipment	6000	2000	1000	0
22	Total				
23					
24	Gross Profit				
25	Donella's Net Profit				
26	Donnella's Gross Profit vs. Income				

Editing Entries

You can edit the active cell by clicking in the Formula bar and making the desired changes. You can also double-click a cell and edit the contents directly there. This technique is known as in-cell editing.

Replacing Entries

Editing an entry is efficient if the entry is so long that retyping it would be time-consuming. Editing can also be helpful when working with complex formulas and other functions that are difficult to recreate. If the entry requires little typing, however, it is usually easier to simply replace it.

Deleting Characters

FROM THE KEYBOARD

Ctrl+Delete to delete text to end of line

Use the Delete and Backspace keys to edit entries in the Formula bar and within a cell. The Delete key removes the character to the right of the insertion point while the Backspace key removes the character to the left of the insertion point.

 Hands-On 2.1   Edit Entries

In this exercise, you will use the Formula bar to revise the contents of cell A2. You will also edit cells B3 and B14 directly in the cells.

Edit in the Formula Bar

1. Open the Income Expense workbook and click cell A2.

2. Follow these steps to edit cell A2 using the Formula bar:

Ⓐ Click in the Formula bar just to the right of the word Expense.

Ⓑ Tap the Spacebar and type **Worksheet**.

X √ *fx*   Income and Expense

Ⓒ Click the Enter button.

Replace an Entry

3. Click cell B14.

4. Type **Quarterly Expenses** and tap Enter.
   The entry Quarterly Expenses replaces the entry Payouts.

Use In-Cell Editing

5. Double-click cell B3 (the cell with the word Income).

6. Use the mouse or the ← key to position the flashing insertion point to the left of the word Income.

7. Type **Quarterly** and tap the Spacebar once.

8. Tap Enter or click Enter ✓ to complete the change.
   The entry should now read Quarterly Income. Notice that part of the word Income spills over into column C. Remember, though, that the entire entry is in column B.

9. Click the Save 🖫 button to update the changes.
   Clicking the Save button automatically saves changes to a workbook that has previously been saved.

Using Undo and Redo

Excel's Undo ↺ button lets you reverse up to your last 16 actions. You can reverse simple actions such as accidentally deleting a cell's content or more complex actions such as deleting an entire row. Most actions can be undone but those that cannot include printing and saving workbooks.

FROM THE KEYBOARD
Ctrl+Z to undo
Ctrl+Y to redo

The Redo ↻ button reverses an Undo command. Use Redo when you undo an action but decide to go through with that action after all.

Undoing and Redoing Multiple Actions

The arrows ▾ on the Undo and Redo buttons display lists of actions that can be undone or redone. You can undo or redo multiple actions by dragging the mouse over the desired actions. You can undo or redo up to 16 actions using this method. However, you must undo or redo actions in the order in which they appear on the drop-down list.

 Hands-On 2.2   Reverse Actions

In this exercise, you will delete the contents of a cell then use Undo to reverse the deletion. When you do, the original data will display in the cell again. You will also use Redo to reverse an Undo command.

Delete the Entry and Use Undo and Redo

1. Click cell A2.
   Notice the cell's content in the Formula bar. The entry is long and although it also appears to be in cell B2, it is entirely in cell A2. Cell B2 is empty.

2. Tap Delete.
   Notice that the entire entry was deleted because it belonged to cell A1.

3. Click Undo ↺ to restore the entry.

4. Click Redo ↻ to delete the entry again.
   Redo always reverses Undo.

5. Click Undo ↺ again to restore the entry.

6. Save the changes but don't close the workbook.

Clearing Cell Contents and Formats

In Excel, you can format cell content by changing the font style, size, and color. You can also add enhancements such as bold, italics, and underline. Cells with numeric data can be formatted as currency, dates, times, percents, and more.

Some simple formatting techniques are introduced in this lesson to demonstrate the functionality of the Clear command. In Lesson 4, Formatting Cell Contents, you will learn about formatting cells in detail.

The Edit→Clear command displays a submenu that lets you clear content, formats, and comments from cells. The submenu also contains an All option that clears all of these items from the selected cell(s).

■ Contents—Clearing the content has the same effect as tapping the Delete key. The cell contents are deleted but any format applied to the cell remains and will be in effect when new data is entered in the cell.

■ Formats—The Formats option removes all text and number formats, leaving unformatted entries in the cell(s).

■ Comments—You can insert comments in cells to document your worksheet. The Comments option also removes comments from the selected cells.

One of the most useful functions of the Edit→Clear command is removing numeric value formats. This is because once a cell is formatted as a particular numeric format, such as a date or currency, Excel remembers that formatting even if the cell contents are deleted.

 ## Hands-On 2.3   Clear Formats

In this exercise, you will enter a number formatted as a date and a number formatted as currency. You will also use the Edit→Clear command to delete cell contents and cell formats.

1. Click cell E1 and enter today's date using dashes between the month, day, and year.
   This cell is formatted as a date because you entered the number with dashes between the month, day, and year. Notice that Excel converts the dashes you typed between the month, day, and year to slashes, the default format. Cell E1 will remain formatted as a date even if the contents are deleted.

TIP! *Dates can be entered using forward slashes or dashes (for example, 1/1/04 or 1-1-04); however, the dashes will be converted to the default format of slashes.*

2. Click cell E1 again and tap Delete.

3. Click cell E2, type **$40**, and click Enter ✓ to complete the entry.
   Notice that Excel formats the number with the Currency format, which includes a dollar sign. The Currency format was applied because you entered the number using a dollar sign.

4. Choose Edit→Clear→Formats.
   The Currency format is cleared.

5. Now choose Edit→Clear→Contents to delete the cell content.
   Notice that this works just like tapping Delete does.

6. When you have finished experimenting, save the changes but don't close the workbook.

Using AutoCorrect

Excel's AutoCorrect feature can improve the speed and accuracy of entering text. AutoCorrect is most useful for replacing abbreviations with a full phrase of up to 255 characters. For example, you could set up AutoCorrect to substitute "as soon as possible" whenever you type "asap." AutoCorrect also automatically corrects common spelling and typographical errors. For example, the word "the" is often misspelled as "teh" and the word "and" is often misspelled as "adn." These and other common spelling mistakes are fixed automatically. AutoCorrect also automatically capitalizes the first letter of a day if you type it in lowercase. For example, if you type "sunday" and complete the entry, AutoCorrect will enter "Sunday" in the cell. Finally, AutoCorrect fixes words that have two initial capital letters by switching the second letter to lowercase.

 TIP! *AutoCorrect entries are shared by all programs in the Microsoft Office Suite so if you've already added some in Word, they are available for you to use in Excel also.*

Expanding AutoCorrect Entries

AutoCorrect goes into action when you type a word in a text entry and tap ⌷Spacebar⌷ or when you complete a text entry. The word or entry is compared to all entries in the AutoCorrect table. The AutoCorrect table contains a list of words and their replacement phrases. If the word you type matches an entry in the AutoCorrect table, a phrase from the table is substituted for the word. This is known as expanding the AutoCorrect entry.

Creating and Editing AutoCorrect Entries

The Tools→AutoCorrect Options command displays the AutoCorrect dialog box. You use the AutoCorrect dialog box to add entries to the AutoCorrect table, delete entries from the table, and set other AutoCorrect options. To add an entry, type the desired abbreviation in the Replace box and the desired expansion for the abbreviation in the With box.

 TIP! *If you create the abbreviation using uppercase letters, it will not work if you type it in lowercase letters later. Type all abbreviations in lowercase so you don't have to remember to type them in uppercase.*

 ## Hands-On 2.4   Using AutoCorrect

*In this exercise, you will use AutoCorrect to fix an **intentional** typo that you will enter into cell A1. It's okay to replace the Donella's Deli entry for now; later in this exercise, you will create an AutoCorrect entry for that title and reinsert it into cell A1.*

Before you begin: The Income Expense workbook should still be open.

Use AutoCorrect

1. Type **adn** (that's "adn," not "and") in cell A1 and tap ⌷Enter⌷.
   Excel corrects the misspelling and enters the word and in the cell.

2. Click cell A1 and type **This adn that**, but don't complete the entry.
   Notice that AutoCorrect fixed the typo immediately after you tapped ⌷Spacebar⌷.

3. Tap ⌷Esc⌷ to cancel the entry.

Create a New AutoCorrect Entry

4. Choose Tools→AutoCorrect Options from the menu bar.

5. Follow these steps to create a new AutoCorrect entry:

A Notice these checkboxes. They instruct AutoCorrect to automatically make the specified corrections in your worksheets.

B Type **dd** in the Replace box.

C Type **Donella's Deli** in the With box.

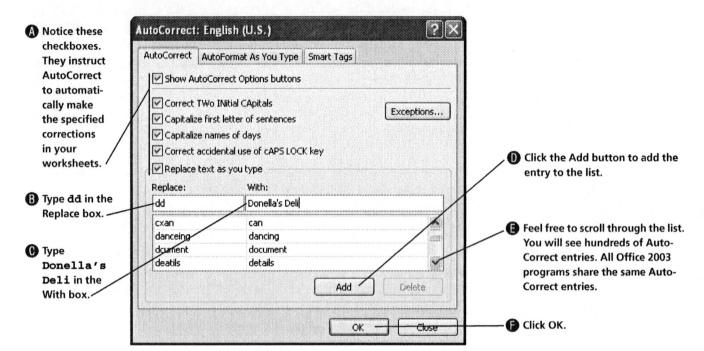

D Click the Add button to add the entry to the list.

E Feel free to scroll through the list. You will see hundreds of Auto-Correct entries. All Office 2003 programs share the same Auto-Correct entries.

F Click OK.

6. Click cell A1, type **dd**, and tap Enter.
AutoCorrect replaces dd with Donella's Deli. Notice that you can use AutoCorrect as a type of shorthand. AutoCorrect can replace abbreviations with phrases you use often, such as your company name or address.

Delete the AutoCorrect Entry

7. Choose Tools→AutoCorrect Options from the menu bar.

8. Scroll through the list of AutoCorrect entries and choose the dd, Donella's Deli entry. You can also type **dd** in the Replace box to rapidly locate the entry.

9. Click the Delete button below the AutoCorrect table then click OK.
The entry is deleted from the AutoCorrect table but the phrase Donella's Deli remains in cell A1.

10. Now type **dd** in cell A2 and tap Enter.
Notice that dd did not change to Donella's Deli.

11. Click the Undo ↺ button to reverse the last action.

Checking the Spelling in a Worksheet

Excel 2003 includes several tools to help you locate errors in worksheets. In this section, you will use Excel's spell checker and in *Microsoft Office Excel 2003: Quick Course 3* you will use the Formula Error Checker to locate errors in formulas.

The Spelling button on the Standard toolbar checks the spelling of all text entries in the current worksheet. The spell checker functions much like the spell checker in Microsoft Word. Excel's spell checker also uses the same main dictionary and custom dictionaries as Word.

QR **QUICK REFERENCE: USING THE SPELLING DIALOG BOX**

Button	Function
Ignore Once	Ignores the misspelled word one time only and prompts you the next time it encounters the same misspelling
Ignore All	Ignores the misspelled word now and for all spell checks during this Excel session
Add to Dictionary	Adds the misspelled word to a custom dictionary
Change	Replaces the misspelled word with the word highlighted on the Suggestions list
Change All	Replaces all occurrences of the misspelled word in this worksheet with the word highlighted on the Suggestions list
AutoCorrect	Corrects then adds the misspelled (and corrected) word to the list of entries in AutoCorrect

 Hands-On 2.5 Check the Worksheet for Errors

In this exercise, you will use the Spelling dialog box to check the worksheet for spelling errors.

Spell Check

1. Click cell A1.
   This forces the spell checker to begin checking at the top of the worksheet.

2. Click the Spelling button on the Standard toolbar.
   The Spelling dialog box will appear and the word Donella's will be marked as Not in Dictionary.

3. Click the Ignore All button to skip the word Donella's.
   Donella's name may not be in the spell checker's dictionary but it is spelled correctly. At this point, the spell checker will scan for any additional misspelled words.

4. Continue to spell check the worksheet using your best judgment when making corrections.
   Notice that you can edit directly in the Not in Dictionary box if the correct word is not listed in the Suggestion box.

Printing Worksheets

Excel gives you many ways to print your work. The method you choose depends on what you want to print. The File→Print command, for instance, offers you print options such as printing specified pages, a selected range, or the entire workbook. Additional choices include printing multiple copies and collating options.

The Print ⎙ button prints one copy of the entire worksheet. For large workbooks in which you frequently want to print only a certain selection you can set a print area, which then becomes the default range for printing when using the Print button. Before printing you can use Print Preview to view what is going to be printed. In *Microsoft Office Excel 2003: Quick Course 2*, you will learn how to change page setup options, such as changing the print orientation, adding headers and footers, printing column headings on every page, and many others.

Print Preview

The Print Preview 🔍 button on the Standard toolbar displays the Print Preview window. Print Preview lets you see exactly how a worksheet will look when printed. Print Preview can save time, paper, and wear and tear on your printer. It is especially useful when printing large worksheets and those with charts and intricate formatting. It is always wise to preview a large or complex worksheet before sending it to the printer. When you display the Print Preview window, the standard toolbars are replaced by the Print Preview toolbar.

 Hands-On 2.6   Use Print Preview

In this exercise, you will view the worksheet in the Print Preview window and explore the zoom commands.

1. Click the Print Preview 🔍 button on the Standard toolbar.

2. Zoom in by clicking anywhere on the worksheet.

3. Zoom out by clicking anywhere on the worksheet.

4. Click the Close button on the Print Preview toolbar to exit without printing.

Print the Worksheet

FROM THE KEYBOARD

Ctrl+P to display the Print box

The Print ⎙ button on the Standard toolbar sends the entire worksheet to the current printer. You must display the Print dialog box if you want to change printers, adjust the number of copies to be printed, or set other printing options such as printing only selected cells. The Print dialog box is displayed with the File→Print command. The following illustration explains the most important options available in the Print dialog box.

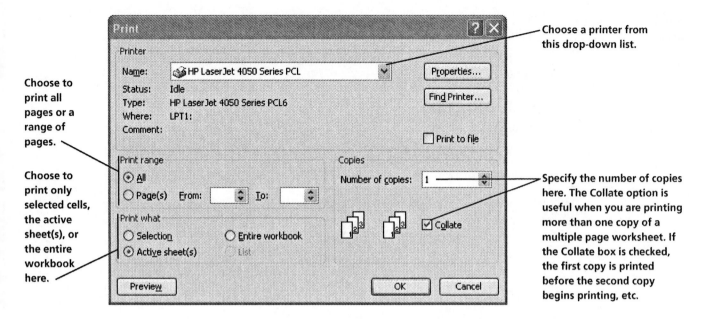

Choose a printer from this drop-down list.

Choose to print all pages or a range of pages.

Choose to print only selected cells, the active sheet(s), or the entire workbook here.

Specify the number of copies here. The Collate option is useful when you are printing more than one copy of a multiple page worksheet. If the Collate box is checked, the first copy is printed before the second copy begins printing, etc.

 Hands-On 2.7   Print the Worksheet

In this exercise, you will view the options in the Print dialog box and print one copy of the entire worksheet.

1. Choose File→Print to display the Print dialog box.

2. Take a few moments to review the box options.

3. When you are ready to print, make sure the options are set as shown in the preceding illustration and then click OK.
   Keep in mind that your printer will probably be different than the one listed in the illustration.

4. Retrieve your worksheet from the printer.

Print Selections

Many times you will want to print only a range of cells. You can do this by selecting the desired cells, choosing File→Print, clicking the Selection button, and clicking OK. You also use this technique to print noncontiguous selections within a worksheet or workbook. For example, use this technique to print two noncontiguous sections of a worksheet or two or more sections on different worksheets. Noncontiguous selections print on separate pages.

To print a selection, you must select the cell range before displaying the Print dialog box. Therefore, if the selection is one that you will be printing frequently, you can save time by setting that selection as a print area. You will learn about print areas in the next topic.

Hands-On 2.8   Print Selections

In this exercise, you will select different portions of the worksheet to print and view them in Print Preview.

Print a Single Selection

1. Select the range A1:E10.
   This selection will allow you to print the main part of the Income section but not rows 11 and 12.

2. Choose File→Print from the menu bar.

3. Choose the Selection option button then click the Preview button at the bottom-left corner of the dialog box.
   Notice that only the selected cells are visible in Print Preview.

4. Click the Close button to exit from Print Preview.

Print Nonadjacent Selections

5. Select the range A3:E10.

6. Press the [Ctrl] key while selecting the range A14:E21.

7. Choose File→Print, choose the Selection option, and click the Preview button.
   Notice that the first selected range is displayed on the first page.

8. Click the Next button on the Print Preview toolbar to view the second page.
   The second selected range should be visible.

9. Click the Close button to exit from Print Preview.

Print Areas

A print area is a range of cells marked for printing. Only the specified area is printed, even when using the Print button. This has the same effect as printing a selection. A print area remains in effect until you clear it.

Print areas are convenient if you intend to print the same area more than once. For example, you may have a report that you print on a weekly or monthly basis. The report may only be a small portion of a large worksheet. Once you set the print area, it is saved with the workbook. This means that every time you open the workbook, the print area for your report is already set and you can simply click the Print button to print it.

 QUICK REFERENCE: SETTING, PRINTING, AND CLEARING PRINT AREAS

Task	Procedure
Set a print area	Select the desired cells and choose File→Print Area→Set Print Area.
Print a print area	Click the Print button.
Clear a print area	Choose File→Print Area→Clear Print Area.

Hands-On 2.9   Set, Preview, and Clear a Print Area

In this exercise, you will set the print area for the entire Income section of the worksheet and view it in Print Preview. You will also clear a print area.

1. Select the range A3:E12.

2. Choose File→Print Area→Set Print Area from the menu bar.

3. Click in the worksheet to deselect the cells.
   Notice that a dashed line surrounds the range A3:E12. This is the current print area.

4. Click the Print Preview ⬚ button.
   Notice that only cells A3:E12 are visible in Print Preview, even though they are no longer selected in the worksheet. A print area remains in effect until you clear or reset it.

5. Close Print Preview and choose File→Print Area→Clear Print Area from the menu bar.

6. Click the Print Preview ⬚ button and notice that the entire worksheet is displayed.

7. Close Print Preview, save the changes to your workbook, and close the workbook.

Using Online Help

Excel's online Help puts a complete reference book at your fingertips. You can get the help you need for just about any topic you can imagine—immediately and right on your Desktop. Plus, if you have an Internet connection, additional Help is available directly from the Microsoft Website. When you are connected to the Internet and search for a Help topic, Help automatically searches for the requested topics at Microsoft.com and displays a results list from which to choose the desired topic.

Locating Help Topics

Your goal when using online Help is to locate topics. Several search methods are available for you to use to locate topics. All Help topics have keywords that identify them. For example, a Help topic that discusses printing workbooks can probably be located by including the keyword "printing" in your search. Once you locate the desired topic, you can display it and follow the instructions in the topic or print it.

Accessing Help

In Excel 2003, you can display the Help window using any of the following methods:

■ Click the Help ⓘ button on the Standard toolbar.

■ Press F1.

■ Choose Help→Microsoft Excel Help from the menu bar.

The following Quick Reference table describes the various methods for locating Help topics.

Search Method	Procedure
Table of Contents	This method is useful if you aren't sure how to describe a topic. The Table of Contents method lets you navigate through a series of categories.
Search Box	This method lets you search for topics with keywords. You choose the desired topic from a list generated by your keyword. This method is most useful if you know the name of the topic or feature for which you are searching.
Type a Question Box	This method allows you to type a phrase into a search box. You choose the desired topic from a list that displays on the screen.

The Help Window Toolbar

The Help window contains a toolbar to assist you with online Help. The following illustration describes the buttons on the Help toolbar.

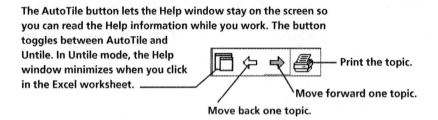

The AutoTile button lets the Help window stay on the screen so you can read the Help information while you work. The button toggles between AutoTile and Untile. In Untile mode, the Help window minimizes when you click in the Excel worksheet.

Print the topic.

Move forward one topic.

Move back one topic.

Hands-On 2.10 Use Online Help

In this exercise, you will search for Help topics on how to create functions in Excel.

Use the Search Box

1. Choose Help→Microsoft Excel Help from the menu bar.
   The Help window will appear.

2. Click the Start Searching ➡ button after typing the word **function** in the Search box.

3. Locate the About the Syntax of Functions topic and then click it to display the information.
   A new pane opens and displays the topic.

4. Take a moment to read the help information. Notice the blue phrases, such as Cell References, scattered throughout the topic.

5. Click the Cell References phrase and notice the definition that appears.

6. If the Help window containing the list of help topics and the Search For box is no longer displayed, click the AutoTile ☐ button on the Help toolbar.

Experiment with Help

7. Try using the Search For method to locate additional Help topics. You can type keywords in the Search For box, click the Start Searching button, and click the desired topic. Try locating Help topics for Excel features you have already learned or for new features to be covered later in this book.

8. Try using the Table of Contents link, located below the Search For box, to locate topics. You must click closed books in the list to locate topics.
You may need to click the Back button at the top of the Search Results task pane to return to the Excel Help task pane.

9. When you have finished, click the Close [X] button on the Help window.

Concepts Review

True/False Questions

1. The Undo button lets you reverse up to the last 16 actions.   TRUE   FALSE

2. Double-clicking in a cell lets you revise the contents of the cell without replacing the entire contents.   TRUE   FALSE

3. When you delete the contents of a cell using the [Delete] key on the keyboard, the formatting remains.   TRUE   FALSE

4. After typing an AutoCorrect abbreviation, you can tap [Enter] to replace it.   TRUE   FALSE

5. You can add new words to the existing spell check dictionary.   TRUE   FALSE

6. You cannot delete the formats in a cell without deleting the contents.   TRUE   FALSE

7. You cannot add new AutoCorrect entries in the Spell Check dialog box.   TRUE   FALSE

8. You can print a group of cells without printing the entire worksheet.   TRUE   FALSE

9. You can use uppercase characters for an AutoCorrect abbreviation.   TRUE   FALSE

10. You can search online for Help topics.   TRUE   FALSE

Multiple Choice Questions

1. What happens when you enter text in a cell that already contains an entry?
   a. The text replaces the original entry.
   b. Excel rejects the new entry, keeping the original entry intact.
   c. The cell contains both the original entry and the new entry.
   d. None of the above

2. Where do you find the command to create an abbreviation for a frequently used phrase?
   a. Insert→AutoCorrect Options
   b. Tools→AutoCorrect Options
   c. Format→AutoCorrect Options
   d. Edit→AutoCorrect Options

3. How do you print a certain area of your worksheet?
   a. Select the range then click Print, Selection, OK.
   b. Select the range, click File→Print Area→ Set Print Area, then click the Print button.
   c. Click the Print ☐ button.
   d. Both a and b

4. How do you clear the date format out of a cell?
   a. Select the cell and tap [Delete].
   b. Click Edit→Clear→Formatting.
   c. Right-click the cell and choose Delete from the pop-up menu.
   d. Click Edit→Delete→All then click OK.

Skill Builders

Skill Builder 2.1   Edit a Worksheet

In this exercise, you will edit a worksheet. This exercise demonstrates that sometimes it is easier to replace entries while at other times it is easier to edit them.

Replace Several Entries

1. Start Excel and click the Open ⬚ button on the Standard toolbar.

2. Open the workbook named Customers.

3. Click cell A4.

4. Type **Ralph** and tap Enter.
   Notice that it was easy to replace the entry because the name Ralph is easy to type.

5. Replace the name Calvin in cell A6 with the name **Steven**.

Edit Using the Formula Bar

6. Click cell C4.

7. Click in the Formula bar just in front of the telephone prefix 333.

8. Tap Delete three times to remove the prefix.

9. Type **222** and complete ✔ the entry.

10. Change the area code in cell C8 from 814 to **714**.

Use In-Cell Editing

11. Double-click cell D4.
    The flashing insertion point appears in the cell.

12. Use → to position the insertion point in front of the word Lane.

13. Use Delete to remove the word Lane.

14. Type **Reservoir** and complete the entry.

15. Edit the next five addresses using either the Formula bar or in-cell editing. The required changes appear bold in the following table.

Cell	Make These Changes
D5	2900 **Carlton** Drive, San Mateo, CA 94401
D6	**2300** Palm Drive, Miami, FL 33147
D7	888 Wilson Street, Concord, CA **94518**
D8	320 Main Street, **Pittsburgh**, PA 17951
D9	132nd Street, Los Angeles, CA **90045**

16. When you have finished, choose File→Close from the menu bar and click the Yes button when Excel asks if you wish to save the changes.

Skill Builder 2.2   Use AutoCorrect

In this exercise, you will edit a worksheet. You will create, use, and delete AutoCorrect entries.

Create AutoCorrect Entries

1. Open the file named Benefits Plan.

2. Click Tools→AutoCorrect Options.

3. In the Replace box, type **q1** and tap the Tab key.
   Remember to type the abbreviation in lowercase.

4. In the With box, type **First Quarter**.

5. Click the Add button.
   Do not click the OK button right now because you are going to make a few more AutoCorrect entries.

6. Make the following three entries. Click OK when you are finished.

q2	**Second Quarter**
q3	**Third Quarter**
q4	**Fourth Quarter**

   AutoCorrect entries can be used in any worksheet.

Use AutoCorrect Entries

7. Click cell B3.

8. Type **q1** and press the [Spacebar].
First Quarter should appear in the cell.

9. Tab the [Tab] key to move the highlight to cell D3.

10. Type **q2** and press the [Spacebar].

11. Using AutoCorrect, enter the last two quarters in row 3 and enter the quarters in columns B, D, F, and H.

Delete AutoCorrect Entries

12. Click Tools→AutoCorrect Options.

13. In the Replace box, type **q1**.
The First Quarter AutoCorrect entry appears in the With box next to the q1 abbreviation in the Replace box.

14. Click the Delete button under the AutoCorrect entry list.

15. Delete the AutoCorrect entries for q2, q3, and q4.

16. When you finish deleting all four entries, click OK.
The AutoCorrect Options dialog box closes.

17. Save the changes and close the workbook.

Skill Builder 2.3   Spell Checking a Worksheet

In this exercise, you will open a workbook and run spell check, making the necessary corrections.

1. Open the workbook named Database Spelling.

2. Click the Spelling 🗹 button.

3. The first problem the spell check comes to is in cell A3, which contains the entry, Firstname.
It is a good practice to not use spaces in column headings; however, since this spelling is not in the Spell Check dictionary, it doesn't like it. We want to leave it like it is.

4. Click the Ignore Once button in the dialog box.

5. Continue spell checking the entire worksheet, using your best judgment on corrections.
If you are in a classroom using this book, do not use the Add or AutoCorrect buttons. If you are using this book on your own, feel free to add items to your dictionary and AutoCorrect list.

 # Assessments

Assessment 2.1   Edit and Print a Worksheet

In this exercise, you will edit and print a worksheet. You will also use AutoFill to extend the months through June.

1. Open the workbook named Bonuses.

2. Edit the title in cell A1 to read **Computer Depot Sales Bonuses**.

3. AutoFill the months February through June in cells C3:G3.

4. Edit the label in cell A4 to **Employee**.

5. Change the name Mary Johnson in cell A5 to **Sally Adams**.

6. Edit the label in cell A9 to read **Grand Total**.

7. Print the completed worksheet, save the changes, and close the workbook.

Assessment 2.2   Edit, Spell Check, and Print a Worksheet

In this exercise, you will run spell check and make the appropriate corrections. Then you will print the worksheet.

1. Open the Credit Limits workbook.

2. Use the following guidelines to edit the worksheet:
   - Replace the word Lines with **Limits** in cell A1.
   - Delete the word New in cell F3.
   - Revise the value in cell C7 to **235**.

3. Clear the formatting from cells A11:F11.

4. Click cell A1 to start the spell check at the top of the worksheet.

5. Click the Spelling ![Spelling button] button on the toolbar to check the worksheet for errors. Make the appropriate changes.

6. When you have finished, click the Print ![Print button] button on the Standard toolbar to print the worksheet.

7. Save the changes and close the workbook.

Assessment 2.3   Work with AutoCorrect

In this exercise, you will create several AutoCorrect entries and use them in the worksheet. You will also edit and delete AutoCorrect entries.

1. Click the New ☐ button to start a new workbook.

2. Create the following AutoCorrect entries:

Replace	With
dd	Donella's Deli
cus	Customer
gl	Georgina Liverman
ww	Wolanda Wakowski
lr	LaVerne Reever
bb	Billy Bob Bodacious

3. Follow these guidelines to create the following worksheet:
   - Use the dd AutoCorrect entry to enter the title in cell A1.
   - Enter the remainder text and telephone numbers, using AutoCorrect abbreviations where appropriate. For example, use cus to enter Customer, lr to enter LaVerne Richardson, etc.

	A	B	C
1	Donella's Deli		
2	Phone List		
3			
4	Customer		Phone Number
5	LaVerne Reever		739-6235
6	Wolanda Wakowski		255-0300
7	Billy Bob Bodacious		235-5522
8	Georgina Liverman		639-7832

4. Edit the entry in cell A2 to read **Phone List**.

5. Change **Reever** in cell A5 to Richardson.

6. Replace **Richardson** for Reever in the lr AutoCorrect entry you made earlier.

7. When finished, save the workbook as **Phone Numbers**.

8. Print and close the workbook.

Critical Thinking

Critical Thinking 2.1   On Your Own

Fred Watson is the owner of Fred's Quality Lawn Care service. Fred has provided high-quality lawn care and landscaping services for more than 25 years. Recently, Fred purchased a personal computer with Office 2003 preinstalled. He intends to use his new computer and Office 2003 to improve his customer service, conduct mailings, computerize his billing processes, and increase his profits. Fred recently took an Excel class at a local community college. He wants to use Excel to track his activities and help maximize his profits so he asks you to clean up a job log that he has created. You will also be responsible for updating and maintaining it.

The worksheet assigns a number to each job. It includes the customer name, day of the week, type of work performed, number of hours required to complete the activity, and other important information. Using the Fred's Job Log workbook, examine the worksheet that Fred has created and edit it to match the following illustration. And yes, you better check for spelling errors—you know how Fred types!

	A	B	C	D	E	F
1	Fred's Quality Lawn					
2						
3	Job #	Customer	Day	Work	Hrs. Req.	Amt Billed
4	100	Smythe	Monday	Mowing	2	40
5	101	Jonesby	Monday	General	4	75
6	102	Patrick	Tuesday	Irrigation	4	210
7	102	Benning	Tuesday	Tree Trim	3	140
8	104	Curtis	Wenesday	Irrigation	6	320
9	105	Hacker	Thursday	Mowing	2	40

When you are finished, save your changes and then close the workbook.

Critical Thinking 2.2   On Your Own

Cathy Adams works for Donella's Deli. The deli frequently delivers orders to their customers. Cathy assigns you the task of setting up a worksheet to record mileage, gasoline usage, and other expenses for the deliveries. Cathy provides you with the following information for the worksheet.

Customer	Miles Driven	Gasoline Used (gallons)	Gasoline Expense	Tolls
Billy Bob Bodacious	485	20	$26	$15
LaVerne Richardson	523	19	$25	$16
Georgina Liverman	410	15	$20	$ 9
Wolanda Wakowski	505	24	$31	$15

Use AutoCorrect to enter the name for each customer. Run the spell check and proofread the worksheet. Set the print area to print only the customer names and miles driven. Change the word Gasoline to **Gas** in the column headings. Delete the six AutoCorrect entries you created in Assessment 2.3 and any others you may have created on your own. Save your workbook as **Delivery Expenses**. Print the worksheet and close the file.

Critical Thinking 2.3   On Your Own

Cindy Johnson conducts tests of PC hard drives at Data Storage Incorporated. Cindy has created a worksheet, named Test Results, and asks you to update it for her. Cindy provides you with her notes and asks you to enter the following additional data into the worksheet:

Unit Type	Produced	Passed	Repaired	Destroyed
CX256-256 GB	9500	9200	240	60
CX256-512 GB	8000	7450	350	200
CX512-512 GB	7000	6910	25	65

Cindy also hands you a printed copy of her original worksheet, which she has edited in red ink. She would like you to make the following changes to her data:

- Change the value in cell B5 to **8500**.

- Change the value in cell C5 to **7950**.

- Change the value in cell D5 to **125**.

- Change the value in cell B6 to **7700**.

- Change the value in cell C6 to **7510**.

- Change the value in cell D6 to **125**.

Finally, Cindy wants you to make sure no spelling errors appear in the worksheet. When you finish editing the worksheet, print a copy of it for her. Save the changes and close the workbook.

Critical Thinking 2.4   Web Research

Dominique Aguyo is a senior at West Side High School. She is certain she wants to major in Chemical Engineering when she attends college in the fall. Your task is to help Dominique identify schools that offer Chemical Engineering as a major. Use Internet Explorer and a search engine of your choice to locate at least five universities that offer Chemical Engineering majors. Since you will type the words college and university several times, take the time to create AutoCorrect entries. Record your results in an Excel spreadsheet. Include the school, city and state, size of the student population, and other information you think would help Dominique make her decision. Check your document for spelling errors, and then save it as **CE Colleges** and close it.

Introducing Formulas and Functions

In this lesson, you will learn about creating and modifying formulas. You will also learn about cell references and how they affect formula results when formulas are copied into adjacent cells. In addition, you will be introduced to Excel functions. Excel has hundreds of built-in functions, including AVERAGE, MIN, MAX, and COUNT. Functions are predefined formulas that have been assigned names. These formulas are more advanced than the formulas you have been working with so far, and many are great for analyzing data. And, because a function does a lot of the work for you, using one instead of entering your own formula can save you time and reduce the risk of typing errors in formulas.

Microsoft Office Excel 2003 objectives covered in this lesson

Objective Number	Skill Sets and Skills	Concept Page References	Exercise Page References
XL03S-2-3	Insert and modify formulas	67–68, 72–73	69–72, 74–78
XL03S-2-4	Use statistical, date and time, financial, and logical functions	64, 80–82	64–67, 81, 83–85

Additional learning resources are available at labpub.com/learn/excel03/

Case Study

Stefanie Beloff is the Vice President of Sales and Marketing for Centron Cellular, a nationwide distributor of cellular telephones. Stefanie has instructed her assistant, Cory Richardson, to provide her with a commission report for her sales force and a financial worksheet to help her plan the growth and profitability of the business. Stefanie wants the commission report separated into two regions. She wants to know the monthly sales and commissions for each sales representative as well as the monthly total, average, minimum, and maximum commissions of the representatives in both regions.

The financial worksheet will contain the selling price of the telephones, manufacturing costs, and commission rates of the sales representatives. It will also contain financial information, such as gross and net profit, and let Stefanie perform what-if analyses. Cory will use absolute cell references when setting up this worksheet. These reports would be formidable tasks for most, but Cory is not concerned because he has expert knowledge of Excel 2003. With a little planning and the power of Excel 2003, Cory will produce these worksheets with ease. A portion of each worksheet is shown below.

	A	B	C	D	E
1	Centron Cellular Quarterly Commission Report				
2					
3	Region 1		Sales		
4	Sales Rep	January	February	March	1st Qtr Totals
5	Branston	32,000	32,000	23,000	
6	Barton	15,000	32,000	23,890	
7	Alexander	45,000	8,900	43,000	
8	Alioto	23,000	19,000	10,900	
9	Chin	34,000	34,000	32,000	
10	Total				
11	Average				
12	Maximum				
13	Minimum				

	A	B	C	D	E	F
1	Centron Cellular Financial Report					
2						
3	Projected Units Sold	10,000	50,000	100,000	500,000	1,000,000
4	Revenue					
5	Manufacturing Cost					
6	Marketing					
7	Commissions					
8	Office Expenses					
9	Rent					
10	Consulting Fees					
11						
12	Total Costs					
13	Gross Profit					
14	Net Profit					
15	Gross Profit vs. Revenue					
16						
17	Initial Selling Price	$15		Commission Rate		14%
18	Manufacturing Setup Cost	$30,000		Tax Rate		35%
19	Initial Manufacturing Unit Cost	$10		Office Expenses		0.50%

Working with Formulas and Functions

The power of Excel is most apparent when you use formulas and functions. The most common type of calculation is summing a column or row of numbers. In fact, this calculation is so common that Excel provides the AutoSum function and a toolbar button specifically for this purpose. Many other functions will be introduced later: date and time functions in Lesson 5, Working with Dates and Text Features, and Restructuring Worksheets, financial functions in *Microsoft Office Excel 2003: Quick Course 2*, and logical functions in *Microsoft Office Excel 2003: Quick Course 3*. In addition to AutoSum, you will use many other formulas in Excel. In fact, many worksheets, such as financial reports, require hundreds or even thousands of complex formulas.

Using AutoSum

FROM THE KEYBOARD
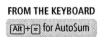 for AutoSum

The AutoSum Σ button on the Standard toolbar automatically sums a column or row of numbers. When you click AutoSum, Excel proposes a range of numbers. You can accept the proposed contiguous range or drag in the worksheet to select a different range. AutoSum first looks above the selected cell for two or more values in the column to total. If it doesn't find any, it looks to the left of the cell for two or more values in the row. When you complete the entry, Excel inserts a SUM function in the worksheet, which adds the numbers in the range. The result then appears in the cell, while the formula itself appears in the Formula bar.

Other Functions Available through the AutoSum Button

The AutoSum drop-down Σ ▾ button displays a function list. Some of the functions on the list include SUM, AVERAGE, MIN, and MAX. Functions are predefined formulas that perform calculations. You will learn how to use these later in this lesson.

 Hands-On 3.1   Use AutoSum

In this exercise, you will use AutoSum to calculate several totals for Centron's commission report, which contains three separate worksheets. Keep in mind that this section introduces functions. You will learn more about formulas as you progress through this lesson.

Calculate a Column Total

1. Open the Quarterly Reports workbook.

2. Click cell B10.

3. Click the AutoSum Σ button.

4. Follow these steps to review the formula and complete the entry:

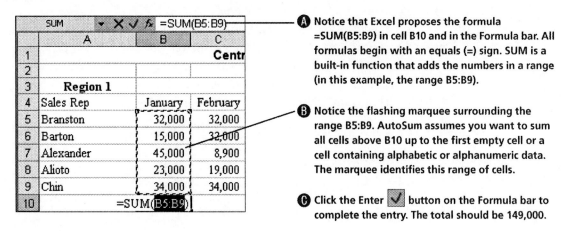

A Notice that Excel proposes the formula =SUM(B5:B9) in cell B10 and in the Formula bar. All formulas begin with an equals (=) sign. SUM is a built-in function that adds the numbers in a range (in this example, the range B5:B9).

B Notice the flashing marquee surrounding the range B5:B9. AutoSum assumes you want to sum all cells above B10 up to the first empty cell or a cell containing alphabetic or alphanumeric data. The marquee identifies this range of cells.

C Click the Enter ☑ button on the Formula bar to complete the entry. The total should be 149,000.

5. Click cell C10.

6. Click AutoSum Σ and complete ☑ the entry.

TIP! *If you know the range to sum contains no blank cells, you can simply double-click the AutoSum button to complete the entry.*

7. Use the preceding technique to calculate the column total in cell D10.

Calculate Several Totals with One Command

8. Select the range B23:D23 (the cells requiring totals in row 23).

9. Click the AutoSum Σ button.
The column totals for cells B23, C23, and D23 should be calculated automatically. AutoSum displays the marquee and requires confirmation only when you are calculating a single total.

Total Rows with AutoSum

10. Click cell E5.

11. Click AutoSum Σ and Excel will propose the range B5:D5, which includes all numbers in row 5.

12. Complete ☑ the entry.
The row sum should total 87,000.

13. Now calculate the row total in cell E6.

Override the Range AutoSum Proposes

14. Click cell E7 then click AutoSum **Σ**.

Notice that Excel assumes you want to sum the cells E5 and E6, above E7. This assumption is incorrect. Excel made this assumption because two cells are above E7, which is enough to make a range. Excel always proposes a column summation if it has a choice between a column and row summation. A blank cell directly above the total cell could change the logic. A good rule of thumb is to always check the position of the marquee to determine if you want to accept or override Excel's decision.

15. Follow these steps to override the proposed range:

Ⓐ Position the mouse pointer in cell B7 and drag to the right to select the range B7:D7.

| 7 | Alexander | | 45,000 | 8,900 | 43,000 | =SUM(B7:D7) |

Ⓑ Notice that the new range B7:D7 appears in the formula.

16. Complete ✔ the entry.

The row sum should total 96,900.

17. Use the preceding technique to calculate the totals in cells E8, E9, and E10.

Calculate Several Row Totals with One Command

You can eliminate the problem of AutoSum proposing the incorrect formula by summing a range of row totals with one command. You also used this technique to sum the column totals.

18. Select the range E18:E23, as shown in the following illustration.

	A	B	C	D	E
16	Region 2				
17	Sales Rep	January	February	March	1st Qtr Totals
18	Richardson	18,000	54,000	36,790	
19	Thomas	12,000	35,900	45,678	
20	Carter	56,000	34,900	72,490	
21	Williams	39,000	54,000	21,000	
22	Jones	23,000	89,000	38,900	
23	Total	148,000	267,800	214,858	

19. Click the AutoSum **Σ** button.

The January, February, and March commissions are summed for each row. Your completed worksheet should match the following illustration.

	A	B	C	D	E
1				Centron Cellular Quarterly Co
2					
3	**Region 1**		**Sales**		
4	Sales Rep	January	February	March	1st Qtr Totals
5	Branston	32,000	32,000	23,000	87,000
6	Barton	15,000	32,000	23,890	70,890
7	Alexander	45,000	8,900	43,000	96,900
8	Alioto	23,000	19,000	10,900	52,900
9	Chin	34,000	34,000	32,000	100,000
10	Total	149,000	125,900	132,790	407,690
11	Average				
12	Maximum				
13	Minimum				
14					
15					
16	Region 2				
17	Sales Rep	January	February	March	1st Qtr Totals
18	Richardson	18,000	54,000	36,790	108,790
19	Thomas	12,000	35,900	45,678	93,578
20	Carter	56,000	34,900	72,490	163,390
21	Williams	39,000	54,000	21,000	114,000
22	Jones	23,000	89,000	38,900	150,900
23	Total	148,000	267,800	214,858	630,658

20. Take a few minutes to examine the formulas in the worksheet.

21. When finished, save the changes and continue with the next topic.

Creating and Modifying Formulas

By now you should be comfortable computing totals with AutoSum. AutoSum is convenient for summing a range of numbers; however, Excel has many other types of formulas.

All formulas, even functions, begin with an equals (=) sign and include one or more arithmetic operators. The result of a formula appears in the cell. The formula itself appears in the formula bar. You create a formula by typing it in the cell (or formula bar) or by pointing and clicking in the cells to be referenced in the formula. When creating or modifying a formula, each cell reference and its corresponding cell's border is displayed in a different color.

Cell and Range References

Formulas derive their power from the use of cell and range references. For example, in the previous exercise you used AutoSum to insert the formula =SUM(B5:B9) in cell B10. Because the range reference (B5:B9) was used in the formula, you could have copied the formula across the row with the fill handle. There are two important benefits to using references in formulas:

- Formulas can be copied to other cells.

- Formula results are automatically recalculated when the data in the referenced cell(s) changes.

Order of Operation

Excel formulas follow the algebraic hierarchy. This means that the formula completes multiplication and division operations before addition and subtraction operations. You can change this sequence by using parentheses. Thus, if you require a formula to perform the addition or subtraction first, you must enclose that portion of the formula in parentheses. For example, the formula = B7/(C4–C2) will first subtract the value in C2 from the value in C4 and then divide the result by B7. Without the parentheses, the formula would first divide the value in B7 by the value in C4 and then subtract the value in C2, which would yield the wrong result.

Arithmetic Operators and Spaces

Formulas include the standard arithmetic operators shown in the following table. Notice that each formula in the table begins with an equals (=) sign. Also, keep in mind that formulas are entered into the cell in which you want the answer to appear.

Parentheses change the order of calculations

QUICK REFERENCE: USING ARITHMETIC OPERATORS IN FORMULAS		
Operator	**Example**	**Comments**
+ (addition)	=B7+B11	Adds the values in B7 and B11
– (subtraction)	=B7-B11	Subtracts the value in B11 from the value in B7
* (multiplication)	=B7*B11	Multiplies the values in B7 and B11
/ (division)	=B7/B11	Divides the value in B7 by the value in B11
^ (exponentiation)	=B7^3	Raises the value in B7 to the third power (B7*B7*B7)
% (percent)	=B7*10%	Multiplies the value in B7 by 10% (.10)
( ) (calculations)	=B7/(C4-C2)	Subtracts the value in C2 from the value in C4 then B7 would be divided by the result

Hands-On 3.2   Use the Keyboard to Enter Formulas

In this exercise, you will enter a formula by typing in a cell. You will calculate the total of the Retail Sales Subtotal and the Business Sales Subtotal.

1. Click the IncExp sheet tab at the bottom of the window.

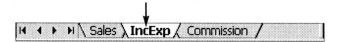

2. Click cell B13.

3. Type **=B7+B12** and tap ⎵Enter⎵ to complete the formula.
   The result should be 297000. This is the summation of the two subtotals in cells B7 and B12.

 Cell references in formulas are not case sensitive so you don't have to capitalize the column reference when typing a formula.

4. Click cell C13.

5. Type **=C7+C12** and complete the entry.
   The result should be 393700.

Point Mode

One potential danger that can occur when typing formulas is accidentally typing the incorrect cell reference. This is easy to do, especially if the worksheet is complex. Point mode can help you avoid this problem. With point mode, you can insert a cell reference in a formula by clicking the desired cell as you are typing the formula. Likewise, you can insert a range reference in a formula by dragging over the desired cells. You will use point mode in the following exercise.

 Hands-On 3.3   Use Point Mode to Enter Formulas

In this exercise, you will create formulas by clicking in the cells to be referenced in the formula. You will calculate the total income for the fourth quarter and calculate the gross profit, net profit, and ratio of gross profit to income.

1. Click cell D13.

2. Type **=**.
   Notice that Excel begins building the formula by entering the equals (=) sign in the Formula bar.

3. Click cell D7.
   Notice that Excel adds the reference D7 to the formula in the Formula bar.

4. Type **+** (try tapping the plus ⊞ key on the numeric keypad).

5. Click cell D12.
   The Formula bar should contain the formula =D7+D12.

6. Complete the entry.
   The total should be 347648.

7. Be sure the highlight is in cell D13 then drag the fill handle one cell to the right.
   The formula is copied to cell E13. The result should be 1038348.

8. Click cell E13 and notice the formula =E7+E12 in the Formula bar.
   The references were updated to reflect the new formula location.

Calculate the Gross Profit

In this portion of the exercise, you will create a formula to find the gross profit, which is calculated by subtracting the total expenses from the total income.

9. If necessary, scroll down until rows 12–26 are visible.

10. Click cell B25.
   Cell B25 will contain a formula to calculate the gross profit. The formula will be =B13–B23, which you will create in the next few steps using point mode.

11. Type **=** and click cell B13.

12. Type **–**, click cell B23, and complete the entry.
   The gross profit should equal -10800. As you can see, Centron Cellular was not profitable in its first month.

13. Copy the formula to the next three cells by dragging the fill handle to the right.

Calculate the Net Profit

You will calculate the net profit in the next few steps. You will use a simplified net profit calculation; that is, the gross profit minus income taxes. You will assume that Centron Cellular will not pay taxes in Q1 and Q2. This is because they lost money in Q1 and their gross profit was only $26,310 in Q2. You will also assume Centron's tax rate will be 15% for Q3 and the YTD. The formula is Net Profit = Gross Profit * (1–Taxrate). For example, if the tax rate is 15%, Centron will keep 85% of their gross profit. So the Net Profit = Gross Profit * 0.85.

14. Click cell B25.
   In the Formula bar, notice that the gross profit is B13-B23. In the next few steps you will attempt to copy the gross profit formula from cell B25 to cell B26.

15. Drag the fill handle down to cell B26.

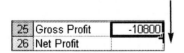

16. Click cell B25 and notice that the gross profit formula in the Formula bar is =B13-B23.

17. Click cell B26 and notice that the net profit formula is =B14-B24.

18. Look at cells B14 and B24 in the worksheet. They are empty.
The formula result is 0 because cells B14 and B24 are empty. This example demonstrates that you must be careful when copying formulas. Excel updated the cell references when you copied the formula. This produced an incorrect result because the formula is referencing incorrect cells.

19. Click Undo 🔄 to reverse the copy procedure.

20. Click cell B26, type the formula **=B25**, and complete the entry.
This simple formula makes cell B26 equal to cell B25.

21. Click cell C26, type the formula **=C25**, and complete the entry.
Once again, the net profit and gross profit should be equal in Q2 because Centron has no tax liability in the second quarter.

22. Click cell D26 and enter the formula **=D25*.85**.
The result should be 62110.35. We are assuming a tax rate of 15% in Q3, so Centron gets to keep 85% of its gross profit.

23. Click cell E26 and enter the formula **=E25*.85**.
The result should be 75293.85. Keep in mind that you can either type the formulas or use point mode and the Formula bar. From this point forward, you will simply be instructed to enter a formula. Use whichever method works best for you.

Calculate the Ratios

Stefanie wants to determine the ratio of gross profit to total income, or GP/TI. This ratio is important in determining the health of a business. It will show how quickly Centron can grow by reinvesting the money it earns. This ratio will show Stefanie the amount of profit Centron will earn from each dollar of product it sells.

24. Click cell B27 and enter the formula **=B25/B13**.
The result should be -0.03636. You will learn about formatting cells in Lesson 4, Formatting Cell Contents.

25. Use the fill handle to copy the formula to cells C27, D27, and E27.
The results should match the following example.

27	Gross Profit vs. Income	-0.03636	0.066828	0.210187	0.08531

26. Click cell C27 and notice the formula =C25/C13.
Once again, Excel updated the cell references when the formula was copied. In this case, it is good that the references were updated because the formula now refers to the correct gross profit and total income in cells C25 and C13.

27. Click the Save 💾 button to save the changes.

Revising Formulas

You can revise any formula by editing it directly in the cell or making the desired editing changes in the Formula bar. You can complete an edited formula by tapping Enter on the keyboard or clicking the Enter button on the Formula bar.

 Hands-On 3.4   Edit Formulas

In this exercise, you will edit values in the ratio formulas for Q3 and YTD.

1. Click in cell D26.

2. Click in the Formula bar at the end of the formula.

3. Tap the Backspace key twice to erase the 85.

4. Type **90** and tap Enter.

5. In cell E26, change the .85 to **.80**.

6. Take a few minutes to look over all the formulas in this worksheet.

7. When finished, save the changes and close the workbook.

Using Cell References in Formulas

A cell reference identifies which cell or range of cells contains the values to use in a formula. Cell references are one of three types: relative, absolute, or mixed. All formulas use relative cell references unless you specifically instruct Excel to use another type. You used relative cell references in the formulas you created for the Quarterly Reports worksheet. As this lesson continues, you will learn about the other two types of formulas.

Relative Cell References

A relative cell reference means the cell is **relative** to the cell that contains the formula. For example, when you create a formula in cell C3 to subtract A3 minus B3, Excel finds the first value is two cells to the left of the formula. The second value is one cell to the left of the formula.

When you copy a formula, the cell references update automatically and refer to new cells relative to the new formula cell. For example, if you copied the formula mentioned in the previous paragraph down to cell C4, the new formula would be A4 minus B4. The first and second values are still relative to the same number of cells to the left of the formula cell.

Absolute Cell References

You have been using relative references thus far in this course. Relative references are convenient because they update automatically when formulas are moved or copied. Moving and copying are covered in Lesson 4, Formatting Cell Contents. In some situations you may not want references updated when a formula is moved or copied. You must use absolute or mixed references in these situations. Absolute references always refer to the same cell, regardless of which cell the formula is moved to or copied to. You can refer to cells on other worksheets or in other workbooks. In *Microsoft Office Excel 2003: Quick Course 2*, you will learn about referring to cells in other locations.

Creating Absolute References

You create absolute references by placing dollar signs in front of the column and row components of the reference: for example, $C$1. You can type the dollar signs as you enter a formula or add them later by editing the formula. The following illustration shows an example of how absolute references are used in formulas.

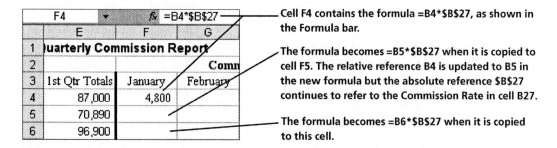

Cell F4 contains the formula =B4*$B$27, as shown in the Formula bar.

The formula becomes =B5*$B$27 when it is copied to cell F5. The relative reference B4 is updated to B5 in the new formula but the absolute reference $B$27 continues to refer to the Commission Rate in cell B27.

The formula becomes =B6*$B$27 when it is copied to this cell.

Mixed References

You can mix relative and absolute references within a reference. For example, the reference $C1 is a combination of an absolute reference to column C and a relative reference to row 1. Mixed references are useful when copying many types of formulas.

Using the F4 Key

You make a reference absolute or mixed by typing dollar signs while entering the reference. You can also click in front of a reference in the Formula bar and use the F4 key to insert the dollar signs. The first time you tap F4, dollar signs are placed in front of both the column and row components of the reference. If you tap F4 again, the dollar sign is removed from the column component, thus creating a mixed reference. If you tap F4 a third time, a dollar sign is placed in front of just the column component.

In this exercise, you will enter formulas using absolute cell references. You will also copy formulas.

Enter a Formula with Relative References

1. Open the workbook named Financial Report.
   Take a few moments to study the workbook. In particular, notice that rows 4 through 15 will contain formulas. Many of the formulas require absolute references, which will refer to the variables in rows 17–19. When this project is completed, you will be able to apply a what-if analysis by quickly changing the Initial Selling Price, Manufacturing Setup Cost, and other variables. The worksheet will be recalculated each time you change a variable.

2. Click cell B4.
   The Revenue in cell B4 is equal to the Projected Units Sold in B3 multiplied by the Initial Selling Price in B17. In the next step, you will enter a formula that uses relative references.

3. Type the formula **=B3*B17** and complete the entry.
   The result should be 150,000.

4. Use the fill handle to copy the formula one cell to the right.
   Cell C4 should display a blank result.

5. Click cell C4 and notice the formula =C3*C17 in the Formula bar.
   Notice that cell C17 is empty. The formula in cell B4 uses relative references so Excel updated the references in cell C4 when you copied the formula. This is incorrect because you want cell C4 to continue to refer to the Initial Selling Price in cell B17. In the next few steps, you will convert the reference in cell B4 to an absolute reference.

6. Click Undo 🔄 to reverse the copy.

Edit and Copy the Formula

7. Click cell B4 and follow these steps to convert the B17 reference to absolute:

   Ⓐ Click in the Formula bar just in front of the B17 reference.

   Ⓑ Tap the F4 key and notice that Excel inserts dollar signs in front of the B and the 17.

8. Complete the entry.
   The result should still be 150,000.

9. Use the fill handle to copy the formula one cell to the right.
   Cell C4 should now have the correct result of 750,000.

10. Click cell C4 and notice the formula =C3*$B$17 in the Formula bar.
    Notice that the relative reference B3 was updated to C3. This is correct because the formula should refer to the Projected Units Sold in cell C3. The absolute reference $B$17, however, continues to refer to the Initial Selling Price in cell B17. This is also correct.

11. Use the fill handle to copy the formula in cell C4 across the row to cells D4, E4, and F4.

Apply a Discount Percentage

This worksheet assumes that the selling price decreases as the number of units sold increases. This is because Stefanie depends on large distributors to sell many cellular phones. Initially, they will sell their phones through small outlets at $15 per unit. However, they will need large distributors if they ever want to sell 1,000,000 units. These distributors will demand large discounts.

12. Click cell D4.

13. Click in the Formula bar just to the right of the formula.
    Notice that Excel changes the color of the cell references and the corresponding worksheet cells. This makes identifying which cells the formula is referencing easy.

14. Type ***80%** to make the formula =D3*$B$17*80%.
    The new formula will reduce the selling price to 80% of the initial selling price.

15. Complete the entry.
    The result should be 1,200,000.

16. Click cell E4 and use the technique in the preceding steps to multiply that formula by **65%**.
    The result should be 4,875,000.

17. Multiply the formula in cell F4 by **50%**.
    The result should equal 7,500,000. Fifty percent is the maximum discount that Centron offers.

Experiment with What-If Analyses

In the next few steps, you will adjust the initial selling price in cell B17. When you do this, the formulas will be recalculated in row 4. Formulas with cell references allow you to apply what-if analyses and determine the outcome of various scenarios.

18. Click cell B17.

19. Type **20** and complete the entry.
    Notice that the numbers in row 4 have been recalculated. The number displayed in cell B4 should be 200,000, the number in cell B5 should be 1,000,000, etc.

20. Change the number in B17 to **10** and watch the numbers recalculate again.
    You can now determine the impact of initial selling price on revenue.

21. Change the number in B17 back to **15**.

Calculate the Manufacturing Costs in Row 5

The manufacturing cost of Centron's cell phone is composed of an initial setup and a per unit cost for each additional phone manufactured. The setup cost is fixed unless Stefanie can find a manufacturer with lower setup fees. The per unit cost decreases as the volume increases. For example, Stefanie can expect much lower per unit manufacturing costs at 1,000,000 units sold than at 10,000 units sold. In the next few steps, you will enter the formulas to calculate this situation.

22. Click cell B5.

23. Type **=$B$18+B3*$B$19** exactly as shown, including the dollar signs.

24. Complete the entry.
    The result should be 130,000.

25. Take a few moments to study the formula you just entered.
Notice that the formula adds the manufacturing setup cost in cell B18 to the product of the units sold in B3 and the initial manufacturing unit cost in B19 (a multiplication operation). The B18 and B19 references are absolute because you will copy the formula across the row in the next few steps. You will want the copied formulas to continue to refer to those cells.

26. Use the fill handle to copy the formula across the row to cells C5 through F5.

27. Take a moment to study the results.
Notice that Centron's manufacturing costs are greater than the revenue when the projected units sold reaches 500,000 in column E. Manufacturing costs should decrease as the projected units sold increases. You will apply the necessary discount percentages in the next few steps.

Apply the Discount Percentages

28. Click cell C5.

29. Click in the formula bar and type ***90%** at the end of the formula.
*The new formula =$B$18+C3*$B$19*90% will reduce the manufacturing cost of each unit to 90% of the initial manufacturing cost.*

30. Complete the entry.
The result should be 480,000.

31. Click cell D5 and use the technique in the preceding steps to multiply that formula by **80%**.
The result should be 830,000.

32. Multiply the formula in cell E5 by **50%** and multiply the formula in cell F5 by **35%**.

Calculate the Marketing Costs

The marketing costs in row 6 will include a $100,000 charge for developing an infomercial to promote Centron's cell phones. Marketing costs also include a component equal to 3% of the revenue. This 3% covers the cost of running an infomercial and developing and mailing product literature.

33. Click cell B6.

34. Enter the formula **=100000+B4*3%** (five zeros).
The result should be 104,500. You didn't have to use absolute references in this formula because you are not referencing the variables in rows 17, 18, and 19. In fact, you want B4 to be a relative reference because you will change it to B5, B6, etc. when you copy the formula across the row.

35. Use the fill handle to copy the formula to cells C6 through F6.

Calculate the Commissions

36. Click cell B7.

37. Enter the formula **=B4*$F$17**.
The result should be 21,000.

38. Use the fill handle to copy the formula to cells C7 through F7.

39. Click in each cell in row 7 and notice the formulas in the Formula bar.
Excel updates the relative reference B4 but leaves the absolute reference $F$17 as it is.

Calculate the Office Expenses

You will calculate the total office expenses with the same type of formula you used to calculate the commissions. Office expenses are calculated as ½% of the revenue. Once again, these are approximations. You will apply what-if analyses with these percentages later in this lesson.

40. Click cell B8.

41. Enter the formula **=B4*$F$19**.

42. Copy the formula across the row to cells C8 through F8.

Enter the Rent and Consulting Fees

Stefanie believes Centron can achieve a unit volume of 100,000 before opening an additional office and warehouse. Their rent payment is $12,000 per year ($1,000 per month). She assumes an office and warehouse will cost $36,000 per year. Likewise, she expects to spend $5,000 on consulting fees when the unit sales are below 100,000 and $15,000 when sales are above 100,000. In the next step, you will enter these numbers into rows 9 and 10 of the worksheet. You do not need formulas in these rows.

43. Enter the following numbers into rows 9 and 10:

	B	C	D	E	F
9 Rent	12,000	12,000	12,000	36,000	36,000
10 Consulting Fees	5,000	5,000	5,000	15,000	15,000

Calculate the Total Costs

44. Click cell B12.

45. Click the AutoSum **Σ** button and notice that Excel proposes the incorrect formula =SUM(B3:B11).
This formula includes the projected units sold and revenue in rows 3 and 4, which is incorrect.

46. Select the range B5:B10 and complete the entry.
The result should be 273,250.

47. Use the fill handle to copy the formula across the row.

Calculate the Gross Profit

The gross profit is calculated as the revenue in row 4 minus the total costs in row 12.

48. Click cell B13 and enter the formula **=B4−B12**.
The result should be -123,250 or (123,250). As you can see, the result shows that Centron won't do well if it sells only 10,000 units.

49. Use the fill handle to copy the formula across the row.

Calculate the Net Profit

*The net profit is equal to the gross profit minus taxes. You will assume a flat tax rate of 35%, as shown in cell F18. The net profit formula is Net Profit = Gross Profit * (1-TaxRate). For example, if the tax rate is 35%, then (1-TaxRate) = 65%. Centron will retain 65% of the profit and 35% will be paid in taxes. You will use absolute references in the net profit formula when referencing the tax rate in cell F18. You will also use parentheses to change the order of the calculations.*

50. Click cell B14 and enter the formula **=B13*(1-$F$18)** exactly as shown.
    The result should be -80,113 or (80,113). This result doesn't make sense because Centron won't pay taxes if it loses money. However, you will leave the result for now. Notice that parentheses were required in the formula. You want Excel to subtract the Tax Rate in F18 from the number 1 first then multiply the result by cell B13. The parentheses instruct Excel to perform the subtraction calculation first.

51. Use the fill handle to copy the formula across the row.

Calculate the Gross Profit versus Revenue

The gross profit versus revenue ratio can help determine the health of a business. You will calculate this ratio in the following steps.

52. Click cell B15 and enter the formula **=B13/B4**.
    The result should be -1 or (1). Notice that you didn't need absolute references in this formula.

53. Use the fill handle to copy the formula across the row.
    Cells C15 through F15 should contain zeros. This is because the ratio returns a number between 0 and 1.

54. Select cells B15:F15 and click the Percent Style **%** button.
    Notice that the numbers have been converted to percentages with one click. You will learn more about formatting numbers in Lesson 4, Formatting Cell Contents.

55. Save the changes to your workbook.
    At this point, your worksheet should match the following example.

	A	B	C	D	E	F
1	**Centron Cellular Financial Report**					
2						
3	Projected Units Sold	10,000	50,000	100,000	500,000	1,000,000
4	Revenue	150,000	750,000	1,200,000	4,875,000	7,500,000
5	Manufacturing Cost	130,000	480,000	830,000	2,530,000	3,530,000
6	Marketing	104,500	122,500	136,000	246,250	325,000
7	Commissions	21,000	105,000	168,000	682,500	1,050,000
8	Office Expenses	750	3,750	6,000	24,375	37,500
9	Rent	12,000	12,000	12,000	36,000	36,000
10	Consulting Fees	5,000	5,000	5,000	15,000	15,000
11						
12	Total Costs	273,250	728,250	1,157,000	3,534,125	4,993,500
13	Gross Profit	(123,250)	21,750	43,000	1,340,875	2,506,500
14	Net Profit	(80,113)	14,138	27,950	871,569	1,629,225
15	Gross Profit vs. Revenue	-82%	3%	4%	28%	33%
16						
17	Initial Selling Price	$15		Commission Rate		14%
18	Manufacturing Setup Cost	$30,000		Tax Rate		35%
19	Initial Manufacturing Unit Cost	$10		Office Expenses		0.50%

Displaying Formulas

Excel normally displays the results of formulas in worksheet cells. However, you may need to display the actual formulas from time to time. Displaying the formulas can be helpful, especially in complex worksheets like the Centron Cellular financial worksheet. Displaying formulas can help you understand how a worksheet functions. It can also be used to "debug" the worksheet and locate potential problems. To display formulas, use the Tools→Options command to open the Options dialog box. The Options dialog box contains a View tab with a Formulas checkbox. Checking the Formulas box will display the formulas in all worksheet cells. The Options dialog box can be used to set numerous other global options.

FROM THE KEYBOARD
Ctrl+` to display or hide formulas

 Hands-On 3.6   Display Formulas and Perform a What-If Analysis

In this exercise, you will display formulas instead of the results in the cells. You will also edit cell contents and view how the change affects the formula result.

1. Choose Tools→Options and make sure the View tab is active.

2. Check the Formulas box and click OK.
   Excel will widen the worksheet columns to display the formulas. If the Formula Auditing toolbar appears, just ignore it. You will learn about this in Microsoft Office Excel 2003: Quick Course 3.

3. Feel free to browse through the worksheet and review the formulas.
   Notice how useful this technique is for understanding how a worksheet functions. It's also useful for locating problems in formulas.

4. Click the Print Preview button.

5. In a multiple page worksheet, the Next and Previous buttons allow you to navigate through the pages.
   Notice that you could print the formulas if desired.

6. Click the Close button to exit Print Preview.

7. Choose Tools→Options from the menu bar.

8. Uncheck the Formulas box and click OK to remove the formulas display.

Perform a What-If Analysis

9. Take a close look at the gross profit in row 13 and the gross profit versus revenue in row 15. Can you draw any conclusions from the numbers? Will Centron Cellular's business be healthy if the projected units sold number is less than 100,000?
   After analyzing the worksheet, Stefanie realizes that Centron will flourish if everything goes right and the company sells 500,000 units or more. However, she realizes this may not happen and she needs to make the business profitable even if only 10,000 units are sold. Her goal is a gross profit versus revenue ratio of 10% at 10,000 units sold and 20% at 50,000 units and above.

10. Click cell B6.
    Look at the Formula bar and notice the $100,000 cost for developing the infomercial. Stefanie realizes the $100,000 infomercial is a bad idea. She decides to cancel the infomercial and concentrate on hiring sales people. You will make the necessary adjustments in the next few steps.

11. Enter the new formula **=B4*2%** in cell B6.

   The result should be 3,000. You reduced the percentage from 3% to 2% because Stefanie is not airing the infomercial.

12. Use the fill handle to copy the formula across the row.

   Notice that eliminating the $100,000 infomercial has a huge impact on gross profit and gross profit versus revenue. This is especially true when the units sold are 100,000 or less. However, the gross profit versus revenue is still less than 20% when the units sold are less than 100,000. Stefanie realizes that the manufacturing setup cost in cell B18 is prohibitively high. Also, the initial manufacturing unit cost of $10 is high, especially when the units sold is small. Stefanie decides to locate another manufacturer to help reduce these costs.

13. Click cell B18.

14. Enter the number **15000** and watch the impact this change has on the worksheet.

   The entire worksheet is recalculated. Pay close attention to the numbers in rows 13 and 15.

15. Now enter the number **10000** and notice the impact this change has.

16. Change the initial manufacturing cost in cell B19 from $10 to **$9**.

   This should have a huge impact on the profitability of the business. As you can see, the worksheet has shown us that keeping manufacturing costs low is extremely important. Also, notice that the worksheet no longer contains negative numbers.

17. Click cell F17 and change the commission rate from 14% to **10%**.

   What type of impact does this change have? Will reducing the commission rate have an impact on the number of units sold? As you can see, many of the variables are interdependent. However, the worksheet shows us the impact of changing one or more variables.

18. Take a few minutes to experiment with the worksheet.

   Feel free to change any of the values in rows 17 through 19.

19. When finished, save the changes and close the workbook.

Using Statistical Functions

Excel has more than 400 built-in functions. Functions are predefined formulas that perform calculations. You construct functions using a set of basic rules known as syntax. Fortunately, most functions use the same or similar syntax. The following illustration defines the syntax of the SUM function. This syntax also applies to the MIN, MAX, AVERAGE, and COUNT functions, which are discussed in the Quick Reference table that follows the illustration.

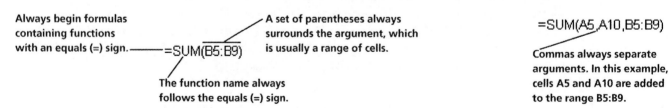

Always begin formulas containing functions with an equals (=) sign.

=SUM(B5:B9)

The function name always follows the equals (=) sign.

A set of parentheses always surrounds the argument, which is usually a range of cells.

=SUM(A5,A10,B5:B9)

Commas always separate arguments. In this example, cells A5 and A10 are added to the range B5:B9.

QUICK REFERENCE: UNDERSTANDING COMMON FUNCTIONS

Function	What it Does	Syntax Example
MIN	Returns the minimum value of a range	=MIN(B5:B9)
MAX	Returns the maximum value of a range	=MAX(B5:B9)
AVERAGE	Returns the average of values in a range	=AVERAGE(B5:B9)
COUNT	Determines the number of cells in a range	=COUNT(B5:B9)

You can count numbers, dates, and formulas.

Entering Functions with the Keyboard

You can type a function and its argument(s) directly in the desired cell. You can also click in the desired cell and type the function in the Formula bar. If you choose to type a function, you can use point mode to assist you in entering the function arguments.

 Hands-On 3.7   Entering Functions with the Keyboard

In this exercise, you will create AutoSum and Average functions.

Do a Little Detective Work and Use AutoSum

1. Open Quarterly Reports and display the Commission sheet.

2. Notice that the worksheet has a January column under the Commissions heading.
   The commissions in column F are calculated with a simple formula.

3. What commission rate is used to calculate sales representatives' commissions?
   You can determine this by clicking a commission cell in column F and reviewing the formula in the Formula bar.

4. Click cell F9, click AutoSum **Σ**, and complete the entry.
   The total commissions for January should equal 22,350.

5. Look at the Formula bar and notice that AutoSum placed the function =SUM(F4:F8) in the cell.
   The SUM function uses the standard function syntax discussed at the beginning of this topic.

Type the AVERAGE Function

6. Click cell F10, type the function **=AVERAGE(F4:F8)**, and complete the entry.
   The result should equal 4,470. This is the average of the values in the range F4:F8. Notice that the syntax is the same as the SUM function syntax except that it uses the function name AVERAGE instead of SUM.

7. Select the SUM and AVERAGE functions in cells F9:F10, and then use the fill handle to copy them to columns G and H.

8. Using the technique outlined above, calculate the average monthly commissions for Region 2 in row 23.

Inserting Functions

The Insert Function f_x button on the Formula bar displays the Insert Function box. The Insert Function box provides access to all built-in functions. The Insert Function box lets you locate a function by typing a description or searching by category. When you locate the desired function and click OK, Excel displays the Function Arguments box. The Function Arguments box helps you enter arguments in functions. The Insert Function box and the Function Arguments box are shown in the following illustrations.

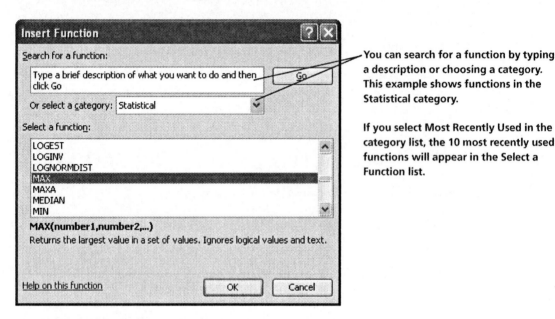

You can search for a function by typing a description or choosing a category. This example shows functions in the Statistical category.

If you select Most Recently Used in the category list, the 10 most recently used functions will appear in the Select a Function list.

The Function Arguments box appears when you choose a function and click OK.

You can type the argument (typically a range) in this box or select the desired range in the worksheet.

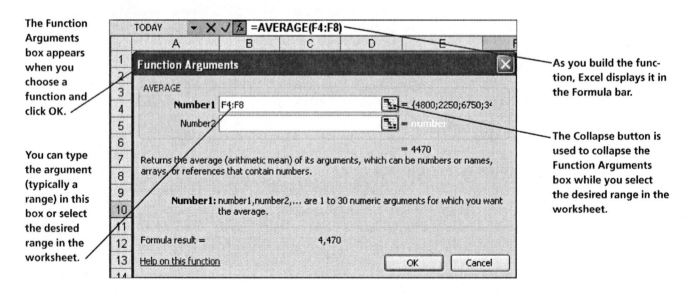

As you build the function, Excel displays it in the Formula bar.

The Collapse button is used to collapse the Function Arguments box while you select the desired range in the worksheet.

In this exercise, you will insert MAX and MIN functions in your worksheet.

Insert the MAX Function

1. Click cell F11 then click the Insert Function fx button on the Formula bar.

2. Follow these steps to choose the MAX function:

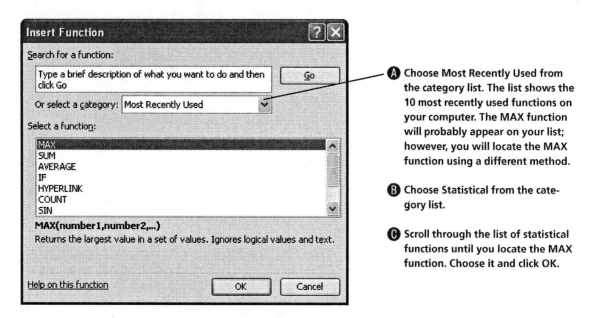

Ⓐ **Choose Most Recently Used from the category list. The list shows the 10 most recently used functions on your computer. The MAX function will probably appear on your list; however, you will locate the MAX function using a different method.**

Ⓑ **Choose Statistical from the category list.**

Ⓒ **Scroll through the list of statistical functions until you locate the MAX function. Choose it and click OK.**

Notice that the MAX(F10) function appears in the Formula bar. This is the correct function but the range F10 is incorrect. You could type the correct range, F4:F8, in the Formula bar or the Function Arguments box. However, you will insert the range by dragging in the worksheet in the following steps.

3. Click this collapse button in the Function Arguments box.

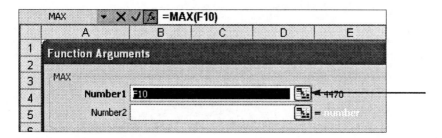

4. Follow these steps to select the appropriate range of cells and restore the Function Arguments box:

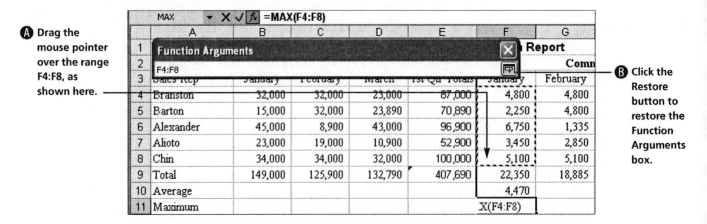

Take a moment to review the formula in the Formula bar. It should be =MAX(F4:F8).

5. Complete the function by clicking OK on the Function Arguments box.
The result should equal 6,750.

6. Use the fill handle to copy the formula to G11 and H11.

7. Using the preceding technique, calculate the maximum monthly commissions for Region 2 in row 24.

Use Point Mode to Enter the MIN Function

8. Click cell F12 and type **=min(**.
If you type a function in lowercase, Excel will convert it to uppercase when you complete the entry. Remember, you must always type the opening parenthesis when entering a function in point mode.

9. Drag the mouse down the range F4:F8.

10. Type a closing parenthesis **)**.
The formula should be =min(F4:F8).

11. Complete the entry.
The result should equal 2,250. In this exercise, you used two different methods to create functions. You can also insert functions by typing them directly into the cell or the Formula bar. In the future, use whichever method you prefer.

12. Use the fill handle to copy the formula to G12 and H12.

13. Using the technique outlined above, calculate the minimum monthly commissions for Region 2 in row 25.

Change the Values

You may be wondering why you used the MIN and MAX functions in this worksheet when it is relatively easy to see which sales representatives had the minimum and maximum commissions. The benefit of using functions becomes apparent when the values change or when you have many rows. The functions automatically recalculate the SUM, AVERAGE, MAX, and MIN when values in the worksheet change.

14. Click cell B5, change the sales number from 15000 to **30000**, and complete the entry. *Notice that the functions in cells F9, F10, and F12 recalculate the sum, average, and minimum.*

15. Click Undo to change the number back to **15000**.

16. For extra practice, feel free to calculate any remaining average, maximum, or minimum functions for the monthly sales in each region.

17. Save the changes but keep the worksheet open.

Using AutoCalculate

The AutoCalculate box on the Status bar lets you view the sum of a range of numbers without actually inserting a SUM function in the worksheet. You can also right-click the AutoCalculate box to see the average, minimum, or maximum of the selected range. The following illustration highlights these concepts.

To use AutoCalculate, first select a range. Excel displays the sum in the AutoCalculate box on the Status bar.

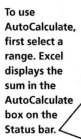

If desired, right-click the AutoCalculate box and choose another function from the context menu.

Hands-On 3.9   Use AutoCalculate

In this exercise, you will experiment with the AutoCalculate feature.

1. Select any range of numbers in your worksheet.

2. Locate the AutoCalculate box on the Status bar. The sum of the selected numbers should be displayed.

3. Right-click the AutoCalculate box and notice that the context menu appears.

4. Choose Average from the context menu to display the average of the numbers in the Auto-Calculate box.

5. Select another range to display the average in the AutoCalculate box.

6. Right-click the AutoCalculate box and choose Sum from the context menu.

7. Save the changes and close the workbook.

Concepts Review

True/False Questions

1. All formulas begin with an equals (=) sign. TRUE FALSE

2. You can double-click the AutoSum button to enter a formula. TRUE FALSE

3. AutoSum can total a range of cells that contains blanks. TRUE FALSE

4. MIN and MAX are examples of functions. TRUE FALSE

5. Function arguments are always surrounded by quotation marks (" "). TRUE FALSE

6. You can calculate several totals with one AutoSum command. TRUE FALSE

7. You can use more than one arithmetic operator in a formula. TRUE FALSE

8. When you type a cell reference in a formula, you must type the column in uppercase. TRUE FALSE

9. You use F5 to make a cell absolute. TRUE FALSE

10. You can use AutoFill to copy a formula. TRUE FALSE

Multiple Choice Questions

1. Which button displays the Function Arguments dialog box?
   a. Function Argument
   b. Insert Function
   c. AutoSum
   d. None of the above

2. Which function calculates the highest value in a selection?
   a. Count
   b. Minimum
   c. Maximum
   d. None of the above

3. Which arithmetic operators can you use in a formula?
   a. +
   b. *
   c. /
   d. All of the above

4. How do you complete a formula?
   a. Tap Enter on the keyboard
   b. Click in a cell outside of the formula cell
   c. Click the Enter button
   d. Both a and c

Skill Builders

Skill Builder 3.1   Use the AUTOSUM Function

In this exercise, you will use AutoSum to compute totals.

1. Open the Benefit Plan workbook.

2. Click cell C10, and then click the AutoSum Σ button.
   Notice that Excel proposes the formula =SUM(C8:C9). Excel proposes this incorrect formula because there are empty cells in the range you are to sum.

3. Drag the mouse pointer over the range C5:C9. The flashing marquee will surround the range C5:C9, as shown to the right.

4. Complete the entry.
   The total should equal 650.

5. Use the techniques described in the preceding steps to compute the totals in cells E10, G10, and I10.

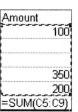

6. Save the changes to your workbook and close it.

Skill Builder 3.2   Create Simple Formulas

In this exercise, you will create formulas using the keyboard as well as the point and click method.

1. Open the Orders And Returns workbook.

2. Click cell B18.

3. Type **=**.

4. Click in cell B4 and type **+**.

5. Click in cell B9 and type **+**.

6. Click in cell B14 and tap Enter.

7. Use AutoFill to copy the formula to cells C18 and D18.

8. Using the techniques described in the preceding steps, create a formula in cell B19 that totals the exchanges from all three stores.

9. Create another formula in cell B20 that totals the returns from all three stores.

10. Use AutoFill to copy the formulas into the appropriate cells.

11. Take a few minutes to examine the formulas in the Formula bar.

12. When finished, save and close the workbook.

Skill Builder 3.3   Use the AVERAGE Function

In this exercise, you will calculate averages by typing the function into the cells. You will also create a simple formula to calculate the differences between two years.

1. Open the workbook named Greeting Cards.

2. Click cell B8.

3. Begin typing the formula **=average(**.

4. Click and drag over the range B3:B6, type **)**, and complete the entry.
   The result should equal 33.

5. Use the fill handle to copy the formula across row 8.

6. Click cell B17.

7. Type the function **=average(b12:b15)** and complete the entry.
   The result should equal 23.5. Once again, you can type the function name and arguments in lowercase and Excel will convert them to uppercase.

8. Use the fill handle to copy the formula across row 17.

9. Click cell B20.

10. Enter the formula **=b7–b16** and complete the entry.
    The result should be 38.

11. Use the fill handle to copy the formula across row 20.

12. Save and close the workbook.

Skill Builder 3.4   Use Absolute References

In this exercise, you will create a worksheet that calculates commissions as Total Sales * Commission Rate. You will change the Commission Rate to see the impact this change has on the Total Sales. You will use an absolute reference when referencing the commission rate.

1. Start a new workbook and set up the following worksheet. Type all numbers as shown.

	A	B	C
1	January Commission Report		
2			
3	Commission Rate		10%
4			
5		Total Sales	Commission
6	John	42000	
7	Ned	38000	
8	Ellen	65000	
9	Helen	18000	
10	Bill	29000	

2. Click cell C6 and enter the formula **=B6*$C$3**.
   The result should be 4200. Cell C3 needs an absolute reference because you will copy the formula down the column and the new formulas must also reference cell C3.

3. Use the fill handle to copy the formula down the column to cells C7 through C10.

4. Click cell C3 and change the percentage to **15%**.
   By this time, you should see the benefit of setting up values first (such as the commission rate) and referencing them in formulas. It allows you to perform what-if analyses. In most cases, you will need absolute references when referencing variables in this manner. Absolute references are necessary whenever you copy a formula that references a variable in a fixed location.

5. Change the commission percentage back to **10%**.

6. Save the workbook as **January Commissions** and close it.

 **Assessments**

Assessment 3.1   Create Simple Formulas

In this exercise, you will develop a worksheet with simple formulas.

1. Start a new workbook.

2. Follow these guidelines to create the following worksheet:
   - Enter all text and number entries.
   - Use formulas in columns D and F to calculate subtotals and new balances. Calculate each subtotal as Previous Balance plus New Charges. Calculate each new balance as Subtotal minus Payment Amount.
   - Use AutoSum to calculate totals for the range B11:F11.

3. Use Print Preview to view your completed worksheet, and then print it.
   Some of the columns in the following illustration have been widened so you can see what to type. Some of your text will not appear because your columns are not wide enough. Don't worry; you will learn how to widen columns in the next lesson.

	A	B	C	D	E	F
1	Donna's Deli - Customer Credit Lines					
2						
3	Customer	Previous Balance	New Charges	Subtotal	Payment Amount	New Balance
4	George Lopke	100	50	150	150	
5	Wanda Watson	230	85	315	315	
6	Alicia Thomas	58	100	158	100	
7	Bill Barton	60	35	95	0	
8	Latisha Robertson	140	80	220	0	
9	Amy Chang	200	150	350	350	
10	Dan Long	90	65	155	100	
11	Total Credit					

4. Save your workbook as **Credit Limits** and close it.

Assessment 3.2   Use AVERAGE, MIN and MAX

In this exercise, you will create a new worksheet that includes text and numbers. You will enter formulas and functions. Finally, you will save, print, and close the workbook.

1. Follow these guidelines to create the worksheet shown under step 2:

   - Enter the text and numbers as shown in the following table.
   - Use the formulas in the following table to calculate the interest charge in column E and the new balance in column F. Use parentheses in the Interest Charge formula to change the order of the calculation. You want Excel to subtract the payments from the beginning balance then multiply the result by 1.5%. Don't type the words Beginning Balance, etc. in the formulas; use the appropriate cell references.

   > Interest Charge = 1.5% * (Beginning Balance – Payments)
   >
   > New Balance = Beginning Balance + Purchases – Payments + Interest Charge

   - Use AutoSum to calculate the totals in row 10.
   - Use the MAX and MIN functions to calculate the highest and lowest numbers in rows 11 and 12.

2. Print the worksheet when you have finished.

	A	B	C	D	E	F
1	Bill's Hot Tubs - Accounts Receivable Report					
2						
3		Beginning			Interest	New
4	Customer	Balance	Purchases	Payments	Charge	Balance
5	Zelton	2000	2300	1000		
6	Ranier	2450	1000	2450		
7	Worthings	5400	2190	3000		
8	Alonzo	3400	500	3400		
9	Barton	100	3400	100		
10	Totals					
11	Highest					
12	Lowest					

3. Save the workbook as **Accounts Receivable** then close it.

Assessment 3.3   Use Absolute References

In this exercise, you will create formulas using absolute references.

1. Open the Jan Price Change Worksheet.

2. Follow these guidelines to complete the following worksheet:

   - Enter the text entries as shown. Enter the numbers in column B and the percentage in cell B3.

   - Use a formula to calculate the discounted price in cell C6. Use an absolute reference when referring to the discount rate in cell B3. Remember that you are calculating the discounted price so your formula must subtract the discount rate in B3 from 1. The generic formula is Discounted Price = Original Price * (1–Discount Rate).

   - Copy the formula in cell C6 down the column.

3. Change the percentage in cell B3 to **10%** and watch the worksheet recalculate.

4. Change the percentage in cell B3 to **15%** and watch the worksheet recalculate.

5. Save and close the workbook.

	A	B	C
1	January Price Change Worksheet		
2			
3	January Discount Rate	15%	
4			
5		Original	Discounted
6	Item	Price	Price
7	Track and Walk Footwear	34.50	
8	Action Aerobics Wear	19.00	
9	Designer Jeans	50.00	
10	Sherman Cowboy Boots	67.95	
11	Jensen Back Packs	34.55	
12	Rain or Shine Coats	45.00	
13	Diamond Back Socks	2.95	
14	Steck-Harman Shirts	19.95	
15	Back Country Jeans	24.95	

Assessment 3.4   Create a Financial Report

In this exercise, you will create a worksheet by entering data, creating formulas, and using absolute references. You will also save, print a section of, and close the workbook.

1. Use these guidelines to create the following financial report:

    ■ Type the headings, labels, and numbers as shown in the following illustration.

    ■ Use formulas to calculate the numbers in rows 6–9. The formulas should multiply the revenue in row 4 by the variables in rows 15–19. For example, the employee costs in cell B6 are calculated as the revenue in cell B4 multiplied by the percentage in cell B15. Use absolute references in these formulas when referring to the variables so you can copy the formulas across the rows. You must use absolute references to get full credit for this assessment!

    ■ Use AutoSum to calculate the total costs in row 10.

    ■ Calculate the gross profit in row 12 as Revenue–Total Costs.

    ■ Calculate the net profit in row 13 as Gross Profit * (1–Tax Rate). Once again, use absolute references when referring to the tax rate in cell B19.

2. Apply what-if analysis to your worksheet by changing the percentages in rows 15–19. Make sure the report recalculates correctly when the values are changed.

3. Print the worksheet.

4. Set a print area for the range A1:E13 and print just that area.

5. Save the workbook as **2004 Projected Income** then close it.

	A	B	C	D	E
1	2004 Projected Income				
2					
3		Q1	Q2	Q3	Q4
4	Revenue	345000	390000	480000	500000
5					
6	Employee Costs				
7	Capital Expenditures				
8	Manufacturing				
9	Marketing & Sales				
10	Total Costs				
11					
12	Gross Profit				
13	Net Profit				
14					
15	Employee Costs	18%			
16	Capital Expenditures	22%			
17	Manufacturing	17%			
18	Marketing & Sales	16%			
19	Tax Rate	40%			

Critical Thinking

Critical Thinking 3.1   On Your Own

Stacy Sanchez is a freelance graphic designer and Website developer. She specializes in helping small businesses establish corporate identities. Stacy's computer skills allow her to transform creative ideas into stunning visual designs that win over customers and earn her lucrative contracts. She wants to focus her energies on customers who produce the highest rates of return. Stacy asks you to set up a worksheet to help her analyze her customer base. She provides you with the following initial data:

Company Type	Number of Projects	Total Billings	Total Hours
Consulting	14	$25,900	235
Technology	23	$81,420	679
Manufacturing	6	$16,200	171
Food Service	8	$15,200	179
Retail Sales	12	$30,480	311

Calculate the total number of projects, total billings, and total hours. Calculate the average billings per project for each company type. Calculate the average hourly billing rate for each company type. Use the AVERAGE function to calculate the average total billings and the average hourly rate for all company types combined. Save the workbook as **Customer Analysis**.

Critical Thinking 3.2   On Your Own

Marina Berkman is a manager in the research department of CTA, Inc. CTA prepares studies on consumer buying habits for companies and organizations throughout the United States. Marina asks you to prepare a worksheet to record the food-buying habits of consumers. The worksheet must record on a daily basis the amount of money spent on groceries, breakfast out, lunch out, dinner out, and snacks out. The worksheet should record the information for one person over an entire week. Enter the data you desire and include totals of all expenditures for each day of the week and expenditure type. Use the AVERAGE function to calculate the average daily expenditures for each expenditure type. Save your workbook as **Buying Habits**.

Critical Thinking 3.3   On Your Own

John Jennings is the founder and owner of Crispy Crust Pizza. He started Crispy Crust in a stall in his local shopping mall and has had so much success that he wants to expand by opening three more stores over the next 18 months. John thinks he can increase the profit margin of Crispy Crust by opening these stores. He figures that the combined sales volume of the four stores will allow him to lower his food and packaging costs. In addition, he will be able to allocate his advertising, management, and overhead costs over the four stores. John hires you to prepare an income and expense worksheet.

Use Excel to set up a financial worksheet for Crispy Crust Pizza using the following information for the original (first) store. In addition, calculate the pretax profit and the profit versus revenue for the original store. The pretax profit is simply the revenue minus total costs and expenses.

First Store Forecasted Revenue	$200,000
Food costs as a percentage of revenue	12%
Packaging costs as a percentage of revenue	2%
Advertising expenses as a percentage of revenue	14%
Management expenses as a percentage of revenue	13%
Overhead costs as a percentage of revenue	22%

Set up a variable section in the worksheet with the following initial percentages:

- Per store sales increase: 10%
- Food cost savings: 4%
- Packaging savings: 16%
- Advertising savings: 38%
- Management cost savings: 23%
- Overhead savings: 12%

Calculate the revenue, expenses, pretax profit, and pretax profit versus revenue for two, three, and four stores. Assume the revenue and expenses are equal to the original store revenue and expenses multiplied by the number of stores. Adjust the revenue and expenses using percentages in the variable section. For example, imagine John has three stores. The revenue would be equal to the revenue of the original store multiplied by three (three stores), plus an additional 10% of the revenue for the three stores. John assumes the additional revenue will result from crossover traffic between stores. Use absolute references in formulas that refer to the variable section of the worksheet. Copy formulas whenever possible and use absolute references where necessary so you can copy formulas. Save your completed worksheet as **Pizza Report**.

Critical Thinking 3.4   Web Research

David is a junior in high school with a 4.0 GPA and a bright future. David's parents want him to attend Harvard University. They ask you to set up an expense worksheet for a four-year stay at Harvard. Use Internet Explorer and a search engine of your choice to locate Harvard University's Website. Determine the approximate tuition, fees, room, board, and personal expenses for a full-time undergraduate student. The purpose of your worksheet is to determine the out-of-pocket expenses for which David's parents must plan. Use the following payment sources for the first year of attendance:

■ David's contribution (first year): $3,500

■ Scholarship contribution (first year): $12,500

■ Student loans (first year): $5,700

Use formulas to calculate the amount that David's parents will need to contribute for each of the next four years. Use formulas to adjust the expenses and payment sources for David's sophomore, junior, and senior years as shown below.

■ Tuition, fees, room, board, and personal expenses: 5% annual increase

■ David's contribution: 15% annual increase

■ Scholarships: No change ($12,500 each year)

■ Student loans: 10% annual increase

When you have finished, save your workbook as **Harvard Costs**.

LESSON 4

Formatting Cell Contents

In this lesson, you will use several types of formatting features to enhance your worksheets. You will also learn powerful tools and techniques, such as AutoFormat and the Format Painter. By the end of this lesson, you will have developed the skills necessary to produce professional-looking worksheets.

IN THIS LESSON

Microsoft Office Excel 2003 and Microsoft Office Excel 2003 Expert objectives covered in this lesson

Objective Number	Skill Sets and Skills	Concept Page References	Exercise Page References
XL03S-3-1	Apply and modify cell formats	100–103, 106–108, 111, 113, 116	101–102, 104–105, 107–109, 111–112, 114–117
XL03S-3-3	Modify row and column formats	105	106
XL03S-5-2	Insert, delete, and move cells	117–118, 120, 124	118–119, 121–125
XL03E-5-3	Modify Excel default settings	109	110

Additional learning resources are available at labpub.com/learn/excel03/

Case Study

Beverly Richardson is the owner of her own beauty salon, Beverly's Secret—A House of Beauty. Beverly knows the importance of keeping accurate financial records. When she first opened the salon, she knew very little about Excel; however, she knew enough to keep track of important data such as her income, expenses, and commissions. She now wants to expand her salon and must seek financing. Although she has the data entered in a worksheet, she realizes it is difficult to read. After taking an Excel class, she now feels ready to format her worksheet into a professional-looking document. Beverly will use Excel's powerful and easy-to-use formatting tools to produce her worksheets.

	A	B	C	D	E
1	Beverly's Secret - A House of Beauty - Income Statement				
2					
3	Income				
4	Services	First Quarter	Second Quarter	Third Quarter	Fourth Quarter
5	Hair	21,500	28,900	32,750	42,000
6	Nails	8,000	16,000	25,000	56,000
7	Subtotal				
8	Other Income				
9	Gratuities	4,625	6,981	8,750	15,000
10	Products	1,500	500	500	500
11	Subtotal				
12	Total Income				
13					
14	Expenses				
15	Description	First Quarter	Second Quarter	Third Quarter	Fourth Quarter
16	Lease Payment	3,000	3,000	3,000	3,000
17	Utilities	400	310	290	380
18	Advertising	800	800	800	800
19	Salaries	12,000	12,000	14,000	14,000
20	Beauty Supplies	15,000	15,500	18,000	24,000
21	Equipment	6,000	2,000	1,000	500
22	Total Expenses				

Applying Number Formats

Excel lets you format numbers in a variety of ways. Number formats change the way numbers are displayed though they do not change the actual numbers. Once a number formatting has been applied to a cell, it remains with the cell—even if the contents are deleted. The following Quick Reference table describes the most common number formats.

QUICK REFERENCE: UNDERSTANDING NUMBER FORMATS

Number Format	Description
General	Numbers are formatted with the General Style by default. It does not apply any special formats to the numbers.
Comma	The Comma Style format inserts a comma between every third digit in the number. It also inserts a decimal point and two decimal places, which can be removed if desired.
Currency	The Currency Style format is the same as the Comma format except it adds a dollar ($) sign in front of the number.
Percent	A percent (%) sign is inserted to the right of the number in the Percent Style. The percentage is calculated by multiplying the number by 100.

 NOTE! *In Lesson 2, Expanding on the Basics, you learned that the Currency Style is applied automatically when you type an entry beginning with a dollar sign.*

The following table provides several examples of formatted numbers.

Number Entered	Format	How the Number Is Displayed
1000.98	General	1000.98
1000.98	Comma with 0 decimal places	1,001
	Comma with 2 decimal places	1,000.98
1000.98	Currency with 0 decimal places	$1,001
	Currency with 2 decimal places	$1,000.98
.5366	Percent with 0 decimal places	54%
	Percent with 2 decimal places	53.66%

Using the Formatting Toolbar

The Formatting toolbar contains buttons that allow you to apply the Currency, Comma, and Percent number styles—the most common number styles. The Formatting toolbar also includes buttons that allow you to increase and decrease the number of displayed decimals. The following illustration shows the number formatting buttons on the Formatting toolbar.

FROM THE KEYBOARD

Ctrl+Shift+$ for Currency Style
Ctrl+Shift+% for Percent Style
Ctrl+Shift+! for Comma Style
Ctrl+Shift+~ for General Style

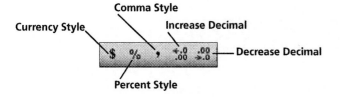

The Increase Decimal and Decrease Decimal buttons change the number of displayed decimal places. For example, if you enter the number 100.37 and decrease the decimals to 0, the number would display as 100. The actual number remains as 100.37, however, and is used in any calculations that reference the cell.

 Hands-On 4.1   Format Numbers

In this exercise, you will use the Currency, Comma, and Percent buttons on the Formatting toolbar. You will also decrease decimals on selected cells.

Apply the Currency Style

1. Open the Inc Statement workbook.

2. Select the four subtotals in row 7 (be careful not to drag the fill handle).
   Remember, the fill handle is not used to select cells. It is only used to copy cells and expand series. Be sure your pointer has the thick white cross shape whenever you wish to select cells.

3. Click the Currency Style $ button and notice that the cells are formatted as shown here.

7	Subtotal	29500	44900	57750	98000

Notice that Currency Style adds a dollar sign in front of the number, a comma after every third digit, and a decimal point with two decimal places.

TIP! *After you format a numeric cell, number signs (#####) may fill the cell. This means the column is not wide enough to fit the entry. You will learn how to widen columns later in this lesson.*

Decrease the Decimals

4. Be sure the four cells you just formatted are selected.

5. Click the Decrease Decimal 🔲 button twice to remove the displayed decimals.
   Notice that the dollar signs ($) are positioned on the left side of the cells. You will adjust this alignment later in the lesson.

6. Select the subtotal and total income cells in rows 11 and 12, as shown here.

| 11 | Subtotal | 6125 | 7481 | 9250 | 15500 |
| 12 | Total Income | 35625 | 52381 | 67000 | 113500 |

7. Click the Currency Style 🔲 button then decrease the decimals to 0.

8. Format the numbers in rows 22, 24, and 25 as Currency Style with 0 decimals.
   Remember to use the ⎡Ctrl⎤ key to select noncontiguous ranges.

Apply the Comma Style

9. Select the numbers in rows 5 and 6.

10. Click the Comma Style 🔲 button then decrease the decimals to 0.
    Notice that Comma Style looks like Currency Style without the dollar sign. Also notice that the numbers now line up with the currency formatted numbers in the subtotal row.

11. Format the numbers in the ranges B9:E10 and B16:E21 as Comma Style with 0 decimals.

Apply the Percent Style

12. Select the numbers in the last row of the worksheet.

13. Click the Percent Style 🔲 button.
    The numbers should be formatted as Percent Style with 0 decimal places. Percent Style does not display decimals. You can always use the Increase Decimal button to display decimals.

14. Click the Increase Decimal 🔲 button twice to display two decimal places.

15. Click Undo 🔲 twice to remove the decimals.

Using the Format Cells Dialog Box

FROM THE KEYBOARD
⎡Ctrl⎤+⎡1⎤ to display Format Cells dialog box

The Format→Cells command displays the Format Cells dialog box. This dialog box provides built-in number styles not available on the Formatting toolbar. You can format numbers with one of these built-in styles by displaying the dialog box and choosing the desired style. You can even create your own customized number styles to suit your needs. The Format Cells command is also available from a context menu when you right-click on a selected cell.

Using Accounting and Currency Styles

The dollar signs in the Inc Statement worksheet currently have a fixed format. In other words, they are fixed on the left side of the cells. You can use the Format Cells dialog box to choose a number style that floats the dollar signs next to the numbers. Two number styles apply currency symbols (such as dollar signs) to numbers.

■ Accounting Style—The Currency Style **$** button on the Formatting toolbar actually applies the Accounting Style to numbers. This lines up dollar signs and decimal points in columns. The dollar signs appear fixed at the left edges of the cells.

■ Currency Style—The Currency Style floats dollar signs next to the numbers. Like the Accounting Style, the Currency Style displays a comma after every third digit as well as decimals and a decimal point.

Displaying Negative Numbers

Negative numbers can be displayed either preceded by a minus sign or surrounded by parentheses. You can also display negative numbers in red. The Currency option and Number option in the Format Cells dialog box let you choose the format for negative numbers.

The negative numbers format you choose affects the alignment of numbers in cells. If the format displays negative numbers in parentheses, a small space equal to the width of a closing parenthesis appears on the right edge of cells containing positive numbers. Excel does this so the decimal points are aligned in columns containing both positive and negative numbers. These concepts are described in the following illustrations.

	A	B	C
15	Description	First Quarter	Second Quar
16	Lease Payment	3000	3000
17	Utilities	400	310
18	Advertising	800	800
19	Salaries	12000	12000
20	Beauty Supplies	15000	15500
21	Equipment	6000	2000
22	Total Expenses	37200	33610
23			
24	Gross Profit	(1575)	18771
25	Net Profit	(1575)	18771

Notice the slight space between positive numbers and the right edge of the cells.

Notice that the closing parenthesis of negative numbers is flush with the right edge of the cell.

	A	B	C
15	Description	First Quarter	Second Quar
16	Lease Payment	3000.00	3000.00
17	Utilities	400.00	310.00
18	Advertising	800.00	800.00
19	Salaries	12000.00	12000.00
20	Beauty Supplies	15000.00	15500.00
21	Equipment	6000.00	2000.00
22	Total Expenses	37200.00	33610.00
23			
24	Gross Profit	(1575.00)	18771.00
25	Net Profit	(1575.00)	18771.00

When the numbers are displayed with decimals, this slight shift of the positive numbers lines up the decimal points of both the positive and negative numbers.

Hands-On 4.2   Use the Format Cells Dialog Box

In this exercise, you will use the Format Cells dialog box to apply a currency format, set the number of decimal places, and set the negative number style.

1. Select the numbers with the Currency Style in row 7.

2. Choose Format→Cells from the menu bar.

3. Be sure the Number tab at the top of the dialog box is active.

4. Notice that the Custom option is chosen at the bottom of the Category list.
   The Custom option is chosen because you modified the number style when you decreased the decimal places in the previous exercises, creating a custom number format.

5. Follow these steps to format the numbers with floating dollar signs:

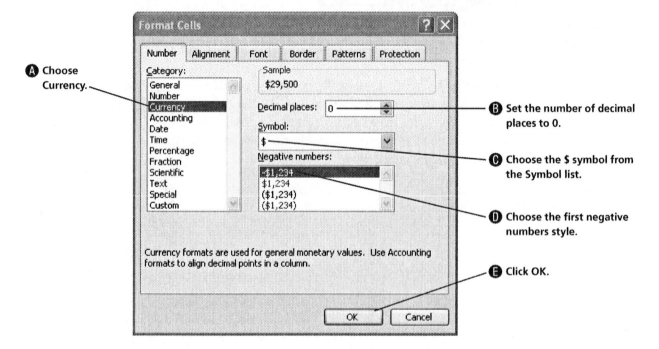

Notice that the dollar signs are now floating just in front of the numbers. Also notice that the numbers are now shifted slightly to the right and no longer line up with the numbers above them. This is because of the Negative Numbers option you set. You will adjust the Negative Numbers option in the next step.

Adjust the Negative Numbers Option

6. Be sure cells B7:E7 are still selected.

7. Right-click on the selected cell and choose Format→Cells from the context menu.

8. Notice the various Negative Numbers formats.
   Red formats display negative numbers in red. Also notice that some of the formats are surrounded by parentheses. Formats with parentheses cause positive numbers to shift to the left, as discussed earlier.

9. Choose the third Negative Numbers format ($1,234) and click OK.

   The numbers should now be right aligned with the numbers in rows 5 and 6. The numbers in rows 5 and 6 are formatted with Comma Style. Comma Style displays negative numbers in parentheses. This is why the positive numbers in rows 5 and 6 are shifted slightly to the left.

Check Out the Accounting Style

10. Be sure cells B7:E7 are still selected and choose Format→Cells from the menu bar.

11. Choose the Accounting category.

12. Be sure the symbol type is set to $ and the decimal places are set to 0.

13. Click OK and notice that the dollar signs once again have a fixed placement on the left side of the cells.

    This was how the numbers were formatted when you first clicked the Currency Style button in Hands-On 4.1. The Currency Style button actually applies the Accounting Style to numbers.

14. Click Undo 🔄 to restore the Currency Style.

Explore other Number Styles

15. Choose Format→Cells from the menu bar.

16. Take a few minutes to browse the various number styles in the Category list.

    Feel free to choose a style and read the description that appears at the bottom of the dialog box.

17. Click the Cancel button when you have finished exploring.

    You will continue to format numbers in a later exercise.

18. Save the changes to the document and continue with the next topic.

Arranging Data

Many features for arranging data in a worksheet are available. For example, you can align the data within cells left, right, or center; indent data within a cell; change the column width; and merge cells. You will explore these features in this section. In Lesson 5, Working with Dates and Text Features, and Restructuring Worksheets, you will learn about other ways to arrange worksheets, including wrapping text, inserting extra lines, and setting vertical alignment.

Aligning Entries

The Align Left 🔳, Center 🔳, and Align Right 🔳 buttons on the Formatting toolbar let you align entries within cells. By default, text entries are left aligned and number entries are right aligned. To change alignment, select the cell(s) and click the desired alignment button.

Hands-On 4.3   Align Text Entries and Widen Columns

In this exercise, you will align the entries in row 4 and widen columns A, C, D, and E.

1. Select the range B4:E4.

> First Quarter | Second Quart | Third Quarter | Fourth Quart

2. Click the Center ☰ button on the Formatting toolbar.
   Each entry in the range should appear centered within its cell.

Adjust Column Widths

In the next few steps, you will adjust the width of columns A, C, D and E. A complete discussion of adjusting column widths is presented in Lesson 5, Working with Dates and Text Features, and Restructuring Worksheets.

3. Follow these steps to adjust the width of column A:

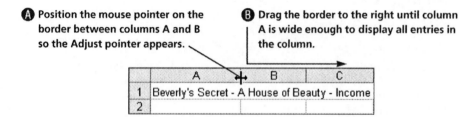

Ⓐ Position the mouse pointer on the border between columns A and B so the Adjust pointer appears.

Ⓑ Drag the border to the right until column A is wide enough to display all entries in the column.

4. Widen column C until the word Quarter is completely visible in cell C4.
   You will need to drag the border between the column headings C and D.

5. Widen columns D and E until the word Quarter is completely visible within cells D4 and E4.

6. Click the Save 💾 button to save the changes.

Merging and Splitting Cells

Excel's merge cells option lets you combine cells. Merged cells behave as one large cell and you can merge cells both vertically and horizontally. The merge cells option is useful if you want to place a large block of text (such as a paragraph) in the worksheet. You merge cells by selecting the desired cells, issuing the Format→Cells command, and checking the Merge Cells box on the Alignment tab. Likewise, you can split a merged cell into the original cell configuration by removing the checkmark from the Merge Cells box.

The Merge and Center ⊞ button merges selected cells and changes the alignment of the merged cell to center. This technique is often used to center a heading across columns. You split a merged and centered cell the same way you split any other merged cell. The following illustration shows a heading centered across columns A–E.

	A	B	C	D	E
2					
3			Income		
4	Services	First Quarter	Second Quarter	Third Quarter	Fourth Quarter

The Income heading is centered above columns A–E.

 ## Hands-On 4.4   Use Merge and Center

In this exercise you will center a heading across a range of cells.

Merge Cells

1. Select the range A3:E3.
   Notice that this range includes the heading you wish to center (Income) and the range of cells you wish to center this heading across (A3:E3). Make sure that you do not select the entire row. If you accidentally choose the row 3 header and merge and center, the Income heading will be centered over all 256 columns of the spreadsheet!

	A	B	C	D	E
2					
3	Income				

2. Click the Merge and Center 🔲 button (near the middle of the Formatting toolbar).
   Notice that the cells have been merged and the Center button on the Formatting toolbar is highlighted.

3. Click the Align Left 🔲 button and the entry will move to the left side of the merged cell.

4. Click the Center 🔲 button to center the entry in the merged cell.

Split Cells

5. Choose Format→Cells from the menu bar.

6. Click the Alignment tab on the Format Cells dialog box.
   Notice that the Merge Cells box is checked. It is checked whenever cells are merged.

7. Remove the checkmark from the Merge Cells box and click OK.

 TIP! *Another way to split a merged cell, once it is selected, is to simply click the Merge and Center button again.*

8. Click anywhere to deselect the cells and notice that they are no longer merged.
   You use this technique to split merged cells.

9. Click Undo 🔲 to restore the merged cell.

10. Select the range A1:E1.

11. Click the Merge and Center 🔲 button to center the title.

Indenting Entries

The Increase Indent 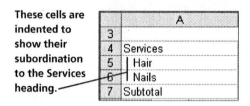 button and Decrease Indent button on the Formatting toolbar let you offset entries from the left edges of cells. Indenting is useful for conveying the hierarchy of entries. The following illustration shows indented cells.

These cells are indented to show their subordination to the Services heading.

 ## Hands-On 4.5   Indent Entries

In this exercise, you will use the Increase Indent and Decrease Indent buttons on the Formatting toolbar.

1. Click cell A5.

2. Click the Increase Indent button twice.
   Notice that the entry is indented slightly each time you click the button.

3. Click the Decrease Indent button once.

4. Click cell A6 and increase the indent once.

5. Select cells A9 and A10.

6. Press and hold down the [Ctrl] key while selecting the range A16:A21.
   The range A16:A21 contains the Lease Payment, Utilities, etc. subheadings below the Description heading in column A.

7. Increase the indent once.

Formatting Data

FROM THE KEYBOARD
[Ctrl]+[B] for Bold
[Ctrl]+[U] for Underline
[Ctrl]+[I] for Italic

In Excel and other Office programs, you can format text by changing the font, font size, and color. You can also apply various font enhancements, including bold, italic, and underline. To format cells, select the desired cells and apply formats using buttons on the Formatting toolbar. You can also choose formats and set a new default font from the General tab of the Tools→Options dialog box.

You can choose a font from the font list or click the drop-down button and type the desired font name to rapidly scroll the list.

Font size

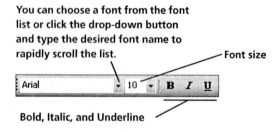

Bold, Italic, and Underline

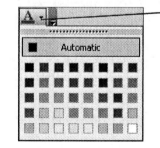

The Font Color button is on the right edge of the Formatting toolbar. The color palette appears when you click the drop-down button. Once you choose a color, it is displayed on the button. From that point forward, you can rapidly apply the color by clicking the button.

Hands-On 4.6   Format Entries

In this exercise, you will change the style, size, and color of the title in cell A1 and the column headings in row 4. You will also add bold and italic enhancements to various cells.

Enhancing Data

1. Click cell A1.

2. Click the drop-down arrow on the Font Size 10 button on the Formatting toolbar and choose 14.

3. Click the Bold **B** button on the Formatting toolbar.
   Notice that the entire title is formatted. Once again, the entire title belongs to cell A1, even though it also appears that it is in columns B–E.

4. Click the drop-down button on the Font Color **A** button located at the right edge of the Formatting toolbar.

5. Choose one of the dark blue shades from the color palette.
   Notice that the color you chose is now displayed on the Font Color button. You can now apply the same color to other cells by selecting the cells and clicking the button.

6. Select cell A3, and then click the Font Color **A** button and notice that the same color is applied to the Income cell.

7. Increase the font size of the Income cell to 12 and apply bold formatting.

8. Select the First Quarter through Fourth Quarter headings in row 4.

9. Apply bold formatting then click the Italic *I* button.
   Bold and italic enhancements are made to the headings in row 4.

10. Choose a different color from the Font Color **A** button's color palette.
    Later in this lesson, you will use the Format Painter to copy font and number formats to other cells.

11. Widen column C and E so the entire entries are displayed.

12. Save the changes and close the workbook.

Setting a New Default Font

When you start Excel, a blank workbook with default characteristics based on a template called Normal.dot opens. The Normal.dot template contains a set of defaults that every new workbook inherits. The font style and size are just two of those defaults. The default font is Arial with a point size of 10. You can change the font defaults using the General page in the Tools→Options dialog box. Once you change the defaults, every new workbook you create will use the new characteristics.

Hands-On 4.7   Set Default Font

In this exercise, you will change the default font style and size then start a new workbook and view the changes. You will then reset the defaults to the Excel standards.

1. Click the New button.
   Notice that the font style is Arial and the font size is 10.

2. Click Tools→Options in the menu bar.

3. Follow these steps to change the default font:

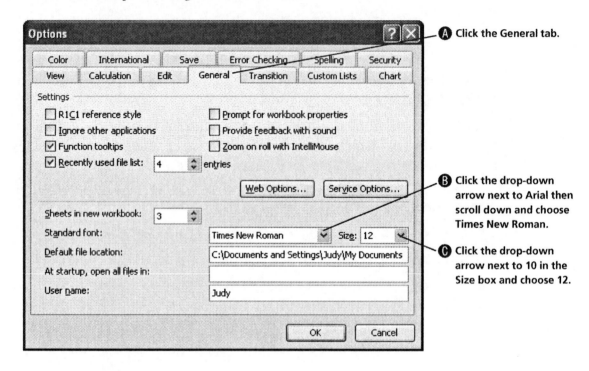

Ⓐ Click the General tab.

Ⓑ Click the drop-down arrow next to Arial then scroll down and choose Times New Roman.

Ⓒ Click the drop-down arrow next to 10 in the Size box and choose 12.

Spend a few minutes looking at the options.

If you don't recognize an option, click the Question mark ❓ *button in the upper-right corner of the dialog box then click the option. A context menu will appear with a description of the option. Click anywhere on the screen to hide the context menu.*

4. Click OK to close the dialog box, and then click OK in the message box that appears then close and restart Excel.
   Notice that the font settings for the new worksheet are Times New Roman, 12pt.

5. Using the same technique described in step 3, change the default font back to Arial, 10pt.

6. Close and restart Excel.
   The font should now be Arial, 10pt.

Using the Format Painter

 Copying text and number formats is easy with the Format Painter. It copies all formats from the source cell to the target cell(s). The Format Painter saves time and helps create consistent formatting throughout a workbook.

QUICK REFERENCE: USING THE FORMAT PAINTER

To copy...	Procedure
formats to one other cell or range	■ Click the cell that has the format(s) you wish to copy. ■ Click the Format Painter once. ■ Select the cell or range to which you want to copy the format(s).
formats to multiple locations	■ Click the cell that has the format(s) you wish to copy. ■ Double-click the Format Painter. ■ Select the cells or ranges to which you want to copy the format(s) then click the Format Painter one time to turn it off.

TIP! *Since you double-clicked the Format Painter, you can copy the formats to multiple ranges and even scroll through the workbook to reach the desired location(s).*

 Hands-On 4.8 **Use the Format Painter**

In this exercise, you will use the Format Painter to copy formats already applied to other cells.

Copy Text Formats

1. Open Inc Statement, and then click cell A3 (the merged cell with the Income heading).

2. Click the Format Painter button on the Standard toolbar and notice that a paintbrush icon is now attached to the mouse pointer.

3. Click cell A14.
   The text formats should be copied to that heading. The paintbrush icon vanishes because you clicked the Format Painter button just once in the previous step. If you want to copy formats to multiple locations, you must double-click the Format Painter.

4. Click cell B4.
   This cell should contain the heading First Quarter.

5. Click the Format Painter button.

6. Select the range B15:E15 to copy the formats to those cells, as shown here.

15	Description	First Quarter	Second Quarter	Third Quarter	Fourth Quarter

Copy Number Formats

7. Select the cells containing numbers in row 7 and apply bold formatting to them.

   Notice that the numbers in row 7 have the Currency Style with floating dollar signs. In the next few steps, you will use the Format Painter to copy both the number and the text formats to the numbers in rows 11, 12, and 22–25. Notice that these rows currently have fixed dollar signs on the left edges of the cells.

8. Click cell B7.

9. Double-click the Format Painter ✏ button.

10. Select the range B11:E12 to copy the formats to those cells, as shown here.

| 11 | Subtotal | $ | 6,125 | $ | 7,481 | $ | 9,250 | $ | 15,500 |
| 12 | Total Income | $ | 35,625 | $ | 52,381 | $ | 67,000 | $ | 113,500 |

11. Select the range B22:E26 to copy the formats to those cells, as shown here.

22	Total Expenses	$	37,200	$	33,610	$	37,090	$	42,680
23									
24	Gross Profiit	$	(1,575)	$	18,771	$	29,910	$	70,820
25	Net Profit	$	(1,575)	$	18,771	$	25,424	$	53,115
26	Gross Profit vs. Income	$	(0)	$	0	$	0	$	1

12. Click the Format Painter ✏ button to turn it off.

    You had to turn off the Format Painter this time because you double-clicked it initially. Also, notice that the Percent number style in row 26 has been removed. In this example, you wanted to copy the Bold text style to row 26 but not the Currency Style. Keep in mind that the Format Painter copies both text formats and number formats.

13. Select the numbers in row 26 and use the Percent Style % button to reapply the Percent Style.

14. Save the changes and continue with the next topic.

Applying Borders and Colors

The Borders ⊞ ▾ button on the Formatting toolbar lets you add borders to cell edges. When you click the Borders drop-down button, a tear-off palette of popular border styles appears. You apply a style to all selected cells by choosing it from the palette. You can also use the Format→Cells command to display the Format Cells dialog box. The Borders tab on the dialog box lets you apply additional border combinations. You can also choose a color from the dialog box to apply colored borders.

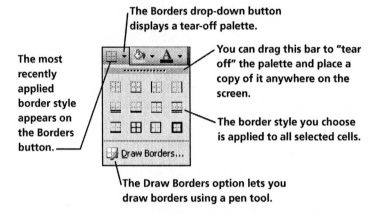

The Borders drop-down button displays a tear-off palette.

You can drag this bar to "tear off" the palette and place a copy of it anywhere on the screen.

The border style you choose is applied to all selected cells.

The most recently applied border style appears on the Borders button.

The Draw Borders option lets you draw borders using a pen tool.

Applying Fill Colors and Patterns

The Fill Color ⬛ button on the Formatting toolbar lets you fill the background of selected cells with color. Just like with the Borders drop-down button, when you click the Fill Color drop-down button, a tear-off palette of colors appears. You can apply a color to all selected cells by choosing it from the palette. The fill color is independent of the font color used to format text and numbers. The Format Cells dialog box has a Patterns tab that lets you apply fill colors and a variety of patterns.

Hands-On 4.9   Add Borders and Fill Colors

In this exercise, you will apply borders, fill colors, and font colors to selected cells.

Format the Title Cells

1. Select cell A1 and click the Borders drop-down button.

2. Follow these steps to put a thick border around the range:

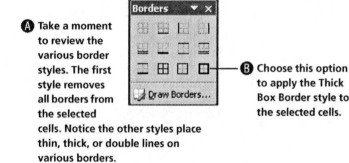

Ⓐ Take a moment to review the various border styles. The first style removes all borders from the selected cells. Notice the other styles place thin, thick, or double lines on various borders.

Ⓑ Choose this option to apply the Thick Box Border style to the selected cells.

3. Be sure cell A1 is selected, click the Fill Color drop-down button, and choose the Light Yellow color.

4. Be sure cell A1 is still selected and click the Font Color drop-down button.

5. Choose a color that will provide adequate contrast to the yellow color you chose in step 4.

6. Click outside the range so you can see the formats.
   The lines on the top and left sides of the range may not be visible because the column and row headings are blocking them. Notice that the fill color fills the range while the font color only affects the text. Also notice that the colors and line style you chose now appear on the buttons. If desired, you could apply these same colors and line style to other selected cells by clicking the buttons.

7. Click the Print Preview button.

8. If necessary, click anywhere on the worksheet to zoom in.
   The lines on the top and left sides of the range should now be visible.

9. Click the Close button to exit from Print Preview.

Add Additional Borders

10. Select the range A3:E12.
This range includes all cells in the Income section.

11. Click the Borders drop-down ⏷ button.

12. Choose the All Borders ⊞ style (second style on the bottom row).

13. Click the Print Preview 🔍 button.
Having a border on every cell is too busy. You will change the borders in the next few steps.

14. Close the Print Preview window.

Remove Borders and Reapply Borders

15. Be sure the range A3:E12 is still selected.

16. Click the Borders drop-down ⏷ button and choose the Thick Box Border ⬚ style.

17. Click the Print Preview 🔍 button.
A thick border has been applied to the outside of the range but the inside borders have not been removed.

18. Close the Print Preview window.

19. Click the Borders drop-down ⏷ button and choose the No Borders ⬚ style (first button).
The borders are removed from the selected range.

20. Click the Borders drop-down ⏷ button and choose the Thick Box Border ⬚ style.

21. Click the Print Preview 🔍 button, review the results, and close Print Preview.

Apply Fill Color and Font Color

22. Select the range A14:E22.
This range includes all cells containing entries in rows 14–22.

23. Click the Fill Color 🪣 button (not the drop-down button) to apply the same fill color that was applied to the large merged cell at the top of the worksheet.

24. Click the Font Color 🅰 button (not the drop-down button) to apply the same font color that was applied to the merged cell.

25. Apply the same fill color and font color to the range A24:E26.

26. Save the changes to your workbook.

27. Take a few moments to experiment with borders and fill colors. Use Undo to reverse any changes you make.

Applying AutoFormats

The Format→AutoFormat command lets you choose from a variety of predefined formats. These predefined formats automatically apply number formats, borders, fill colors, font colors, font sizes, and other formats to a selected range. You may be pleasantly surprised when you see the professional formatting that AutoFormat can apply.

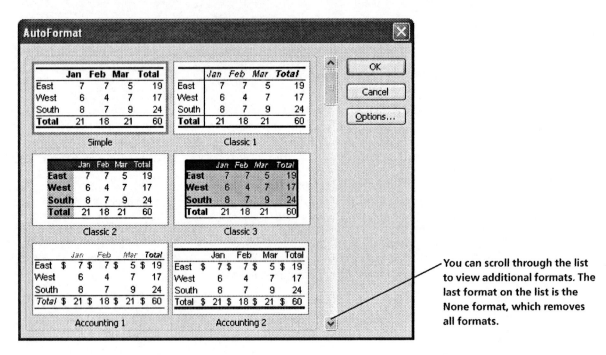

The Auto-Format box shows previews of the available formats.

You can scroll through the list to view additional formats. The last format on the list is the None format, which removes all formats.

 NOTE! *You must select a range before applying an AutoFormat.*

Hands-On 4.10   Use AutoFormat

In this exercise, you will apply built-in AutoFormats to separate sections of the worksheet.

Use AutoFormat on Region 1

1. Select the range A3:E12, which includes all cells for Income.

2. Choose Format→AutoFormat from the menu bar.

3. Click the Options button just below the Cancel button on the right side of the box.
   Checkboxes will appear at the bottom of the dialog box. These boxes determine the formats that Auto-Format will apply. Be sure all of the boxes are checked.

4. Scroll through the list and notice the various formats.

5. Scroll to the top of the list and choose Classic 3 style.

6. Click OK and click anywhere outside the selection to view the formats.
   Notice that AutoFormat detected rows containing formulas and formatted those rows differently than the body and header rows. AutoFormat makes formatting decisions by determining which rows and columns have text, numbers, and formulas.

Remove the AutoFormats

7. Select the range A3:E12 (the range you just formatted).

8. Choose Format→AutoFormat from the menu bar.

9. Scroll to the bottom of the list and choose the None format.

10. Click OK and notice that the formats are gone.
    You can use this technique to remove all formats, whether or not they were applied with AutoFormat.

Format Other Ranges

11. Click the Undo 🔄 button to restore the AutoFormats to Income.

12. Select the range A14:E26, which includes all cells for the remainder of the worksheet.

13. Choose Format→AutoFormat and apply the Classic 3 style.

14. Click in the large merged cell at the top of the worksheet.

15. Apply the Classic 3 AutoFormat to the merged cell.

16. Increase the font size of the merged cell to 12 and remove the italics.

17. Save the changes to your workbook.

18. Feel free to experiment with AutoFormat then continue with the next topic.

Moving and Copying Cells and Formats

The Cut, Copy, and Paste options are available in all Office 2003 applications. With Cut, Copy, and Paste you can move and copy cells within a worksheet, between worksheets, and between different Office applications. For example, you can use the Copy command to copy a range from one worksheet and the Paste command to paste the range into another worksheet or even a Word document. Cut, Copy, and Paste are most efficient for moving or copying cells a long distance within a worksheet or between worksheets. Cut, Copy, and Paste are easy to use if you remember the following concepts.

■ Select the cells before issuing a Cut or Copy command.

■ Position the highlight at the desired location before issuing the Paste command. This is important because the range you paste will overwrite any cells in the paste area.

When you move or copy you can use the formats from the source selection or those of the destination cells. You access these options through the Paste Options button. Additional paste commands are available when using the Paste Special feature, which is discussed in *Microsoft Office Excel 2003: Quick Course 3.*

QUICK REFERENCE: USING CUT, COPY, AND PASTE

Command	Description	Procedure
Cut	The Cut command removes entries from selected cells and places them on the Office Clipboard.	Click the Cut [✄] button or press [Ctrl]+[X]
Copy	The Copy command also places entries on the Office Clipboard but leaves a copy of the entries in the original cells.	Click the Copy [⧉] button or press [Ctrl]+[C]
Paste	The Paste command pastes entries from the Office Clipboard to worksheet cells beginning at the highlight location.	Click the Paste [📋] button or press [Ctrl]+[V]

Using the Office Clipboard

The Office Clipboard lets you collect items from any Office document or program and paste them into any other Office document. For example, you can collect a paragraph from a Word document, data from an Excel worksheet, and a graphic from a PowerPoint slide then paste them all into a Word document. The Office Clipboard can also be used within an application like Excel to collect several items and paste them as desired. The Office Clipboard can hold up to 24 items.

How It Works

You can place items on the Office Clipboard using the standard Cut and Copy commands; however, the Office Clipboard must first be displayed in the task pane. You display the Office Clipboard with the Edit→Office Clipboard command. Once the Office Clipboard is displayed, choose an item (or all items) and paste it into your worksheet.

 Hands-On 4.11   Use Copy and Paste

In this exercise, you will copy and paste data using the buttons on the Standard toolbar.

Copy the Commission Formula to Cell E5

1. Click the Commissions sheet tab then click cell C5 and take a moment to review the formula in the Formula bar.

Your objective is to copy this formula to the February and March commission columns. You can't do this with the fill handle because the cells are not adjacent to cell C5.

2. Click the Copy [⧉] button on the Standard toolbar.
   Notice the flashing marquee in cell C5. This indicates that the sales commission formula has been copied and is ready to be pasted.

3. Click cell E5 then click the Paste ![icon] button.

The formula will be pasted and will calculate the commission as 4800. The flashing marquee in cell C5 indicates that the formula is still available for pasting into other cells.

4. Notice the Paste Options ![icon] button next to the pasted cell in the worksheet.

The Paste Options button provides several options that allow you to control how the data is pasted. You will learn more about Paste Options later in this lesson.

Paste to a Range

5. Select the range E6:E9.

6. Click the Paste ![icon] button on the Standard toolbar (not the Paste Options button) to paste the formula.

You can always copy a single cell and paste it into a range of cells.

7. Select the range G5:G9 and paste the formula into those cells.

You can continue to paste as long as the marquee is flashing.

8. Tap [Esc] on the keyboard to dismiss the marquee and the Paste Options button.

You can always turn off the flashing marquee with the [Esc] key.

9. Click any cell you just pasted into and review the formula in the Formula bar.

Excel updates the references in the formulas to reflect the new formula locations.

Paste to Multiple Ranges

10. Click cell C10 and click the Copy ![icon] button.

11. Click cell E10.

12. Press and hold the [Ctrl] key and click cell G10.

Both cells E10 and G10 should be selected.

13. Click the Paste ![icon] button to paste the formula into both cells.

14. Use the preceding techniques to copy the AVERAGE, MAX, and MIN functions from column C to columns E and G. You can copy the functions one at a time or select all three functions and copy and paste them simultaneously.

Copy the Heading Rows

15. Select all entries in rows 3 and 4 by dragging over the cells.

16. Click the Copy ![icon] button then click cell A16.

In the next step, you will paste the range to cell A16. You should always paste a large range like this to one cell (A16 in this case). Excel will use cell A16 as the starting location of the pasted range. Be careful when using this technique because Excel will overwrite any cells in the pasted range.

17. Click the Paste ![icon] button.

In the next exercise, you will continue to copy cells with the drag and drop technique. For now, continue with the editing task in the next step.

18. Change the heading in cell A16 from First Quarter to **Second Quarter**.

Using Drag and Drop for Selected Cells

The Drag and Drop feature produces the same results as Cut, Copy, and Paste. Drag and Drop is efficient when you are moving or copying entries a short distance within the same worksheet. If the original location and destination are both visible in the current window, Drag and Drop is generally easier than Cut, Copy, and Paste. With Drag and Drop, you select the cells you wish to move or copy and then release the mouse button. Then you point to the edge of the selected range and drag the range to the desired destination. If you wish to copy rather than move the range, hold down the Ctrl key while dragging and dropping. Be sure to release the mouse button before releasing the Ctrl key or Excel will move instead of copy the selection.

Using Drag and Drop for Entire Worksheets

An entire worksheet can be moved or copied to a new worksheet or even a different workbook by dragging the sheet tab. The same rules apply for moving and copying worksheets as they do for selected cells. That is, hold down the Ctrl key to copy (instead of move) the sheet. When moving or copying to a different workbook, you must have both workbooks opened.

Using the Right-Drag Method

Right-dragging is a variation of the Drag and Drop technique. Many beginners have trouble with Drag and Drop because they have difficulty controlling the mouse. This difficulty is compounded when they are trying to copy entries using Drag and Drop because copying requires the Ctrl key to be held while the selected range is dragged. With the Right-Drag method, the right mouse button is used when dragging. When the right mouse button is released at the destination, a context menu appears. This menu gives you several options including Move, Copy, and Cancel. This provides more control because you do not have to use the Ctrl key when copying and you can cancel the move or copy if you change your mind about the command.

Hands-On 4.12   Use Drag and Drop

In this exercise, you will use Drag and Drop to move and copy text and formulas in the worksheet. You will also use the right-drag method to copy within the same worksheet and to a new worksheet.

1. Follow these steps to drag and drop text entries:

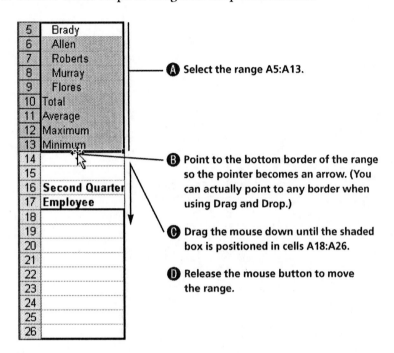

A Select the range A5:A13.

B Point to the bottom border of the range so the pointer becomes an arrow. (You can actually point to any border when using Drag and Drop.)

C Drag the mouse down until the shaded box is positioned in cells A18:A26.

D Release the mouse button to move the range.

Notice how easy it was to move the cells with Drag and Drop. You should use Drag and Drop if the move is a short distance within the same worksheet.

Unfortunately, you should have copied the cells instead of moving them. You will correct this in the next few steps.

2. Click the Undo 🔄 button to reverse the move.

Use Right-Drag

3. Be sure the range A5:A13 is still selected.

4. Position the mouse pointer on the bottom edge of the selected range and press and hold down the **right** mouse button.

5. Drag the mouse down until the range A18:A26 is highlighted, as in step 1, then release the right mouse button.
   A context menu will appear with several choices.

6. Choose Copy Here from the context menu.
   The selected range will be copied.

Use Right-Drag to Copy

7. Follow these steps to copy the January sales data and commission formulas to the Second Quarter:

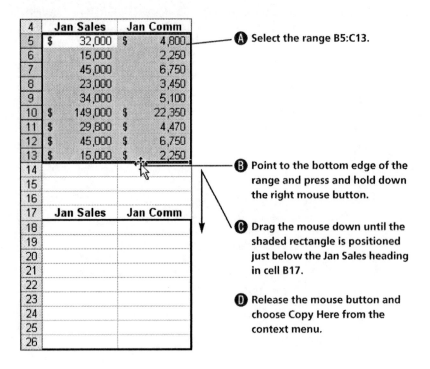

4	Jan Sales	Jan Comm
5	$ 32,000	$ 4,800
6	15,000	2,250
7	45,000	6,750
8	23,000	3,450
9	34,000	5,100
10	$ 149,000	$ 22,350
11	$ 29,800	$ 4,470
12	$ 45,000	$ 6,750
13	$ 15,000	$ 2,250
14		
15		
16		
17	Jan Sales	Jan Comm
18		
19		
20		
21		
22		
23		
24		
25		
26		

A Select the range B5:C13.

B Point to the bottom edge of the range and press and hold down the right mouse button.

C Drag the mouse down until the shaded rectangle is positioned just below the Jan Sales heading in cell B17.

D Release the mouse button and choose Copy Here from the context menu.

8. Use the right-drag method to copy the February and March sales data and commission formulas to the Second Quarter.
You need to delete the cells for all the sales values for the second quarter. Don't delete the formula though.

9. Follow these steps to select the sales value for January, February, and March:

	B	C	D	E	F	G
17	Jan Sales	Jan Comm	Feb Sales	Feb Comm	Mar Sales	Mar Comm
18	$ 32,000	$ 4,800	$ 32,000	$ 4,800	$ 23,000	$ 3,450
19	15,000	2,250	32,000	$ 4,800	23,890	$ 3,584
20	45,000	6,750	8,900	$ 1,335	43,000	$ 6,450
21	23,000	3,450	19,000	$ 2,850	10,900	$ 1,635
22	34,000	5,100	34,000	$ 5,100	32,000	$ 4,800
23	$ 149,000	$ 22,350	$ 125,900	$ 18,885	$ 132,790	$ 19,919
24	$ 29,800	$ 4,470	$ 25,180	$ 3,777	$ 26,558	$ 3,984
25	$ 45,000	$ 6,750	$ 34,000	$ 5,100	$ 43,000	$ 6,450
26	$ 15,000	$ 2,250	$ 8,900	$ 1,335	$ 10,900	$ 1,635

A Select the range B18:B26.

B Hold down the Ctrl key and select the ranges D18:D26 and F18:F26.

10. Tap the [Delete] key to delete the data.

11. Save the changes to your workbook.

    Notice that all the commission cells now display dashes and dollar signs. The formulas have not been deleted; they are empty until data is entered in the sales columns.

    At this point, your worksheet should match the following illustration.

	A	B	C	D	E	F	G
1			Commission Report				
2							
3	First Quarter						
4	Employee	Jan Sales	Jan Comm	Feb Sales	Feb Comm	Mar Sales	Mar Comm
5	Brady	$ 32,000	$ 4,800	$ 32,000	$ 4,800	$ 23,000	$ 3,450
6	Allen	15,000	2,250	32,000	$ 4,800	23,890	$ 3,584
7	Roberts	45,000	6,750	8,900	$ 1,335	43,000	$ 6,450
8	Murray	23,000	3,450	19,000	$ 2,850	10,900	$ 1,635
9	Flores	34,000	5,100	34,000	$ 5,100	32,000	$ 4,800
10	Total	$ 149,000	$ 22,350	$ 125,900	$ 18,885	$ 132,790	$ 19,919
11	Average	$ 29,800	$ 4,470	$ 25,180	$ 3,777	$ 26,558	$ 3,984
12	Maximum	$ 45,000	$ 6,750	$ 34,000	$ 5,100	$ 43,000	$ 6,450
13	Minimum	$ 15,000	$ 2,250	$ 8,900	$ 1,335	$ 10,900	$ 1,635
14							
15							
16	Second Quarter						
17	Employee	Jan Sales	Jan Comm	Feb Sales	Feb Comm	Mar Sales	Mar Comm
18	Brady		$ -		$ -		$ -
19	Allen		-		$ -		$ -
20	Roberts		-		$ -		$ -
21	Murray		-		$ -		$ -
22	Flores		-		$ -		$ -
23	Total	$ -		$ -		$ -	
24	Average	$ -		$ -		$ -	
25	Maximum	$ -		$ -		$ -	
26	Minimum	$ -		$ -		$ -	

Use Drag and Drop to Copy Worksheets

12. Follow these steps to copy the entire Commission worksheet to a new worksheet:

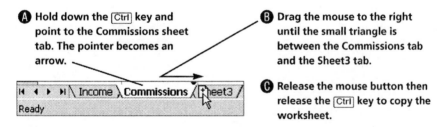

Ⓐ Hold down the [Ctrl] key and point to the Commissions sheet tab. The pointer becomes an arrow.

Ⓑ Drag the mouse to the right until the small triangle is between the Commissions tab and the Sheet3 tab.

Ⓒ Release the mouse button then release the [Ctrl] key to copy the worksheet.

Notice the new sheet tab named Commissions(2). In Microsoft Office Excel 2003: Quick Course 2, *you will learn how to rename the sheet tabs to make them easier to recognize.*

Move Data to Other Worksheets

Beverly decides she would like to have the commissions for each quarter on separate worksheets. When you move or copy a portion of a worksheet, you cannot use Drag and Drop; you must use Cut, Copy, and Paste.

13. Click the Commissions sheet tab.

14. Select the range A16:G26.
    You will copy this range to a new worksheet using the buttons on the Standard toolbar since Drag and Drop will not work here.

15. Click the Copy ⬚ button.

16. Click the Sheet3 tab at the bottom of the worksheet.

17. Be sure cell A1 is selected then click the Paste ⬚ button.

18. Widen columns A–G.
    You will learn about other ways to work with columns in Lesson 5, Working with Dates and Text Features, and Restructuring Worksheets.

19. Change the word Second to **Third** in cell A1.

20. Save the changes but don't close the workbook.

Using Paste Options

The Paste Options button contains additional formatting options, such as whether to use formatting from the source data or the destination cells, and whether to keep the same column width as the source.

Hands-On 4.13 Use Paste Options

In this exercise, you will copy and paste selected cells into a new worksheet and use the Keep Source Column Widths paste option.

1. Click the Commissions sheet, select the range A1:G11, and click the Copy button.

2. Click the Sheet4 tab and click the Paste button.
   Notice that the columns in the destination sheet are not wide enough. The Paste Options box at the bottom-right corner of the pasted selection will make changing the columns in this new sheet very easy.

3. Follow these steps to format the new sheet with the column widths from the Commissions sheet:

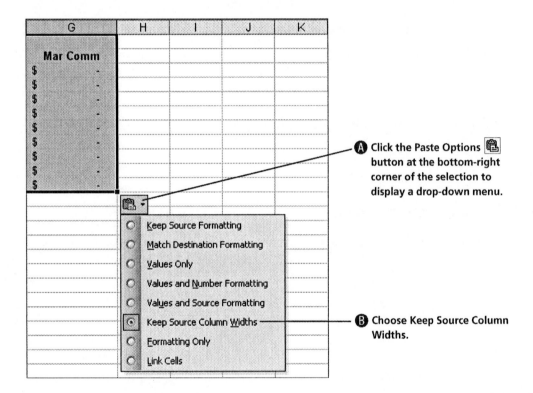

A Click the Paste Options button at the bottom-right corner of the selection to display a drop-down menu.

B Choose Keep Source Column Widths.

Notice that the column widths expanded automatically to match the column widths of the Commissions sheet.

4. Save the changes and close the workbook.

Concepts Review

True/False Questions

1. Accounting Style lines up dollar signs at the left edges of cells.   TRUE   FALSE

2. The Merge and Center button can only be used with numbers.   TRUE   FALSE

3. The Comma Style inserts a dollar sign in front of numbers.   TRUE   FALSE

4. The Format Painter copies text formats but not number formats.   TRUE   FALSE

5. You can change a font's style and size but not its color.   TRUE   FALSE

6. You cannot move or copy cells to other worksheets.   TRUE   FALSE

7. You can keep the column widths from the source sheet when pasting into a new worksheet.   TRUE   FALSE

8. Formulas cannot be copied.   TRUE   FALSE

9. With one click on the Format Painter, you can copy formats into multiple locations.   TRUE   FALSE

10. Titles can be centered across multiple columns.   TRUE   FALSE

Multiple Choice Questions

1. Which keystroke combination copies selected cells?
   a. Shift + C
   b. Ctrl + X
   c. Alt + V
   d. Ctrl + C

2. Which command displays a dialog box that can be used to set the default Font?
   a. Format→Cells
   b. Edit→Cells
   c. Tools→Options
   d. None of the above

3. What must you do before clicking the Merge and Center button?
   a. Click the cell that contains the entry you wish to center.
   b. Select the cells you wish to center the entry across, making sure the entry is included in the selection.
   c. Select the entire row that contains the entry you wish to center.
   d. None of the above

4. How is the dollar sign positioned with the Accounting Style?
   a. It floats to the immediate left of the number.
   b. It is fixed on the left edge of the cell.
   c. The Accounting Style does not place a dollar sign in front of numbers.
   d. The answer depends on whether the number has a decimal point.

Skill Builders

Skill Builder 4.1   Use Copy and Paste

In this exercise, you will use toolbar buttons to copy and paste data. You will also create and copy AutoSum and Average formulas.

1. Open the workbook named Postcards.

2. Select the range A1:E9.

3. Click the Copy ![button] button.

4. Click cell A11 then click the Paste ![button] button.

5. Change the month January in the pasted heading to **February**.

6. Use the AutoSum **Σ** button to compute the total in cell B8.

7. Click cell B9 and enter the function **=AVERAGE(B4:B7)**.

8. Use the Copy ![button] and the Paste ![button] buttons to copy the AutoSum and AVERAGE formulas across rows 8, 9, 18, and 19.
   You can safely copy these formulas to rows 8, 9, 18, and 19 because the range in the functions includes four cells (B4:B7). The formulas in rows 8 and 18 require SUM functions that add the values in four cells. The formulas in rows 9 and 19 require AVERAGE functions that average four cells.

9. Save and close the workbook.

	A	B	C	D	E
1	Client Greetings, Inc. - January				
2					
3	Division	Christmas	Easter	Valentines	Thanksgiving
4	Boston	27	43	14	34
5	Los Angeles	31	47	19	39
6	New York	35	51	24	44
7	St. Louis	39	55	29	49
8	Total	132	196	86	166
9	Average	33	49	21.5	41.5
10					
11	Client Greetings, Inc. - February				
12					
13	Division	Christmas	Easter	Valentines	Thanksgiving
14	Boston	27	43	14	34
15	Los Angeles	31	47	19	39
16	New York	35	51	24	44
17	St. Louis	39	55	29	49
18	Total	132	196	86	166
19	Average	33	49	21.5	41.5

Skill Builder 4.2   Use AutoFormat

In this exercise, you will use AutoFormat to apply an attractive format to the worksheet.

1. Open the workbook named Corporate Budget.

2. Select the range A1:E16, which includes all active cells in the worksheet.

3. Choose Format→AutoFormat from the menu bar.

4. Scroll through the list, choose the List 2 style, and click OK.

5. Click outside the range and review the format.
   The format looks good, although it may be nice to have a slightly larger title.

6. Click cell A1 and increase the size to 12.
   You can always add your own formatting enhancements to a worksheet after AutoFormat has been used.

7. Save and close the workbook.

Skill Builder 4.3   Copy Data and Formats

In this exercise, you will use toolbar buttons to copy and paste data, use the Merge and Center command, and use the Format Painter to copy formats.

1. Open the workbook named Expense Tracking.

2. Select the range A3:E4, which includes all text entries in rows 3 and 4.

3. Click the Copy 🖺 button.

4. Click cell A10 and then paste the entries above the second set of numbers.
   Notice that the text formats (including the coloring) were copied with the text.

5. Click cell A17 and then paste the entries above the third set of numbers.

6. Change the headings to **February** and **March** for the second and third sets of numbers.

7. Select the range A5:A8, which includes the names and Totals heading in Column A.

8. Copy the selection and then paste it to cells A12 and A19.

9. Copy the formulas from the totals row below the first set of numbers.

10. Paste the formulas the second and third sets of numbers.

11. Select the range A1:E1 then click the Merge and Center [⊞] button.
    Notice that the title is now centered across the range of cells.

12. Using the same procedure, center the January entry in cell A3 across columns A through E.

13. Select cell A3 and double-click the Format Painter [🖌] button.

14. Copy the formatting to cells A10 and A17, and then turn off the Format Painter.

15. Save and close the workbook.

Assessments

Assessment 4.1   Format and Enhance a Worksheet

In this exercise, you will format and add enhancements to text and numbers, change the column width, and center the title across worksheet columns. You will also print the worksheet.

1. Open the workbook named Accounts Rec.

2. Follow these guidelines to format the following worksheet:
   - Indent the customer names in column A.
   - Format rows 5, 10, 11, and 12 in Currency Style with 0 decimals using the toolbar buttons.

   Notice that when you use the Currency Style button the dollar signs stay on the left edges of the cells. If you choose the Currency format from the Format Cells dialog box, the dollar signs float next to the numbers.

   - Format rows 6–9 as Comma with 0 decimals.
   - Apply bold formatting to the entries in rows 10–12.
   - Merge and Center the title in cell A1 across the columns.
   - Format the title with Bold and change the font size to 14pt.
   - Format the column and row headings with Bold.
   - Change the column width on column A so all entries are displayed.

3. Print the worksheet when you have finished.

4. Save and close the workbook.

	A	B	C	D	E	F
1			**Atlantic Pools - Accounts Receivable**			
2						
3		Beginning			Interest	
4	Customer	Balance	Purchases	Payments	Charge	New Balance
5	Zelton	$ 2,000	$ 2,300	$ 1,000	$ 15	$ 3,315
6	Ranier	2,450	1,000	2,450	-	1,000
7	Worthington	5,400	2,190	3,000	36	4,626
8	Alonzo	3,400	500	3,400	-	500
9	Barton	100	3,400	100	-	3,400
10	Totals	$ 13,350	$ 9,390	$ 9,950	$ 51	$ 12,841
11	Highest	$ 5,400	$ 3,400	$ 3,400	$ 36	$ 4,626
12	Lowest	$ 100	$ 500	$ 100	$ -	$ 500

Assessment 4.2   Use Copy and Paste and Drag and Drop

In this exercise, you will create and format a worksheet, use Copy and Paste, create formulas, and add enhancements to data.

1. Use these guidelines to create the following worksheet:

   ■ Enter all the numbers and text as shown. Use Copy and Paste or Drag and Drop to copy the text or numbers whenever possible. For example, all three Wilson children were given the same allowances in all four years. Therefore, you can enter the data in row 5 then copy row 5 to rows 10 and 15.

   ■ Use the Increase Indent [icon] button to indent the allowance, saved, and interest earned entries in column A.

   ■ Calculate the interest earned with the formula Interest Earned = Saved * Interest Rate. Use the interest rates shown in the following rate table.

2001	2002	2003	2004
3.5%	4.5%	6.5%	6.5%

   ■ Use AutoSum to calculate the Total Interest in cells F7, F12, and F17.

   ■ Calculate the Total Family Interest in cell F19 as the sum of cells F7, F12, and F17.

   ■ Apply a Currency with 2 decimals format to all cells containing formulas in rows 7, 12, 17, and 19.

   ■ Apply bold formatting to all entries in rows 7, 12, 17, and 19.

   ■ Widen all columns as necessary.

2. Print the workbook, save it as **Family Allowance**, and close it.

	A	B	C	D	E	F
1	Wilson Family Allowances					
2						
3		2001	2002	2003	2004	Total Interest
4	Jason					
5	Allowance	260	300	300	340	
6	Saved	120	110	200	220	
7	Interest Earned					
8						
9	Cindy					
10	Allowance	260	300	300	340	
11	Saved	120	110	200	220	
12	Interest Earned					
13						
14	Betty					
15	Allowance	260	300	300	340	
16	Saved	130	290	280	310	
17	Interest Earned					
18						
19	Total Family Interest 2001 - 2004					

Assessment 4.3   Use AutoFormat

In this exercise, you will open an existing workbook and apply an AutoFormat.

1. Open the workbook named Atlantic Pools.

2. Use the Classic 3 AutoFormat style to format the following worksheet.

3. Print the workbook, save the changes, and close it.

	A	B	C	D	E	F
1	Atlantic Pools - Accounts Receivable					
2						
3	Customer	Beginning Balance	Purchases	Payments	Interest Charge	New Balance
4	Zelton	$ 2,000	$ 2,300	$ 1,000	$ 15	$ 3,315
5	Ranier	2,450	1,000	2,450	-	1,000
6	Worthington	5,400	2,190	3,000	36	4,626
7	Alonzo	3,400	500	3,400	-	500
8	Barton	100	3,400	100	-	3,400
9	Totals	$ 13,350	$ 9,390	$ 9,950	$ 51	$ 12,841
10	Highest	$ 5,400	$ 3,400	$ 3,400	$ 36	$ 4,626
11	Lowest	$ 100	$ 500	$ 100	$ -	$ 500

Critical Thinking

Critical Thinking 4.1   On Your Own

Mary Perkins is the Customer Service Manager at a large retail store that sells everything from potato chips to television sets. Mary asks you to set up a worksheet to track customer returns. The worksheet should include customer name, item name, SKU code, purchase price, purchase date, return date, and reason for return. Enter five items into your worksheet, using your imagination to determine the product names, SKU codes, price, dates, etc. Add your choice of formatting and enhancements. Save your workbook as **Customer Returns**.

Critical Thinking 4.2   Web Research

Use Internet Explorer and a search engine of your choice to locate five Websites that sell music CDs. Choose five of your favorite CDs and set up a worksheet to categorize and analyze the information you find. In particular, include the name of the company Website, the URL, the CD title, the artist, the price of the CD, and the freight costs. Gather this information for all five CDs from all five Websites. Use formats and enhancements to make your worksheet look professional. Use formulas to calculate the total cost of each CD from each Website. Use the MIN and MAX functions to determine the least and most expensive CDs. Format your worksheet as desired. Save your workbook as **CD Titles**.

Critical Thinking 4.3   Web Research

You have been assigned the task of setting up a worksheet that tracks and analyzes an investment portfolio of publicly traded stocks. You are given the following information as a starting point:

Symbol	Purchase Price	Shares Purchased
CORL	1	500
ORCL	12	100
LU	3	200
MSFT	27	300
HAL	24	250

Use Internet Explorer and a search engine of your choice to locate a Website that offers free stock quotes. Use the site you locate and the symbols shown in the preceding table to determine the current price at which the stocks are trading and the company names associated with the symbols.

Set up a worksheet that contains the information shown in the preceding table. Also include the company name and current price of each stock. Use formulas to calculate the initial value of each investment and the current value based on the quotes you receive. Calculate the gain or loss of each stock in dollars as well as percentage. Use the SUM function to calculate the total value of the initial portfolio and the total current portfolio value. Calculate the total gain or loss for the portfolio. Calculate the average gain or loss percentage of the entire portfolio. Sort the rows in alphabetical order based on the symbols. Format the worksheet using the AutoFormat of your choice. You know you will need to track this every month, so go ahead and copy the data and formulas you've created and paste them on separate sheets. Save your workbook as **Stock Info**.

LESSON 5

Working with Dates and Text Features, and Restructuring Worksheets

In this lesson, you will learn fundamental concepts and techniques for working with dates, including inserting dates into worksheets and using dates in formulas. You will also explore several new formatting techniques, including multi-line text entries and additional cell alignment options. In addition, you will learn about text features such as Find and Replace as well as the Research tool. Finally, you will learn how to restructure a worksheet by inserting and deleting, and hiding and unhiding columns and rows.

Microsoft Office Excel 2003 objectives covered in this lesson

Objective Number	Skill Sets and Skills	Concept Page References	Exercise Page References
XL03S-1-1	Enter and edit cell content	138	138
XL03S-1-2	Navigate to specific cell content	155–156	156–158
XL03S-1-3	Locate, select, and insert supporting information	159	159–160
XL03S-2-4	Use statistical, date and time, financial, and logical functions	140	140–141
XL03S-3-1	Apply and modify cell formats	145	139–140, 146–147
XL03S-3-3	Modify row and column formats	142, 145, 147–148, 151, 153–154	142–145, 149–150, 152–155
XL03S-5-2	Insert, delete, and move cells	151	

Additional learning resources are available at labpub.com/learn/excel03/

Case Study

Tamika Jones is the proud owner of her own home-based business—Tamika's Jewelry Exchange. Tamika wants to record her checking transactions electronically to help her manage her money more effectively. She is even considering stock investments, though she knows she should do some research before handing over her money. Tamika has considered purchasing a program such as Microsoft Money to manage her checkbook and finances. However, at this point, Tamika doesn't have the time to learn another program. Since she already knows Excel, Tamika decides it is the best program for her to create a functional, well-designed worksheet. A portion of her worksheet is shown below.

	A	B	C	D	E	F	G
1	Tamika's Jewelry Exchange - Checkbook Register						
2	Today's Date		October 25, 2003				
3							
4	Date	Check Number	Transaction Description	P/B	Amount of Payment (-)	Amount of Deposit (+)	Balance Forward
5							
6	1/1/04	100	Payments to Barbara Jennings for 5-pound supply of jade	B	400.00		
7	1/3/04		Sales from Berkeley, Telegraph Avenue	B		700.00	
8	1/3/04		Sales to Donna Brown of Taylors Emporium	B		250.00	
9	1/7/04	101	Abalone shells from Pacific Abalone Supply	B	175.00		
10	1/9/04	102	Gold from the San Francisco Diamond and Jewelry Exchange	B	850.00		
11	1/10/04		Checks from relatives for Christmas	P		725.00	
12	1/14/04		Sales to Joan Crawfield, San Ramon Jewels	B		900.00	
13	1/16/04		Sales to Sheryl Gresham, Union Sq. Emporium	B		1,200.00	
14	1/18/04	103	Coast Jewelry Symposium	B	650.00		
15	Total Days in use						

Working with Dates

Dates are used in workbooks in two ways. First, you can simply display dates in cells using various formats such as 12/25/04, December 25, 2004, or 25-Dec-04. Second, you can use dates in formulas. For example, you may want to compute the number of days an invoice is past due. You calculate this as the difference between the current date and the original invoice date.

Understanding Serial Numbers

When you enter a date in a cell, Excel converts the date to a serial number between 1 and 2,958,525. These numbers correspond to the 10-millennium period from January 1, 1900 through December 31, 9999. The date January 1, 1900 is assigned the serial number 1, January 2, 1900 is assigned the serial number 2 . . . and December 31, 9999 is assigned the serial number 2,958,525. When dates are converted as numbers you can use the numbers/dates in calculations. Best of all, it's done for you automatically!

Entering Dates

Excel performs the following steps when you enter a date in a cell:

1. It recognizes the entry as a date if you enter it using a standard date format such as 12/25/04, December 25, 2004, or 25-Dec-04.

2. It converts the date to a serial number between 1 and 2,958,525.

3. It formats the serial number entry with the same date format you used when you entered the date.

This roundabout process occurs behind the scenes so you never see it happening. The benefit of converting dates to numbers and then formatting them with a date format is that the dates can be used in calculations.

 Hands-On 5.1   Enter Dates

In this exercise, you will begin developing a checkbook register. You will enter the dates into column A of the register.

Enter a Date

1. Open Excel and enter the following text entries on the blank worksheet:

	A	B	C	D	E
1	Tamika's Jewelry Exchange - Checkbook Register				
2	Today's Date				
3					
4	Date				

2. Click cell A6.

3. Type **1/1/04** and complete the entry.
   Notice that Excel right aligns the entry in the cell. This occurred because Excel recognized your entry as a date and converted it to a number. Excel always right aligns numbers. Also notice that Excel formatted the year 04 as 2004.

Change Date Formats

4. Click cell A6 and choose Format→Cells from the menu bar.

5. Click the Number tab, if necessary.

6. Be sure the Number tab is active then choose the General category and click OK.
   The number 37987 should be displayed in the cell. This is the serial number for the date January 1, 2004. This number will be used in any formulas that reference cell A6. Notice that the General format displays the number with no commas, currency symbols, or other special formats.

7. Choose Format→Cells from the menu bar.

8. Follow these steps to change the date format:

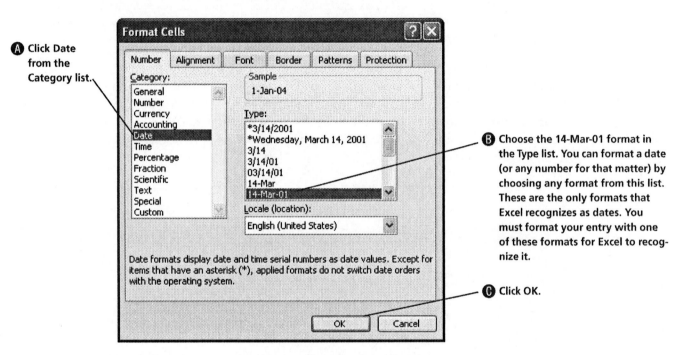

Ⓐ **Click Date from the Category list.**

Ⓑ **Choose the 14-Mar-01 format in the Type list. You can format a date (or any number for that matter) by choosing any format from this list. These are the only formats that Excel recognizes as dates. You must format your entry with one of these formats for Excel to recognize it.**

Ⓒ **Click OK.**

The date should now be formatted with the new format.

9. Use the Format→Cells command to change the format back to 1/1/04 by choosing 3/14/01 from the Type list.

10. Enter the following dates into column A:
    Notice that although you enter dates in cells A7:A10 with only two digits for the year, when you complete each entry the year displays with four digits. You will format the dates in the next few steps.

	A	B	C
1	Tamika's Jewelry Exchange - Ch(		
2	Today's Date		
3			
4	Date		
5			
6	1/1/04		
7	1/3/04		
8	1/3/04		
9	1/7/04		
10	1/9/04		

11. Click cell A6 and click the Align Left button.

12. Use the Format Painter button to copy the date format and left alignment from cell A6 to the other cells with dates in column A.

13. Save the worksheet as **Checkbook Register**.
You will continue to develop the checkbook register as you progress through this lesson.

Inserting Date and Time Functions

In Lesson 3, Introducing Formulas and Functions, you learned about some of Excel's powerful statistical functions. In *Microsoft Office Excel 2003: Quick Course 2* and *Microsoft Office Excel 2003: Quick Course 3*, you will learn about financial and database functions. In this lesson, you will see the value of using date and time functions in Excel.

The current date is often required in worksheets. You may also want to show the date the worksheet was created or printed. You can insert a date function rather than typing the date in a worksheet. Date functions produce the current date and, depending on the specific function, can update automatically. You insert date functions with the Insert Function box or by typing the function in the result cell. Date functions are not case sensitive so you can type the formula in lowercase.

The following Quick Reference table discusses three of the most common date and time functions.

QR **QUICK REFERENCE: UNDERSTANDING DATE AND TIME FUNCTIONS**

Function	Description
TODAY( )	This function displays the current system date and calculates the serial number. The date updates automatically when the worksheet is recalculated or reopened.
NOW( )	This function displays the current system date and time and calculates the serial number. The date updates automatically when the worksheet is recalculated or reopened.
DATE(year,month,day)	This function returns the date entered in the default date format and calculates the serial number. The date does not update when the worksheet is recalculated or reopened.

 Hands-On 5.2 Use the TODAY Function

In this exercise, you will use the TODAY function to display the current date at the top of the checkbook register.

Use the Insert Function Box

1. Click cell C2.

FROM THE KEYBOARD
=TODAY( ) to insert the current date

2. Click the Insert Function button on the Formula bar.
Excel inserts an equals (=) sign in the Formula bar and displays the Insert Function box.

3. Choose the Date & Time category from the category list.

4. Click the various date functions in the Select a Function list and read the descriptions that appear at the bottom of the dialog box.

5. Scroll down, choose the TODAY function, and click OK.
   The Function Arguments box will appear. The syntax =TODAY() is the complete syntax because the TODAY function requires no argument within the parenthesis.

6. Click OK to complete the function.
   Today's date is inserted in cell C2.

Change the Date Format

7. Be sure cell C2 is active and choose Format→Cells from the menu bar.

8. Scroll through the Type list and choose March 14, 2001.

9. Click OK and notice that the new format is applied to the date.
   Notice that you can change the appearance of a date by applying a date format. If you are entering many dates, use a simple format such as 1/1/04. After entering the dates, you can format them using any format you desire.

Use Dates in a Formula

In the next few steps, you will use a formula that subtracts the first date the checkbook register was used (January 1, 2004) from today's date. This will tell you the total number of days that the checkbook register has been in use.

10. Click cell A11 and enter the phrase **Total days in use**.

11. Click cell C11 and type the formula **=C2-A6**.

12. Complete the entry and watch as Excel calculates the difference between the two serial numbers that represent the dates in cells C2 and A6.
    The result in cell C11 will be formatted as a date and time. Cell C11 may be filled with number signs (######) until the format is changed. In the next step, you will use the Format Painter to copy the General format from any blank cell in the workbook to cell C11. All cells in a new workbook have the General format. It will let you see the number of days the checkbook has been in use.

13. Click any blank cell in the workbook.

14. Click the Format Painter ⌗ button, and then click cell C11.
    The General format is copied to the cell.

15. Save the changes and continue with the next topic.

Introducing Text Features

You learned many techniques for arranging data in Lesson 4, Formatting Cell Contents. Now you will expand on that knowledge and learn many new features, including creating link breaks, wrapping text, changing page alignment, and rotating text.

You can add multiple lines to a cell by inserting a line break or setting the Wrap Text option in the Format→Cells dialog box. Use the keystroke combination [Alt]+[Enter] to insert a line break. To delete a line break, click to the right of the last word on the first line and tap [Delete].

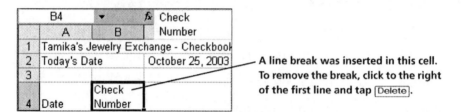

A line break was inserted in this cell. To remove the break, click to the right of the first line and tap [Delete].

Wrapping Text

The Wrap Text option forces text to wrap within a cell as it would in a word processing document. You can turn the Wrap Text option on and off by selecting the desired cell(s), choosing Format→Cells, clicking the Alignment tab, and checking or unchecking the Wrap Text box. Excel wraps text automatically in a cell that contains a line break.

Text will only wrap if the cell is too narrow for the entry. If you want to keep the cell a certain width but still want the text to wrap, you must use the line break method.

 Hands-On 5.3   Create Multiple-Line Text Entries

In this exercise, you will use the [Alt]+[Enter] method to enter data on multiple lines within the same cell. You will also set the Wrap Text option.

Insert a Line Break

1. Click cell B4.

2. Type **Check** and press [Alt]+[Enter].

3. Type **Number** and tap [→] to complete the entry.
   The entry is completed and displays on multiple lines. The insertion point is in cell C4, awaiting the next entry.

4. In cell C4, type **Transaction**.

5. Press [Alt]+[Enter] to insert a line break.

6. Type **Description** and tap [Enter] to complete the entry.

Use the Wrap Text Option

7. Click cell B6.

8. Type the number **100** and tap ⇥ to complete the entry.
The entry is completed and the highlight moves to cell C6.

9. Choose Format→Cells from the menu bar.

10. Choose the Alignment tab at the top of the dialog box.
You will use the various alignment options as you progress through this lesson.

11. Click the Wrap Text checkbox (it should now be checked) and click OK.

12. Type the three-line paragraph shown to the right without pressing
Enter or Alt + Enter . Complete the entry when you have finished.
Keep in mind that the text may wrap differently in your cell because the column width may be different than shown here.

> Payments to Barbara
> Jennings for 5-pound
> supply of jade

13. Widen column C until the text in cell C6 wraps as shown in the preceding illustration.
Don't be concerned if the height of row 6 is higher than the text. You will learn how to adjust the row height later in this lesson.

14. Enter the following data into column C:
The text will flow into the adjacent cells because the Wrap Text option is not set. You will fix this in a moment, using the Format Painter to copy the formatting from cell C6 and make it match this illustration.

	A	B	C	D
1	Tamika's Jewelry Exchange - Checkbook Register			
2	Today's Date		October 25, 2003	
3				
4	Date	Check Number	Transaction Description	
5				
6	1/1/04	100	Payments to Barbara Jennings for 5-pound supply of jade	
7	1/3/04		Sales from Berkeley, Telegraph Avenue	
8	1/3/04		Sales to Donna Brown of Taylors Emporium	
9	1/7/04		Abalone shells from Pacific Abalone Supply	
10	1/9/04		Silver from the San Francisco Diamond and Jewelry Exchange	

15. Click cell C6 then click the Format Painter 🖌 button.
The Format Painter copies any formatting that has been applied to the selected cell.

16. Drag over cells C7:C10 to apply the formatting to wrap the text.
Cells C7:C10 should now match the illustration in step 14.

17. Click cell D4.
    You will type an entry and insert a line break, which will turn on the Wrap Text option.

18. Choose Format→Cells from the menu bar and make sure the Alignment tab is chosen.
    *Notice that the Wrap Text box is **not** checked. This box will be checked automatically when you enter a line break in a cell.*

19. Click the Cancel button without checking the box.

20. Type **Amount of** and press [Alt]+[Enter].

21. Type **Payment (-)** on the second line and tap [Enter] to complete the entry.
    The Payment (-) line is too wide to fit in the cell so Excel wraps the text because the Wrap Text option was activated when you inserted the line break in the cell.

22. Click cell D4, choose Format→Cells, and notice that the Wrap Text box is now checked.

23. Click the Cancel button.

Widen Column D

24. Be sure the highlight is in cell D4 (the Amount of Payment cell).

25. Try to position the mouse pointer on the column heading and notice that it is blocked by the two-line display in the Formula bar.

26. Click cell D3 (which has no entry) and notice that the column headings are visible.

27. Widen column D until the Payment (-) line no longer wraps.
    The first and second lines in cell D4 will remain as two lines regardless of the width of the column. This is because you inserted a line break, thus forcing the second line down.

28. Click cell E4 and use [Alt]+[Enter] to create the entry shown to the right. You will need to widen column E slightly after completing the entry to prevent the second line from wrapping.

    Amount of
    Deposit (+)

29. Enter the phrase **Balance Forward** in cell F4 without inserting a line break.
    Excel will automatically format the entry to fit on two lines. Excel recognized that you were consistently using two-line entries so it formatted the entry by turning on Wrap Text. At this point, rows 1–6 of your worksheet should match the following example (although the date will be different).

	A	B	C	D	E	F
1	Tamika's Jewelry Exchange - Checkbook Register					
2	Today's Date		October 25, 2003			
3						
4	Date	Check Number	Transaction Description	Amount of Payment (-)	Amount of Deposit (+)	Balance Forward
5						
6	1/1/04	100	Payments to Barbara Jennings for 5-pound supply of jade			

Setting Vertical Alignment

While Lesson 4, Formatting Cell Contents, introduced you to aligning cell contents horizontally, this lesson focuses on vertical alignment within cells. Vertical alignment options include top, bottom, center, and justify. The default alignment is Bottom. The Justify option is useful with multiple-line entries. For example, the Justify option evenly distributes unused space between the lines in a multi-line entry. Vertical alignment is set by choosing Format→Cells, clicking the Alignment tab, and choosing the desired alignment from the Vertical box.

 Hands-On 5.4   **Use the Alignment Options**

In this exercise, you will set the vertical alignment for a cell.

1. Click cell A4.
   Notice that the text is currently aligned at the bottom of the cell.

2. Choose Format→Cells and click the Alignment tab.

3. Click the drop-down arrow next to the *Vertical* box, scroll up and choose Top, and then click OK.
   The entry should now be aligned with the top of the cell.

4. Right-click cell A4 and choose Format Cells from the context menu.

5. Change the alignment to Center and click OK.

Rotating Text

Text can be rotated from 0 to 90 degrees using the Orientation option on the Alignment tab in the Format Cells dialog box. Excel automatically increases the row height to accommodate the rotated text. When column headings are extra wide, making the worksheet spread out too far horizontally, you might consider rotating the text to save room.

Hands-On 5.5   **Rotate Text and Enter Text and Formulas**

In this exercise, you will rotate data within a cell and complete the remainder of the worksheet.

1. Be sure the insertion point is in cell A4 and choose Format→Cells from the menu bar.

2. Follow these steps to rotate the Date entry in cell A4:

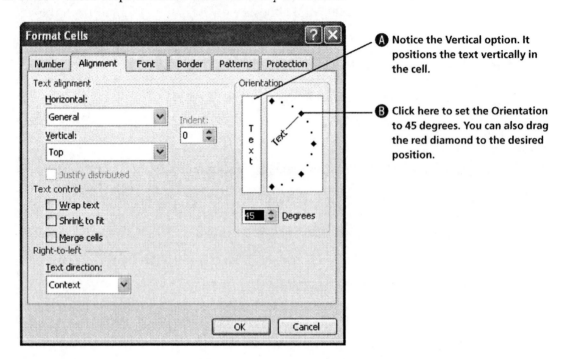

A Notice the Vertical option. It positions the text vertically in the cell.

B Click here to set the Orientation to 45 degrees. You can also drag the red diamond to the desired position.

Notice the other options in this dialog box. You have used all of them except Shrink to Fit, which reduces the font size of an entry until it fits in the cell.

3. Click OK in the Format Cells dialog box.
   The entry is now positioned at a 45 degree angle.

Complete the Remainder of the Worksheet

4. Click cell F5, type **500**, and tap ⌷Enter⌷.
   This is Tamika's beginning balance in her checkbook.

5. Click cell D6, type **400**, and tap ⌷Enter⌷.
   This entry will be subtracted from the Balance Forward when a formula is entered in F6.

6. Click cell F6 and enter the formula **=F5−D6+E6**.
   The result should equal 100. This formula subtracts checks written and adds deposits made to the previous balance forward.

Copy the Formula

7. Click cell F6 then click the Copy 🗐 button.

8. Drag over cells F7:F10.
   All four cells should be selected.

9. Click the Paste ▦ button to copy the formulas to the selected cells.
The results should be 100 in each cell. The cells will be recalculated as soon as you enter the figures in columns D and E.

10. Enter the number **700** into cell E7.
Notice that the formula result in F7 was updated to 800 automatically.

11. Enter the numbers shown in the following illustration to cells B9:B10 and cells D8:E10. **Do not** enter the numbers shown in column F. These numbers are the results of the formula you just copied. Your completed worksheet should match the following example.

	A	B	C	D	E	F
1	Tamika's Jewelry Exchange - Checkbook Register					
2	Today's Date		October 25, 2003			
3						
4	Date	Check Number	Transaction Description	Amount of Payment (-)	Amount of Deposit (+)	Balance Forward
5						500
6	1/1/04	100	Payments to Barbara Jennings for 5-pound supply of jade	400		100
7	1/3/04		Sales from Berkeley, Telegraph Avenue		700	800
8	1/3/04		Sales to Donna Brown of Taylors Emporium		250	1050
9	1/7/04	101	Abalone shells from Pacific Abalone Supply	175		875
10	1/9/04	102	Silver from the San Francisco Diamond and Jewelry Exchange	850		25
11	Total Days in use		83			

Modifying Columns and Rows

As you have seen, many entries do not fit within the default column size. Worksheets can also appear overcrowded with the standard row heights and you may be tempted to insert blank rows between each row to make the worksheet more readable. Inserting blank rows can cause problems down the road, when you begin using some of Excel's powerful automatic features. In this lesson, you will use more timesaving techniques to fix column width and row height issues, such as changing multiple column or rows at the same time and using AutoFit to let Excel decide the best width or height. Both of these commands simply require you to select the multiple columns or rows before issuing the command.

Column Widths and Row Heights

You adjust a column width by dragging the column heading lines, as you learned in Lesson 4, Formatting Cell Contents. Now you will go a few steps farther and adjust multiple columns or rows at the same time, change the standard column width and row height, and let Excel adjust the columns and rows to their best fit. The basic method of dragging the column heading line is often the most efficient way to adjust column widths. To adjust row heights, you can drag the row heading lines. Besides these basic methods, Excel provides additional methods.

AutoFit

You can adjust both column widths and row heights with the AutoFit command. AutoFit adjusts column widths to fit the widest entry in a column. Likewise, AutoFit adjusts row heights to accommodate the tallest entry in a row. The following Quick Reference table discusses AutoFit options and other commands for setting column widths and row heights.

QUICK REFERENCE: CHANGING COLUMN WIDTHS AND ROW HEIGHTS	
Technique	**Procedure**
Set a precise column width	Choose Format→Column→Width and enter the desired width.
Set column widths with AutoFit	Choose Format→Column→AutoFit Selection or double-click the right edge of the column heading. You can also select multiple columns and double-click between any two selected headings. This will AutoFit all selected columns.
Set a precise row height	Choose Format→Row→Height.
Set row heights with AutoFit	Choose Format→Row→AutoFit or double-click the bottom edge of the row heading. You can also select multiple rows and double-click between any two selected headings. This will AutoFit all selected rows.
Manually adjust column widths and row heights	Select the desired columns or rows and drag the column or row heading lines.

Standard Column Widths and Row Heights

Each column in a new worksheet has a standard width of 8.43 characters, where the default character is Arial 10pt. Each row has a standard height of 12.75 points, which is approximately one-sixth of an inch. You can change the standard width of all columns in a worksheet with the Format→Column→Standard Width command. Excel does not have such a command for changing the standard row height.

Hands-On 5.6   Change Column Widths and Row Heights

In this exercise, you will change the column widths and row heights of multiple columns and rows using both the heading lines and the Format→Column commands.

Adjust Column Widths

1. Follow these steps to select columns A–F:

A Position the mouse pointer in column heading A and notice that it turns into a black down arrow.

B Click and drag over all the column headings to column F. The selected columns will all appear shaded, as shown here.

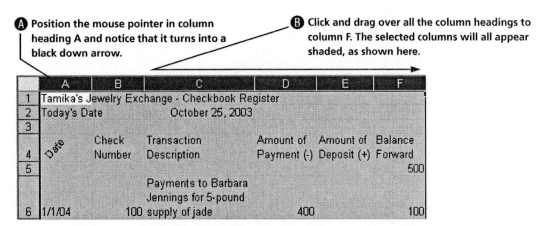

2. Choose Format→Column→AutoFit Selection from the menu bar.
Excel will widen each column to fit the largest entry in the column. Column A should be very wide because the entry in cell A1 is quite long. Also, notice that AutoFit had no impact on the cells in column C, which have the Wrap Text option turned on.

3. Undo 🔄 the AutoFit then select only columns B–F.
Notice that this range does not include the wide entry in cell A1.

4. Position the mouse pointer on the border between columns D and E then double-click when the Adjust pointer appears.

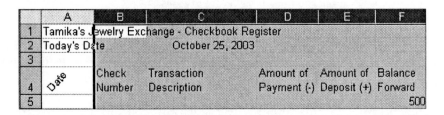

Columns B through F are adjusted to their best fit, which means Excel adjusts the size of each column to display the widest entry.

5. Click anywhere in the worksheet to deselect.
   Notice that AutoFit did a better job this time.

6. Drag the border between columns C and D to the right until each entry in column C has a maximum height of two lines, as shown in the following illustration.

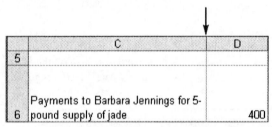

Column C has been widened so cell C6 displays on only two lines.

7. Click anywhere in column C and choose Format→Column→Width from the menu bar.

8. Enter **28** in the box and click OK.
   This will size column C to just the right width.

Adjust Row Heights

9. Follow these steps to adjust the height of row 6:

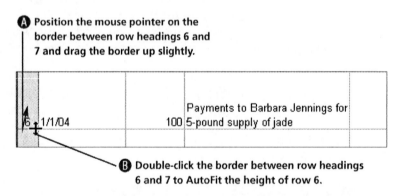

Ⓐ Position the mouse pointer on the border between row headings 6 and 7 and drag the border up slightly.

Ⓑ Double-click the border between row headings 6 and 7 to AutoFit the height of row 6.

10. Position the pointer on row heading 7 then drag down to select row headings 7–10.
    When selecting row headings, be sure to drag with the small, black, right-pointing arrow.

11. Use the double-click technique to AutoFit rows 7–10.

12. Take a few minutes to experiment with the various column width and row height options.
    Try using the double-click AutoFit technique on columns, but be sure to widen the columns first, since they have already been AutoFit.

13. Save the changes to your workbook and continue with the next topic.

Inserting and Deleting Rows and Columns

Excel lets you insert and delete rows and columns. This gives you the flexibility to restructure your worksheets after they have been set up. The following Quick Reference table discusses the various procedures used to insert and delete rows and columns.

QUICK REFERENCE: INSERTING AND DELETING ROWS AND COLUMNS

Task	Procedure
Insert rows	■ Select the number of rows you wish to insert and issue the Insert command. The same number of new rows will be inserted above the selected rows.
	■ Choose Insert→Rows or right-click the selected rows and choose Insert from the context menu.
Insert columns	■ Select the number of columns you wish to insert and issue the Insert command. The same number of new columns will be inserted to the left of the selected columns.
	■ Choose Insert→Columns or right-click the selected columns and choose Insert from the context menu.
Delete rows	Select the desired rows and choose Edit→Delete or right-click a selected row heading and choose Delete from the context menu.
Delete columns	Select the desired columns and choose Edit→Delete or right-click a selected column heading and choose Delete from the context menu.

Inserting and Deleting Cells

You can also insert and delete selected cells, which will shift the position of other cells in the rows or columns where the cells are inserted/deleted. This may cause problems because it alters the structure of your entire worksheet. For this reason, use this feature cautiously.

QUICK REFERENCE: INSERTING AND DELETING SELECTED CELLS

Task	Procedure
Insert cells	■ Select the cells in the worksheet where you want the inserted cells to appear.
	■ Choose Insert→Cells from the menu bar.
	■ Choose the desired Shift Cells option. Other cells will shift position to make room for the inserted cells.
Delete cells	■ Select the cells you wish to delete.
	■ Choose Edit→Delete from the menu bar.
	■ Choose the desired Shift Cells option. The cells will be deleted and other cells will shift position to fill in the space.

Hands-On 5.7 Insert Rows and Columns

In this exercise, you will insert multiple rows and columns in the worksheet and use the Format Painter to copy formats to the new rows and columns.

Insert Rows

1. Select rows 11–14 by dragging the mouse pointer down the row headings.

2. Right-click row heading 12 and choose Insert from the context menu.
   Notice that Excel inserts the same number of rows you selected. You could have right-clicked on any of the selected row headings to make the context menu appear.

3. Click anywhere in the worksheet to deselect the rows.
   Excel formatted the new rows with the same format as the row above them. This will become apparent when you enter data and the text wraps in the cell.

4. Use the fill handle to copy the formula in column F10 to cells F11:F14.
   Until you enter data into columns D and E, cells F11:F14 will all display 25, which was the ending balance in cell F10.

5. Enter the following data in the range A11:E14:

	A	B	C	D	E	F
11	1/10/04		Checks from relatives for Christmas		725	750
12	1/14/04		Sales to Joan Crawfield, San Ramon Jewels		900	1650
13	1/16/04		Sales to Sheryl Gresham, Union Sq. Emporium		1200	2850
14	1/18/04	103	Registration fee for annual West Coast Jewelry Symposium	650		2200

Notice that the formulas in column F automatically recalculate as you enter the data in columns D and E.

Insert a Column

Tamika realizes that she should be keeping track of business versus personal transactions. She wants a new column for this data. You will add a column to track whether an expense is personal or business.

6. Click anywhere in column D.

7. Choose Insert→Columns and a new column will be inserted to the left of column D.
   Notice that the new column has the same width as column C. The cells in this new column have the same text and number formats as the cells to the left of them in column C.

8. Click cell D4 and enter **P/B** for Personal or Business.

9. At this point, all expenses are business-related except cell D11. So, type a **P** in cell D11 and a **B** in the other cells in this column.

10. AutoFit column D by double-clicking the border between column headings D and E. *Column D should be just wide enough to fit the P/B entry.*

11. Select column D and Center ▤ the entries.

Format the Worksheet

12. Select the range A4:G4, which includes all the headings in row 4.

13. Use the Fill Color ⬜▾ button to apply the Aqua (fifth color in the third row) color.

14. Click cell G5 and apply the Light Turquoise (fifth color in the last row) color to that cell.

15. Use the Format Painter ⬜ to copy the format from cell G5 to cells G6:G14. *This will highlight the balances with the same color.*

16. Format cell G5 as Comma Style ⬜ with no decimals.

17. Format the range E6:G14 as Comma Style ⬜ with no decimals.

18. Feel free to format and enhance the worksheet as desired.

19. Save the changes and continue with next topic.

Hiding Columns and Rows

Selected rows and columns are hidden using the Format→Row→Hide command and the Format→Column→Hide command, or the context menu that appears when you right-click the heading(s). Hidden rows and columns are not visible in the worksheet and do not print. However, hidden rows and columns are still part of the worksheet. Therefore, their values and formulas can be referenced by other formulas in the visible rows and columns. Hiding rows and columns is useful when you want to focus attention on other parts of the worksheet.

	A	B	C	D	F
1	Tamika's Jewelry Exchange - Checkbook Register				
2	Today's Date		October 25, 2003		
3					
4	Date	Check Number	Transaction Description	P/B	Amount of Deposit (+)
5					
6	1/1/04	100	Payments to Barbara Jennings for 5-pound supply of jade	B	
7	1/3/04		Sales from Berkeley, Telegraph Avenue	B	700
8	1/3/04		Sales to Donna Brown of Taylors Emporium	B	250

Notice that columns E and G are hidden to draw attention to the deposit column.

Unhiding Columns and Rows

Selected rows and columns can be unhidden using the Format→Row→Unhide command and the Format→Column→Unhide command, or the context menu that appears when you right-click the heading(s). Before unhiding rows, you must select row(s) above and below the hidden rows. Likewise, you must select column(s) on the left and right of hidden columns before issuing the Unhide command.

	A	B	C	D	F	H
1	Tamika's Jewelry Exchange - Checkbook Register					
2	Today's Date		October 25, 2003			
3						
4	Date	Check Number	Transaction Description		P/B	Amount of Deposit (+)
5						
6	1/1/04	100	Payments to Barbara Jennings for 5 pound supply of jade		B	

To unhide column E, you must first select columns D and F.

You could unhide columns E and G at the same time by selecting columns D–H and issuing the Unhide command.

 Hands-On 5.8   Hide and Unhide Rows and Columns

In this exercise, you will hide and unhide two noncontiguous columns.

1. Follow these steps to hide columns E and G:

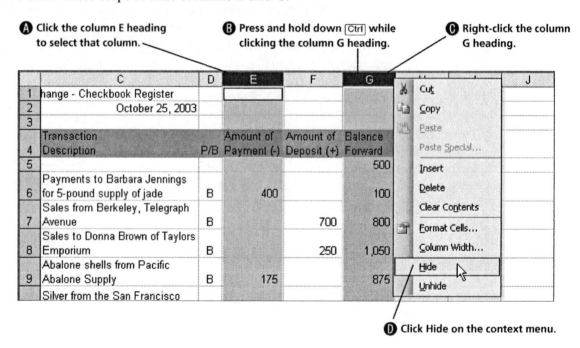

Ⓐ Click the column E heading to select that column.

Ⓑ Press and hold down Ctrl while clicking the column G heading.

Ⓒ Right-click the column G heading.

Ⓓ Click Hide on the context menu.

2. Follow these steps to unhide columns E and G:

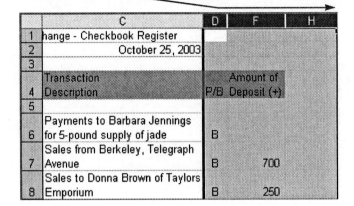

Ⓐ Position the mouse pointer on the column D heading and drag to the right until columns D through H are selected, as shown here.

Ⓑ Choose Format→Column→Unhide from the menu bar.

	C	D	F	H
1	hange - Checkbook Register			
2	October 25, 2003			
3				
4	Transaction Description	P/B	Amount of Deposit (+)	
5				
6	Payments to Barbara Jennings for 5-pound supply of jade	B		
7	Sales from Berkeley, Telegraph Avenue	B	700	
8	Sales to Donna Brown of Taylors Emporium	B	250	

3. Save the workbook when you have finished experimenting and continue with the next topic.

Finding and Replacing Data

Excel's Find command performs searches on a worksheet or an entire workbook. It can search for a particular word, number, cell reference, formula, or format. Find is often the quickest way to locate an item in a workbook. You display the Find box with the Edit→Find command. The Replace box lets you find an item and replace it with a specified item. You display the Replace box with the Edit→ Replace command.

FROM THE KEYBOARD
Ctrl+F for Find
Ctrl+H for Replace

Replacing Cell Formats

Excel 2003 lets you find and replace cell formats. For example, you may want to search all worksheets in a workbook for cells formatted in Currency Style with 0 decimals and replace that format with Currency Style with 2 decimals. Finding and replacing cell formats can be a big timesaver, especially with large worksheets and multiple-sheet workbooks.

You can search for text, values, cell references, or formulas by typing the desired search string in this box.

You can search for a particular cell format by clicking the drop-down arrow on the Format button and choosing the desired format from the Format Cells box. Or, click Choose Format from Cell and click a cell in the worksheet to find cells with the

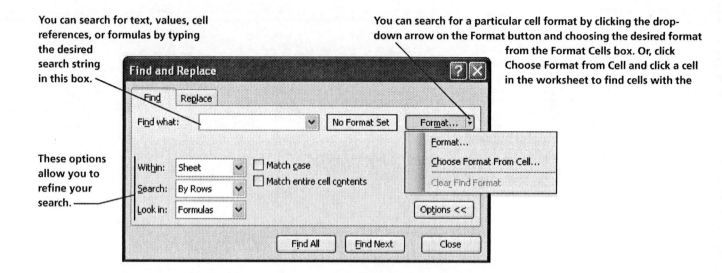

These options allow you to refine your search.

 ## Hands-On 5.9 Use Find and Replace

In this exercise, you will find an entry in the checkbook and replace another entry with new data. You will also replace 0 decimals with 2 decimals in a range of cells.

Find a Word

Tamika is trying to locate a checkbook register transaction involving the purchase of jade.

1. Click in cell A1.

2. Choose Edit→Find from the menu bar.

3. Type **jade** in the Find What box and click the Find Next button.
   The highlight should move to cell C6.

Use Replace

4. Click the Replace tab on the dialog box.
   The Replace With box and two Replace buttons will appear.

5. Select, and then delete the entry in the Find What box. Then, type **silver**.

6. Type **Gold** in the Replace With box. Be sure to capitalize the word.

7. Click the Find Next button and watch the highlight move to cell C10.
   Notice that this cell contains the word silver.

8. Click the Replace button to replace silver with **Gold**.
   In the next few steps, you will replace number formats with formats that display two decimals.

Replace Cell Formats

9. Delete the entries from the Find What and Replace With boxes.

10. Follow these steps to choose a cell with the formats you want to find:

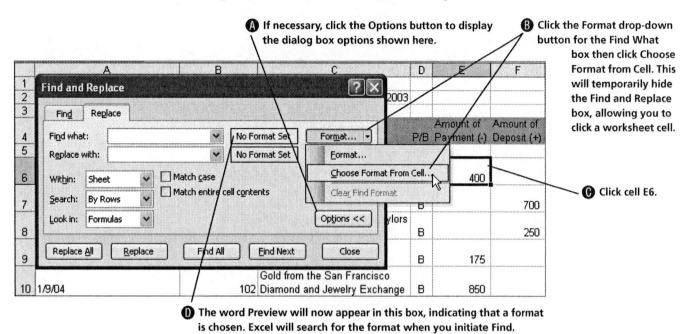

A If necessary, click the Options button to display the dialog box options shown here.

B Click the Format drop-down button for the Find What box then click Choose Format from Cell. This will temporarily hide the Find and Replace box, allowing you to click a worksheet cell.

C Click cell E6.

D The word Preview will now appear in this box, indicating that a format is chosen. Excel will search for the format when you initiate Find.

11. Click the Format button for the Replace With box (not the drop-down button) to display the Replace Format box.

12. Click the Number tab, choose the Number category, be sure the number of decimal places is set to 2, click the box next to *Use 1000 Separator*, and then click OK to complete the format specifications.

13. Click the Replace All button and click OK when Excel informs you of the number of replacements made.

14. Close the Find and Replace dialog box. Notice that the check numbers, total days in use, beginning balance, and cells with light shading did not receive the new format. This is because their format is different than that of cell E6. Only cells with the same format as cell E6 received the new format.

	A	B	C	D	E	F	G
4	Date	Check Number	Transaction Description	P/B	Amount of Payment (-)	Amount of Deposit (+)	Balance Forward
5							500.00
6	1/1/04	100	Payments to Barbara Jennings for 5-pound supply of jade	B	400.00		100.00
7	1/3/04		Sales from Berkeley, Telegraph Avenue	B		700.00	800.00
8	1/3/04		Sales to Donna Brown of Taylors Emporium	B		250.00	1,050.00
9	1/7/04	101	Abalone shells from Pacific Abalone Supply	B	175.00		875.00
10	1/9/04	102	Gold from the San Francisco Diamond and Jewelry Exchange	B	850.00		25.00
11	1/10/04		Checks from relatives for Christmas	P		725.00	750.00
12	1/14/04		Sales to Joan Crawfield, San Ramon Jewels	B		900.00	1,650.00
13	1/16/04		Sales to Sheryl Gresham, Unioni Sq. Emporium	B		1,200.00	2,850.00
14	1/18/04	103	Coast Jewelry Symposium	B	650.00		2,200.00
15	Total Days in use		83				

Replace another Cell Format

15. Choose Edit→Replace to display the Replace box.

16. Click the Format drop-down button on the Find What box and choose Format from Cell.

17. Click cell G5 (the first cell with the light shading).
Both the Find What and the Replace With preview boxes should display the light shading.

18. Click the Format button for the Replace With box (not the drop-down button) to display the Replace Format box.

19. Choose the Number category, make sure the decimals are set to 2, and make sure the Use 1000 Separator box is checked.

20. Click OK then click Replace All on the Replace box.

21. Click OK to acknowledge the number of replacements then close the Find and Replace box.
All shaded cells should now have two decimal places. Keep in mind that in these examples it actually would have been easier to simply select the desired cells and apply or modify the desired formats. However, in a large workbook with multiple sheets, Find and Replace may be much easier.

22. Save the workbook and continue with the next topic.

Using Research Tools

Numerous types of reference information are available to you right at your computer. You can receive stock quotes and other research information with just a few mouse clicks. Using the Tools→Research command, you can search multiple sources, including the Internet. The command displays a Research pane and contains research tools such as a dictionary, thesaurus, encyclopedia, stock quotes, and company information.

 Hands-On 5.10   Research Tools

In this exercise, you will find stock quotes and information on Microsoft Corporation, the stock in which Tamika is considering investing.

1. Select the Sheet2 tab at the bottom of the window.

2. Click Tools→Research to display the Research pane.
   The Research pane lets you look up information in a variety of reference services, which are found in a list when you click the drop-down arrow next to All Reference Books.

3. Follow these steps to display the stock quote for Microsoft Corporation:

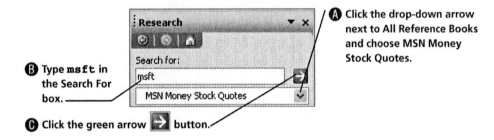

4. Take a few minutes to look at the results of the search.

5. Click cell B3 then click the Insert Price button near the bottom of the Research pane.
   The Last price (meaning the latest price per share shown at the top of the list) is inserted into the selected cell.

6. Click the Detailed Quote link at the bottom of the Research pane.
   Internet Explorer opens and displays the Detailed Quote for Microsoft Corporation.

7. Follow these steps to select the detailed quote so you can copy it into your worksheet:

A Position the mouse pointer right next to the heading Microsoft until it becomes an I-beam.

B Drag to select the entire quote.

8. Right-click anywhere on the selection and choose Copy from the context menu.

9. Click the button on the taskbar for your opened Microsoft Excel file.
You may not be able to see the entire name on the button on the taskbar, depending on how many windows you have open.

10. Click cell A5 and click the Paste button.
The detailed quote is pasted into your worksheet.

11. Try using the Research pane to search for another stock quote.

12. When finished, close the Research pane.

13. Save the changes and close the workbook.

Concepts Review

True/False Questions

1. When you enter a date, Excel converts it to a number.   TRUE   FALSE

2. Excel applies a date format to dates after it converts them to numbers.   TRUE   FALSE

3. You cannot combine a manually inserted line break and automatic text wrapping in the same cell.   TRUE   FALSE

4. The AutoFit command changes the column width to fit the narrowest entry in the column.   TRUE   FALSE

5. Row heights cannot be changed.   TRUE   FALSE

6. Row heights cannot be AutoFit.   TRUE   FALSE

7. New columns are inserted to the left of selected columns.   TRUE   FALSE

8. New rows are inserted above selected rows.   TRUE   FALSE

9. Using the Research task pane, you can download current stock quotes from the Internet.   TRUE   FALSE

10. Hidden columns and rows will print.   TRUE   FALSE

Multiple Choice Questions

1. Which keystroke combination inserts a manual line break?
   a. Shift + Enter
   b. Shift + Tab
   c. Alt + Enter
   d. Ctrl + Enter

2. Which command displays a dialog box for the Wrap Text option?
   a. Format→Cells
   b. Edit→Cells
   c. Format→Text
   d. None of the above

3. Which statement most accurately describes the effect of inserting a row?
   a. The new row uses the formats from the row below it.
   b. The new row uses the formats from the row above it.
   c. The new row contains no formatting.
   d. The formatting in the new row cannot be changed.

4. How many columns are inserted if you select three columns and issue the Insert→ Columns command?
   a. 1
   b. 3
   c. 0
   d. None of the above

Skill Builders

Skill Builder 5.1   Restructure a Worksheet

In this exercise, you will modify a worksheet so it matches the one shown at the end of this exercise.

Add Two New Columns

1. Open the workbook named Defective Items.
   Look at the worksheet at the end of this exercise and notice that it contains two additional columns with the headings Extra Small and Extra Large.

2. Click cell E4 and notice that the formula is =SUM(B4:D4).

3. Click anywhere in column B.

4. Choose Insert→Columns from the menu bar.

5. Now click in column F (the totals column) and insert a column.

6. Click cell G4 and notice that the formula has changed to =SUM(C4:E4).
   The formula should be =SUM(B4:F4). The cell references changed to reflect the new location of cells B4:D4, which are the cells originally referenced in the formula. However, the references did not expand to include the new columns. Be careful when inserting rows and columns because Excel will not always expand the references as you desire. In this example, you inserted columns outside the range referenced in the original formula so Excel did not update the formula references. Excel only updates the references if you insert columns inside the range referenced in the formula. You will repair the Total column formulas later in this exercise.

7. Type the headings **Extra Small** and **Extra Large** in the new columns.
   Notice that both headings have the formatting of the cell to the left of them. The formatting from the column to the left was copied to the inserted columns.

8. Use the Format Painter 🖌 button to copy the formatting from the Small heading to the Extra Small heading in cell B3.

9. Select columns A through G then right-click on any one of the selected headings then choose Insert from the context menu.

10. Click Undo to delete the inserted columns.

Insert Subtotal Rows and Blank Rows

Look at the completed worksheet and notice that it contains a Subtotal row and a blank row after each clothing group.

11. Click cell G14 and notice the formula =SUM(G4:G13) in the Formula bar.

12. Right-click on row heading 6 and use the Insert command to insert a blank row.

13. Click cell G15 and notice that the formula reference has been expanded to =SUM(G4:G14).
    This formula reference was expanded because you inserted a row inside the range G4:G13, which was the original range referenced by the formula.

14. Insert a blank row above row 11.

15. Click cell G16 and notice that the formula is now =SUM(G4:G15).
In the next few steps, you will insert two blank rows above row 16. The formula reference will not expand when you do this because you will insert directly above the row containing the formula.

16. Select rows 16 and 17 by dragging the mouse over the row headings.

17. Choose Insert→Rows and see the two new blank rows.

18. Click cell G18 and notice that the formula reference has not expanded.
Excel does not expand formula references when you insert rows directly above the formulas. You must be aware of this unusual convention and either design your worksheets to accommodate this or manually adjust the formulas after inserting. Notice that this also occurred when you inserted columns earlier in this exercise.

Add Headings, Numbers, and Subtotal Formulas

19. Referring to the illustration at the end of this exercise, enter the numbers in columns B and F and the Subtotal headings and Subtotal formula results shown in rows 6, 11, and 16. The formulas in row 18 should add up the subtotals in each column. You will have to redo all the formulas in column G. These formulas are no longer correct because you inserted columns B and F, which were outside the columns originally referenced by the total formulas.

20. Take a few minutes to proof your worksheet carefully. In particular, make sure all formulas are calculating correctly. Your worksheet should match the following illustration.

	A	B	C	D	E	F	G
1	Ricky's Clothing Store - Defective Items						
2							
3	**Shirts**	Extra Small	Small	Medium	Large	Extra Large	Total
4	Long sleeve	13	12	13	9	11	58
5	Short sleeve	8	9	8	9	8	42
6	Subtotal	21	21	21	18	19	100
7							
8	**Pants**						
9	Blue	6	5	6	4	3	24
10	Khaki	8	7	8	9	4	36
11	Subtotal	14	12	14	13	7	60
12							
13	**Shorts**						
14	White	2	3	2	4	3	14
15	Red	9	1	9	7	6	32
16	Subtotal	11	4	11	11	9	46
17							
18	Total	46	37	46	42	35	206

21. Save and close the workbook.

Skill Builder 5.2   Set Up an Accounts Receivable Report

In this exercise, you will create an accounts receivable aging report that calculates the number of days accounts are past due.

Set Up the Worksheet

1. Click the New Workbook ⬜ button to open a new workbook.

2. Set up the worksheet by typing the headings and numbers shown in the following illustration. Use [Alt]+[Enter] to create the multi-line headings in columns C–F. You will need to widen the columns after typing the headings and you may need to AutoFit row 4 to reduce its height.

	A	B	C	D	E	F
1	Accounts Receivable Aging Report					
2	Report Date					
3						
4	Customer	Invoice #	Invoice Date	Invoice Amount	# of Days Since Invoice Was Issued	# of Days Past Due
5	Wilson	345		123		
6	Arthur	367		980		
7	Bellmont	456		345		
8	Alexander	478		234		
9	Wilmont	489		765		
10	Barton	505		469		

Change the Computer's Date

Later in this exercise, you will use the TODAY function to determine the number of days invoices are past due. In the next few steps, you will change your computer's internal clock so the TODAY function returns the same current date (6/8/2004) as shown later in this exercise.

3. Double-click the clock on the taskbar at the bottom-right corner of your screen. If the clock isn't displayed on the taskbar, click the Start button, choose Settings, choose Control Panel, then double-click the Date and Time icon in the Control Panel.
   The Date/Time Properties dialog box should be displayed.

4. Use the dialog box controls to set the date to June 8, 2004 and click OK.
   There is no need to set the time.

Insert the Current Date and Invoice Dates

5. Click cell C2 and enter the function **=TODAY()**.
   The current date should be displayed in the cell.

6. Enter the invoice dates shown in the following illustration into column C.

	A	B	C
1	Accounts Receivable Aging Report		
2	Report Date		6/8/2004
3			
4	Customer	Invoice #	Invoice Date
5	Wilson	345	1/20/2004
6	Arthur	367	3/12/2004
7	Bellmont	456	3/28/2004
8	Alexander	478	2/4/2004
9	Wilmont	489	1/8/2004
10	Barton	505	2/15/2004

Calculate the Number of Days Since the Invoices Were Issued

7. Click cell E5 and enter the formula **=TODAY()-C5**.
   Enter the formula exactly as shown. Excel will format the result as a date and time.

8. Click any blank cell in the worksheet then click the Format Painter button.

9. Click cell E5 to copy the General Style number format to that cell.
   The result will equal 140. This is the number of days between June 8, 2004 (today's date in this exercise) and the date the invoice was issued.

10. Use the fill handle to copy the formula down the column to cell E10.

11. Click cell F5 and enter the formula **=E5-30**.
    The result will equal 110. This number represents the number of days the invoice is past due, assuming the terms are net 30 days (meaning the invoice will be paid within 30 days).

12. Copy the formula down the column. The worksheet should match the following illustration.

	A	B	C	D	E	F
1	Accounts Receivable Aging Report					
2	Report Date		6/8/2004			
3						
4	Customer	Invoice #	Invoice Date	Invoice Amount	# of Days Since Invoice Was Issued	# of Days Past Due
5	Wilson	345	1/20/2004	123	140	110
6	Arthur	367	3/12/2004	980	88	58
7	Bellmont	456	3/28/2004	345	72	42
8	Alexander	478	2/4/2004	234	125	95
9	Wilmont	489	1/8/2004	765	152	122
10	Barton	505	2/15/2004	469	114	84

Change the System Date Back to Today's Date

13. Use the technique in steps 3 and 4 to change the system date back to today's date.
Notice that the TODAY function does not display today's date in cell C2 and that the dates do not change in the days past due calculations. The date functions refresh only when the workbook is closed and then reopened.

14. Save the workbook as **Rec Aging Report** and close it.

15. Choose File from the menu bar and Rec Aging Report will be displayed at the bottom of the menu.
You can open the most recently used workbooks by choosing them from the menu.

16. Choose Rec Aging Report from the File menu to open the workbook.
Take a moment to review the worksheet and notice that the date in cell C2 is set to today's date. The numbers in column E should also be significantly larger because they are now measuring the number of days past due from today's date. The formula results in column F should also reflect significantly different numbers.

17. Close the workbook and continue with the next exercise.

Skill Builder 5.3   Insert and Delete Rows

In this exercise, you will modify an order entry worksheet by removing and inserting line items.

Open the Workbook and Create the Formulas

1. Open the workbook named Filmore Petroleum.

2. Click cell D4 and enter a formula that calculates the Extended Price as the Quantity multiplied by the Unit Price.
The result should be 239.7.

3. Copy the Extended Price formula down to rows 5–8.

4. Use AutoSum to compute the subtotal for the extended prices in column D.

5. Calculate the Sales Tax as the Subtotal multiplied by **7.75%**.

6. Calculate the Total as the Subtotal plus the Sales Tax.

7. Select all the numbers in columns C–D and increase the decimals to 2.

Delete a Row and Insert a New Row

A customer has decided to cancel his order for electric pencil sharpeners and add toner cartridges.

8. Select row 5 by clicking the row heading and choose Edit→Delete.
   The Subtotal, Sales Tax, and Total should be recalculated.

9. Click anywhere in row 7 and choose Insert→Rows.

10. Add the following item and be sure to use a formula in cell D7:

7	Toner cartridge		10	119.00	1190.00

Insert a Row

11. Click anywhere in row 9 and insert a row above the Subtotal row.

12. Add the following item to the new row and be sure to use a formula in cell D9:

9	Two-line phone		5	145.00	725.00

13. Click cell D10 and notice that Excel has adjusted the formula reference to accommodate the new row.
   Excel adjusted the formula reference because the rows inserted were within the range referenced in the formula.

14. Use the TODAY function to insert the current date in cell E1.

15. Format the date with the date format of your choice.

16. Select columns A through E and use the AutoFit command to adjust the column widths.

17. Save and close the workbook.

Skill Builder 5.4   Find and Replace

In this exercise, you will experiment with finding and replacing contents and formats.

Find and Replace Contents

1. Open the workbook named Quarterly Sales.

2. Choose Edit→Replace from the menu bar.
   Be aware that the formats searched for earlier in the Hands-On exercises may still be in the Find and Replace dialog box. If so, you must clear the formats before completing step 3.

3. Replace Robinson with **Pace**.
   You do not have to use a capital "R" in the Find What box. If you want the replaced text to be capitalized though, you must type it that way in the Replace With box.

Find and Replace Formats

4. Use Ctrl + H to display the Find and Replace box.

5. Delete the entries in the Find What and Replace With boxes.

6. Click the drop-down arrow on the Format button in the Find What row, and then click the Choose Format from Cell command on the menu.

7. Click cell B4.

8. Click the Format button for the Replace With box (not the drop-down button) to display the Replace Format box.

9. Click the number tab, and then choose the Currency category and be sure the decimals are set to 2.

10. Click OK then click Replace All on the Replace box.
    The message should indicate that 10 replacements were made.

11. Click Close to close the Find and Replace box.

12. Save the changes and close the workbook.

 **Assessments**

Assessment 5.1   Restructure an Accounts Receivable Report

In this exercise, you will insert and move columns and rows, create a formula, and apply an AutoFormat to the report.

1. Open the workbook named Accounts Receivable.

2. Use the TODAY function to insert the current date in cell D2.

3. Insert and move rows as necessary to alphabetize rows 5–10.

4. Insert a column between columns A and B and enter the invoice numbers shown in the illustration at the end of this exercise. Also, enter the heading shown in cell B4.

5. Use formulas in column E to calculate the number of days since the invoices were issued as the current date minus the invoice date.

6. Format the entries in column E with the General Style number format.

7. Use formulas in column F to calculate the number of days past due. Assume the terms are net 30 days. Your formulas should subtract 30 from the number of days since the invoice was issued.

8. Use AutoFormat to format the worksheet. The example in this exercise uses the Classic 2 format.

9. Your completed worksheet should match the following illustration. However, the data in columns E and F should be visible in your worksheet.

	A	B	C	D	E	F
1	Accounts Receivable Aging Report					
2	Report Date			5/21/2004		
3						
4	Customer	Invoice Number	Invoice Date	Invoice Amount	# of Days Since Invoice Was Issued	# of Days Past Due
5	Alexander	210	2/4/2004	234		
6	Arthur	155	3/12/2004	980		
7	Barton	246	2/15/2004	469		
8	Bellmont	189	3/28/2004	345		
9	Wilmont	228	1/8/2004	765		
10	Wilson	130	1/20/2004	123		

10. Print the worksheet, save the changes, and close the workbook.

Assessment 5.2   Create a Worksheet with Averages

In this exercise, you will create a worksheet that calculates the number of days between two test dates, the point increase in test scores, the percentage increase in test scores, the average number of days, and the average percentage increase.

1. Enter all text, numbers, and dates as shown in the illustration at the end of this exercise. Follow these guidelines to create the large paragraph shown near the top of the worksheet:
   - Use the Merge and Center button to merge cells A2:C2.
   - Turn on the Wrap Text option.
   - Increase the height of row 2 as shown.
   - Type the text in the large merged cell.

2. Use formulas in column F to calculate the number of days between the two tests.

3. Format the entries in column F with the General Style number format.

4. Use formulas in column G to calculate the point increase between the two test scores.

5. Use formulas to calculate the percentage increase in column H. The percentage increase is calculated as the Point Increase in column G divided by the First Test score in column C.

6. Use the AVERAGE function to calculate the averages in cells F12 and H13.

7. Format all numbers, dates, and text as desired. Adjust row heights and column widths as shown. Format the percent increases in column H as Percent Style with 0 decimals.

8. Print the worksheet when you have finished.

9. Save the workbook as **Performance Evals** and close it.

	A	B	C	D	E	F	G	H
1	**Grade 10 Performance Evaluations**							
2	This worksheet computes the percentage increase in test scores for students who have been receiving special assistance. The average number of days required to achieve the results is also shown.							
3								
4		First Test		Second Test				
5	Student	Date	Score	Date	Score	Number of Days Between Tests	Point Increase	Percentage Increase
6	Lisa Evans	2/3/2004	78	3/30/2004	87			
7	Clara Johnson	2/5/2004	77	3/28/2004	82			
8	Ted Thomas	2/5/2004	65	4/5/2004	80			
9	Brian Wilson	3/10/2004	64	4/1/2004	72			
10	Elizabeth Crawford	3/12/2004	68	4/2/2004	78			
11	Bernice Barton	2/1/2004	72	3/10/2004	88			
12	Average Days							
13	Average Increase							

Critical Thinking

Critical Thinking 5.1   On Your Own

Open the Returns workbook. Insert a column immediately to the right of the Return Date column. Use a formula to calculate the number of days between the Return Date and the Purchase Date. Format the cells in this **Number of Days** column so numbers are displayed with 0 decimal places. Reorganize the columns so the Purchase Price column is to the right of the Number of Days column. Calculate the total value of the returns in cell G9. Adjust all column widths to fit the widest entries in the columns. Save the changes and close the workbook.

Critical Thinking 5.2   On Your Own

Open the Stock Info workbook. Assume the stocks in the portfolio were purchased on the following dates:

Stock Symbol	Date Purchased
CORL	3/5/02
GLC	11/5/01
HAL	11/6/03
LU	8/5/02
MSFT	9/1/03
ORCL	4/25/01

Insert a column to the left of the Purchase Price column and enter the Date Purchased information. Be sure you associate the correct purchase date with the correct stock symbol. Format the dates in the Date Purchased column with a date format. Add another column to the worksheet that calculates the Number of Days the investment has been held as of today's date. The formula should automatically recalculate the number of days whenever the workbook is opened. Format all cells in the Number of Days column to display a number with 0 decimals. Add another column to calculate the Average Daily Dollar Gain for each stock since the purchase date. Use AutoFormat to apply the AutoFormat of your choice to the worksheet. Save the changes and close the workbook.

Critical Thinking 5.3   On Your Own

Janine Carmichael works in the Accounts Payable Department of Data Storage, Inc. This company is in the data warehousing business. With the emergence of the Internet, Data Storage's business has grown rapidly as many new companies have turned to Data Storage to assist them with their data warehousing needs. As with any rapidly growing business, cash flow is important to Data Storage. Janine is responsible for tracking the accounts of delinquent customers and initiating collection activities. Janine asks you to prepare a worksheet that tracks delinquent accounts.

Create a worksheet that includes the customer name, invoice number, invoice date, and invoice amount. Include five fictitious customer accounts in the worksheet. Use a formula to calculate the number of days each account is past due. The formula should count from today's date. It should be dynamic, recalculating the number of days past due each time the workbook is opened. Format the number of days past due cells in General Style. Calculate an interest charge for each past due account. Assume an annual interest rate of 18%. Assume that an interest rate of 18%/365 is charged each day since there are 365 days in a year and 18% is an annualized rate. Calculate the total amount due as the invoice amount plus interest. Use formulas to sum the total invoice amounts, total interest, and total amounts due for all accounts. Use the AVERAGE function to calculate the average days past due for all accounts. Save the workbook as **Delinquent Accts** and close it.

Critical Thinking 5.4   Web Research

Open the Stock Info workbook you updated in Critical Thinking 5.2. Use the Research pane to get quotes on stocks with the symbols CSCO, INTC, and PAYX. Add the stock symbols, company names, and dates purchased to the worksheet. Insert this new information so the rows are in alphabetical order by stock symbol. Assume you are buying 100 shares of each company and that the purchase price and current price are the same. If necessary, copy formulas from other cells to the empty cells in the new rows. Format all cells as necessary. Get a detailed quote for the stock that looks most promising of the three new quotes and copy that detailed quote onto Sheet2. Save the workbook as **New Stock Info**.

Critical Thinking 5.5   Web Research

Open the Delinquent Accts workbook you created in Critical Thinking 5.3. Save the workbook as **Collection Companies**. Use Internet Explorer and a search engine of your choice to locate three companies on the World Wide Web that provide collection services. Add the names of these companies, their Website URLs, and their telephone numbers to Sheet 2. Save and close the workbook.

LESSON 6

Creating an Impact with Charts

In this lesson, you will use Excel's Chart Wizard to create various types of charts. Charting is an important skill to have when using worksheets because comparisons, trends, and other relationships are often conveyed more effectively with charts. You will use the Chart Wizard to create column charts, line charts, and pie charts. In addition, you will learn how to edit and format chart objects.

Microsoft Office Excel 2003 and Microsoft Office Excel 2003 Expert objectives covered in this lesson

Objective Number	Skill Sets and Skills	Concept Page References	Exercise Page References
XL03S-2-5	Create, modify, and position diagrams and charts based on worksheet data	178–179, 182, 184–185, 198	179–193, 198–199
XL03S-3-4	Format worksheets		177
XL03S-5-4	Organize worksheets	176	177
XL03E-2-4	Format charts and diagrams	187–189, 192–194, 196, 199	188–190, 193–197, 199–200

Additional learning resources are available at labpub.com/learn/excel03/

Case Study

Christina Giamo is the founder and CEO of AutoSoft—a rapidly growing software development company. Christina has asked her sales manager, Andy Broderick, to prepare several charts depicting revenue for the 2003 fiscal year. Christina wants charts that compare sales in the various quarters, the growth trend throughout the year, and the contributions of each sales rep to the total company sales. Andy uses Excel's Chart Wizard to produce impressive charts that meet Christina's high standards.

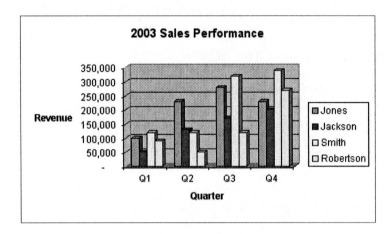

A column chart

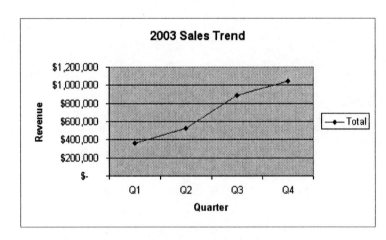

A line chart

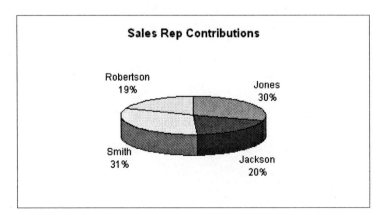

A pie chart

Managing Workbooks

As you begin to work with more advanced topics like charts and create more in depth workbooks, you will need to be comfortable with workbook management and maneuvering around multiple worksheets. In *Microsoft Office Excel 2003: Quick Course 2* you will learn more about working with multiple worksheets. *Microsoft Office Excel 2003: Quick Course 3* expands even further and teaches you how to group worksheets and consolidate their data.

Insert, Delete, Rearrange, and Rename Worksheets

Although Excel displays three worksheets in a new workbook, you can insert as many new worksheets as your available computer memory allows. You can change the default number of worksheets, which you will learn about in *Microsoft Office Excel 2003: Quick Course 2*. This section briefly introduces you to such workbook management topics as inserting, deleting, and moving worksheets; changing the color of worksheet tabs; and renaming sheet tabs. A tab located at the bottom of the sheet identifies each worksheet.

WARNING! *You cannot undo a deleted worksheet.*

QUICK REFERENCE: MANAGING WORKSHEETS	
Task	**Procedure**
Activate a worksheet	Click the desired worksheet tab.
Rename a worksheet	Double-click the worksheet tab, type a new name, and tap [Enter].
Change the worksheet tab color	Click anywhere in the desired worksheet and choose Format→Sheet→Tab Color or right-click the desired sheet tab and choose Tab Color then choose the desired color and click OK.
Insert a worksheet	Click anywhere in the desired worksheet and choose Insert→Worksheet. The new worksheet is inserted to the left of the current sheet.
Delete a worksheet	Click anywhere in the desired worksheet, choose Edit→Delete Sheet, and click OK.
Move a worksheet	Drag the worksheet tab to the desired position in the worksheet order.
Copy a worksheet	Choose Edit→Move or Copy Sheet, choose the desired position in the Before Sheet box, click the Create a Copy box, and click OK.

Hands-On 6.1 Modify Workbooks and Sheet Tabs

In this exercise, you will change the color of and rename a worksheet tab, insert and move a new sheet, and delete a worksheet.

1. Open the workbook named Autosoft Qtrly Sales.

2. Follow these steps to rename Sheet1:

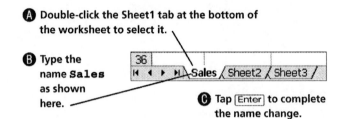

Ⓐ Double-click the Sheet1 tab at the bottom of the worksheet to select it.

Ⓑ Type the name **Sales** as shown here.

Ⓒ Tap Enter to complete the name change.

TIP! *You can click anywhere in the worksheet to complete the name change.*

3. Choose Format→Sheet→Tab Color to display the Format Tab Color box.

4. Choose any color and click OK.
   The color you chose will appear as a thin line at the bottom of the sheet tab as long as the sheet is selected. When you click a different sheet tab, the entire tab will display the color applied.

5. Click any other sheet tab and the colored sheet tab will be fully visible.

6. Follow these steps to move the sheet:

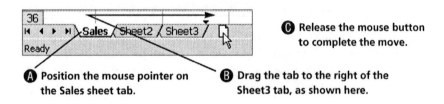

Ⓒ Release the mouse button to complete the move.

Ⓐ Position the mouse pointer on the Sales sheet tab.

Ⓑ Drag the tab to the right of the Sheet3 tab, as shown here.

7. Now drag the Sales sheet back to the first position in the sheet order.

8. Click the Sheet3 tab and choose Edit→Delete Sheet from the menu bar.

9. Try clicking Undo and notice that the sheet cannot be restored.
   Worksheets are permanently deleted when you issue the Edit→Delete Sheet command.

WARNING! *The only way to recover a deleted sheet is to close the workbook without saving and then reopen it.*

10. Choose Insert→Worksheet from the menu bar.
    A new sheet will be inserted to the left of the current sheet.

11. Drag the new sheet to the right of Sheet2 and rename it **Sheet3**.

12. Click the Sales sheet tab and continue with the next topic.

Understanding Charts

Numerical data is often easier to interpret when presented in a chart. You can embed a chart in a worksheet so it appears alongside the worksheet data or you can place the chart on a separate worksheet. Putting the chart on a separate worksheet prevents the chart from cluttering the data worksheet. Regardless of their placement, charts are always linked to the data from which they are created. Thus, charts are automatically updated when worksheet data changes. Charts are made up of individual objects including the chart title, legend, plot area, value axis, category axis, and data series. You can apply many options and enhancements to each object.

Chart Types

Excel provides 14 major chart types. Each chart type also has several subtypes from which you can choose. Excel literally has a chart for every occasion.

Built-In Chart Types

Each chart type represents data in a different manner. You can present the same data in completely different ways by changing the chart type. For this reason, you should always use the chart type that most effectively represents your data. The three most common chart types are column, pie, and line. You will be creating all three types in this lesson.

User-Defined Charts

Excel lets you create and save customized charts to meet your particular needs. For example, you can create a customized chart that contains the name of your company and its color(s) in the background and use it as the basis for all new charts of that type.

Creating Charts with the Chart Wizard

Excel's Chart Wizard guides you through each step of chart creation. You can also edit and enhance a chart after it has been created. The first, and arguably the most important, step in creating a chart is to select the data you want included in the chart. Many beginners find this step to be the most difficult because they are unsure how Excel will interpret the selected data. You will receive plenty of practice selecting data in this lesson.

Column Charts and Bar Charts

Column charts compare values (numbers) using vertical bars. Bar charts compare values using horizontal bars. Each column or bar represents a value from the worksheet. Column charts and bar charts are most useful for comparing sets of values (called data series). Column and bar charts can be created in 2-D or 3-D formats.

Category Axis and Value Axis

The horizontal line that forms the base of a column chart is the category axis. The category axis typically measures units of time such as days, months, and quarters. The vertical line on the left side of a column chart is the value axis. The value axis typically measures values such as dollars. Most chart types (including column and bar charts) have a category and a value axis. The following illustrations show the worksheet data and one of the two column charts you will create in the next exercise. The illustrations show the objects present on most column charts and the corresponding data used to create the chart. Take a few minutes to study these illustrations carefully.

	A	B	C	D	E
1	Autosoft 2003 Quarterly Sales				
2					
3		Q1	Q2	Q3	Q4
4	Jones	100,000	230,000	280,000	230,000
5	Jackson	50,000	130,000	170,000	200,000
6	Smith	120,000	120,000	320,000	340,000
7	Robertson	90,000	50,000	120,000	270,000
8					
9	Total	$ 360,000	$ 530,000	$ 890,000	$ 1,040,000

The following chart was created using the selected data shown here. Notice that the Total row was not included in the selection. The column chart compares the sales numbers for the individual quarters, but it does not include the total sales from row 9.

This is the vertical value axis. Excel created the numbering scale (0–350,000) after it determined the range of values included in the chart.

Notice the chart columns. The columns represent values from the various data series. The first data series is the Jones numbers in row 4. The first column in each quarter represents the Jones numbers.

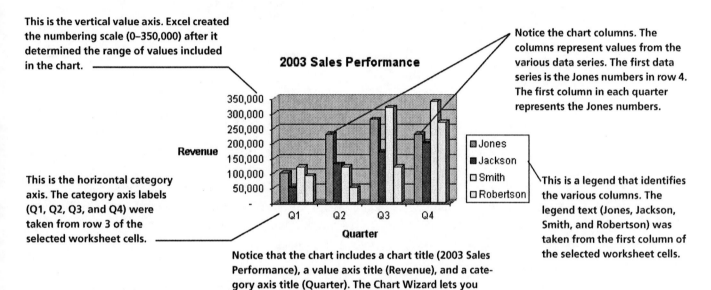

2003 Sales Performance

This is the horizontal category axis. The category axis labels (Q1, Q2, Q3, and Q4) were taken from row 3 of the selected worksheet cells.

This is a legend that identifies the various columns. The legend text (Jones, Jackson, Smith, and Robertson) was taken from the first column of the selected worksheet cells.

Notice that the chart includes a chart title (2003 Sales Performance), a value axis title (Revenue), and a category axis title (Quarter). The Chart Wizard lets you specify the titles when you create the chart.

 Hands-On 6.2   **Create Two Column Charts**

In this exercise, you will create two column charts on separate sheets, one in 2-D format and one in 3-D format. In Hands-On 6.7, you will move the 3-D column chart from its separate sheet and embed it into the worksheet.

Create a 2-D Column Chart on a Separate Chart Sheet

1. Select the range A3:E7.

2. Click the Chart Wizard [⊞] button on the Standard toolbar.
   The Chart Wizard dialog box will appear.

3. Follow these steps to explore the dialog box:

Ⓐ **Click the Custom Types tab. This tab displays built-in chart types that you can modify and save as customized charts.** —

Ⓑ **Click the Standard Types tab and review the various chart types by clicking them on this list. Choose Column when you finish exploring. Also, make sure the first subtype is chosen on the right side of the dialog box.** —

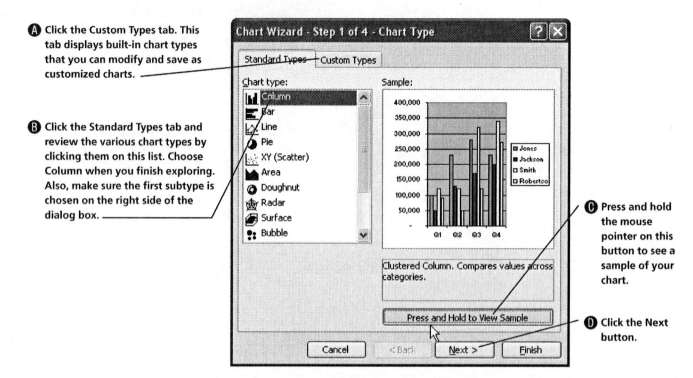

Ⓒ **Press and hold the mouse pointer on this button to see a sample of your chart.**

Ⓓ **Click the Next button.**

The Chart Wizard—Step 2 of 4 box will appear. This box lets you choose a different range of cells. Notice that the range in the dialog box is =Sales!$A$3:$E$7. Sales is the worksheet name, and the dollar signs indicate that these are absolute cell references. For now, just ignore the dollar signs and think of the range as A3:E7.

4. The range Sales!$A$3:$E$7 is correct so click the Next button.
The Step 3 box contains six tabs that let you set various chart options. You will explore these options in the next few steps.

5. Click the Titles tab and note the three available titles.
You will add titles to a chart in the next exercise.

6. Click the Axes tab.
The options on the Axes tab let you hide the labels on the category and value axes. You will typically leave these options set to their default settings.

7. Click the Gridlines tab.
Gridlines help identify chart values. Your chart should display the major gridlines for the value axis. The gridlines are the horizontal lines across the chart.

8. Feel free to click the various gridlines boxes and notice how they appear in the Preview window.
Remove the checkmarks from all checkboxes except the major Gridlines checkbox when you are finished experimenting.

9. Click the Legend tab.
Notice the legend on the right side of the Preview window. It identifies the various columns; for example, the columns for Jones are identified by the color that appears in the legend.

10. Remove the checkmark from the Show Legend box and the legend will vanish.

11. Click the Show Legend box to redisplay the legend.

12. Click the Data Labels tab.
Data labels display the values from the worksheet on top of the columns.

13. Click the Value option to display values at the top of each column.
The numbers will be very crowded in the Preview window.

14. Remove the checkmark from the Value box to remove the data labels.

15. Click the Data Table tab.

16. Click the Show Data Table checkbox and notice the table below the Preview chart.

17. Take a moment to check out the data table then remove the checkmark from the Show Data Table box.

18. Click the Next button to move to Step 4 of 4.

19. Click the As New Sheet option.
This option instructs Excel to create the chart on a separate chart sheet.

20. Click the Finish button.
Look at the sheet tabs and notice that the chart is created on a new sheet named Chart1.

21. Double-click the Chart1 sheet tab.

22. Type the new name **2-D Column Chart** and tap ⌷Enter⌷ to complete the name change.

Create a 3-D Column Chart

23. Click the Sales sheet tab. The range A3:E7 should still be selected.

24. Click the Chart Wizard button.

25. Choose the fourth column chart subtype, as shown to the right.
This subtype is known as a Clustered column with a 3-D Visual Effect.

26. Click the Next button then click Next again on the Step 2 of 4 box.

27. Click the Titles tab and follow these steps in the Step 3 of 4 box:

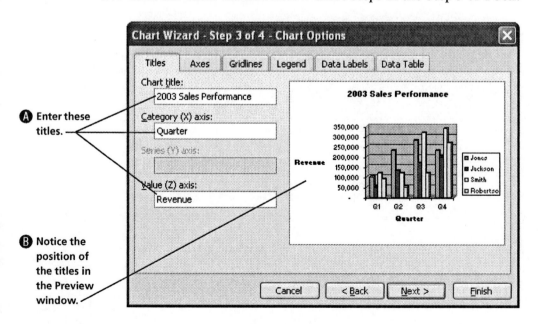

Ⓐ Enter these titles.

Ⓑ Notice the position of the titles in the Preview window.

28. Click the Next button.

29. Click the As New Sheet option and type **3-D Column Chart** in the As New Sheet box.

30. Click Finish.
Excel created a new sheet for your chart. The Chart toolbar will most likely appear as well.

31. Click the Sales tab, and then continue with the next exercise.

Line Charts

Line charts are most useful for comparing trends over a period of time. For example, line charts are often used to show stock market activity where the upward or downward trend is important. Like column charts, line charts have category and value axes. Line charts also use the same or similar objects as column charts. The following illustration shows a line chart that depicts the trend in quarterly sales throughout the year. Take a moment to study the illustration and accompanying worksheet.

	A	B	C	D	E
1	Autosoft 2003 Quarterly Sales				
2					
3		Q1	Q2	Q3	Q4
4	Jones	100,000	230,000	280,000	230,000
5	Jackson	50,000	130,000	170,000	200,000
6	Smith	120,000	120,000	320,000	340,000
7	Robertson	90,000	50,000	120,000	270,000
8					
9	Total	$ 360,000	$ 530,000	$ 890,000	$ 1,040,000

The following chart was created using the selected data shown here. Notice that the data is in two separate ranges. You use the Ctrl key to select these noncontiguous ranges so you can chart just the totals and the Q1–Q4 labels.

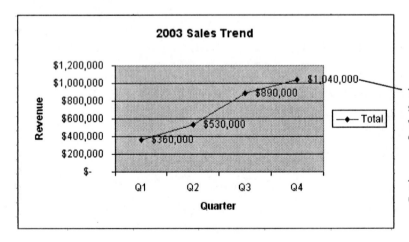

This is a data label. Data labels show the precise value of the various data points. You can use data labels with any chart type.

The line chart clearly depicts the upward trend in sales volume.

Hands-On 6.3   Create a Line Chart

In this exercise, you will create a line chart on a separate sheet.

1. Follow these steps to select the data for the line chart:

	A	B	C	D	E
1	Autosoft 2003 Quarterly Sales				
2					
3		Q1	Q2	Q3	Q4
4	Jones	100,000	230,000	280,000	230,000
5	Jackson	50,000	130,000	170,000	200,000
6	Smith	120,000	120,000	320,000	340,000
7	Robertson	90,000	50,000	120,000	270,000
8					
9	Total	$ 360,000	$ 530,000	$ 890,000	$ 1,040,000

Ⓐ **Select the range A3:E3.**

Ⓑ **Press and hold down** Ctrl **while selecting the range A9:E9. Both ranges should be selected.**

2. Click the Chart Wizard button.

3. Choose Line from the Chart Type list and choose the fourth subtype, as shown to the right.

4. Click Next twice to display the Step 3 of 4 box.

5. If necessary, click the Titles tab on the Step 3 of 4 box.

6. Enter the titles in the Step 3 of 4 box as shown.
When you have completed entering the titles, your sample chart should match the one shown in the following illustration.

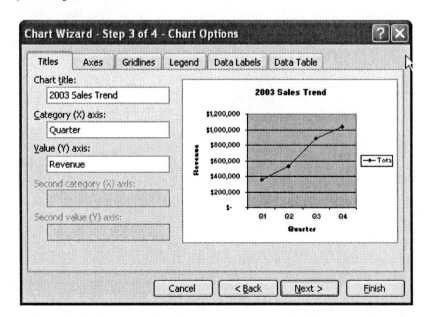

7. Click Next, and then the As New Sheet option and type **Line Chart** in the As New Sheet box.

8. Click the Finish button.
   Line Chart has been assigned to the new sheet tab because you typed this name in the As New Sheet box in step 7.

9. Take a few moments to examine your chart. In particular, notice the relationship between the data and the points on the line.

Pie Charts

Pie charts are useful for comparing parts of a whole. For example, pie charts are often used in budgets to show how they are allocated. You typically select only two sets of data when creating pie charts. You select the values to be represented by the pie slices and labels to identify the slices. The following illustration shows a worksheet and accompanying 3-D pie chart. Notice that the worksheet has a total column. You will create a pie chart based on the total column in Hands-On 6.4.

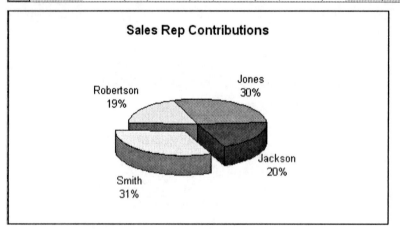

	A	B	C	D	E	F
3		Q1	Q2	Q3	Q4	Totals
4	Jones	100,000	230,000	280,000	230,000	840,000
5	Jackson	50,000	130,000	170,000	200,000	550,000
6	Smith	120,000	120,000	320,000	340,000	900,000
7	Robertson	90,000	50,000	120,000	270,000	530,000

The names in column A will become labels on the pie slices. The numbers in column F will determine the size of the slices.

Sales Rep Contributions

Robertson 19%
Jones 30%
Jackson 20%
Smith 31%

Excel calculates the percentages based on the numbers you select. Notice that the Smith slice is "exploded" out from the pie.

 Hands-On 6.4   Create an Embedded Pie Chart

In this exercise, you will create a pie chart embedded in the Sales worksheet.

1. Click the Sales tab, and then click cell F3 and enter the word **Total**.

2. Select the range F4:F7 and use the AutoSum Σ button to compute the totals for column F.
   The totals calculate the total annual sales for each sales rep. Your totals should match those shown in the preceding illustration.

3. Select the ranges A4:A7 and F4:F7 as shown in the preceding illustration (use [Ctrl] to select the second range).

4. Click the Chart Wizard button.

5. Choose Pie from the Chart Type list and choose the second subtype, as shown to the right.

6. Click Next twice to display the Step 3 of 4 box.

7. If necessary, click the Titles tab on the Step 3 of 4 box.

8. Type **Sales Rep Contributions** as the chart title.

9. Click the Legend tab and remove the checkmark from the Show legend box.
You will add data labels in the next step so you don't need a legend.

10. Click the Data Labels tab and check the Category Name and Percentage boxes.
Each pie slice should have the sales rep name and percentage of total sales displayed.

11. Click the Finish button.
There was no need to click Next on the Step 3 of 4 box because we want the chart embedded in the current worksheet. You can click Finish at any step in the Chart Wizard.

12. Save the changes to your workbook and continue with the next topic.

Moving and Sizing Embedded Charts

You can easily move and size embedded charts and other objects. You must select the chart object before moving, sizing, or modifying it. To select a chart, click anywhere in the chart area. The chart area is the blank area just inside the border of the chart, where no other objects are present. Small black squares called sizing handles appear on the corners and four sides of a selected chart.

QUICK REFERENCE: MOVING AND SIZING EMBEDDED CHARTS	
Task	**Procedure**
Move an embedded chart	Drag the selected chart to a new location.
Change the chart size	Drag any sizing handle.
Change the size of a chart while maintaining original proportions	Press [Shift] while dragging a corner-sizing handle.

Hands-On 6.5   **Move and Size the Embedded Chart**

In this exercise, you will move and resize the embedded pie chart under the worksheet data.

1. Click anywhere outside of the chart to deselect it, if necessary.
   The sizing handles will vanish.

2. Follow these steps to move and size the chart:

Ⓐ Click in the chart area (the blank area inside of the chart border) to make the sizing handles appear.

Ⓑ Position the mouse pointer in the chart area and drag the chart down and to the left to position it under the worksheet data.

Ⓒ Point to the bottom-right corner-sizing handle to make the Adjust pointer appear.

Ⓓ Press and hold down the [Shift] key while dragging the sizing handle to change the width and height proportionally. Adjust the size until the chart has the same width as the worksheet data.

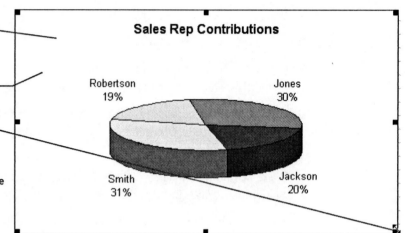

3. Click cell B4.

4. Enter the number **300,000** and watch the pie proportions change.
   Charts are linked to the worksheet data. They always reflect changes in the data even if placed in a separate chart sheet.

5. Click cell B4 again and enter the number **1,000,000**.
   This number is much larger than the other numbers in the worksheet so the other pie pieces are now much smaller.

6. Click cell B4 again and enter the number **100,000**.

7. Save the changes and continue with the next topic.

Previewing and Printing Charts

Use the Print Preview 🔍 and Print 🖨 buttons to preview and print charts. If a chart is on a separate chart sheet, you must first activate it by clicking the sheet tab. If a chart is embedded, you must first select the chart before clicking the Print Preview or Print buttons. In Print Preview the charts display in black and white or in color, depending on the type of printer your computer is connected to.

Hands-On 6.6   Use Print Preview and Print a Chart

In this exercise, you will preview and print the chart.

1. Click anywhere in the worksheet to deselect the chart.

2. Click the Print Preview 🔍 button.
   Notice that both the worksheet and embedded chart are displayed. The chart may appear in black and white while in Print Preview.

3. Click the Close button on the Print Preview toolbar.

4. Click in the blank area near one of the corners of the chart.

5. Click the Print Preview 🔍 button and notice that only the chart is displayed.
   At this point, you could print the chart by using the Print button on the Print Preview toolbar.

6. Click the Close button on the Print Preview toolbar.

7. Click the 2-D column chart worksheet tab to activate that worksheet.

8. Click the Print Preview 🔍 button and notice that the chart is displayed.
   You don't need to select a chart prior to printing if it is on a separate chart sheet.

9. Close the Print Preview window then click the Print 🖨 button.

10. Retrieve your printout from the printer.
    Your chart will be printed in shades of gray unless you have a color printer.

Formatting Charts

You can modify any chart object after the chart has been created. You can change the size, font, color, and placement of titles; format the numbers on the value axis; change the background color of the chart area; and more. You can also add or remove objects, such as legends and data labels. You can even move an embedded chart to a separate chart sheet and vice versa.

Using the Chart Wizard to Modify Charts

You can change the setup of a chart using the Chart Wizard. Simply click the desired embedded chart or click a separate chart sheet then click the Chart Wizard button. You can move through all four screens in the Chart Wizard, choosing options as you do when a chart is first created.

The Chart Menu

When a chart is activated, the menu bar displays a chart item. The first four options on the chart menu display the same screens that appear in the Chart Wizard. You can add, remove, and modify chart objects using the desired screen(s) and change the chart location from embedded to separate sheet and vice versa. The 3-D View option on the Chart menu is useful for changing the elevation and rotation of 3-D charts.

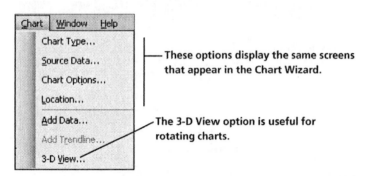

These options display the same screens that appear in the Chart Wizard.

The 3-D View option is useful for rotating charts.

 Hands-On 6.7   Use the Chart Wizard and the Chart Menu

In this exercise, you will move the embedded pie chart to its own sheet. You will also embed the 3-D column chart into the Sales worksheet and display data labels on the chart.

Move the Pie Chart to a Separate Sheet

1. Click the Sales sheet tab.

2. Click in the chart area of the pie chart to make sizing handles appear on the chart borders.
   Notice that the Chart option now appears on the menu bar because a chart is selected.

3. Choose Chart→Location from the menu bar.
   The dialog box that appears is the same one that appears in Step 4 of the Chart Wizard.

4. Choose the As New Sheet option and type **Pie Chart** in the As New Sheet box.

5. Click OK to move the chart to a separate chart sheet.
   Notice that the Chart option is available on the menu bar even though the chart is not selected. The Chart option is always available in chart sheets.

6. Choose Chart→Location from the menu bar.

7. Choose the As Object In option and choose Sales from the drop-down list of sheet names.

8. Click OK to move the chart back into the Sales sheet as an embedded chart.

9. Now move the chart back to a separate chart sheet named **Pie Chart** as you did in steps 2–5.

Embed the 3-D Column Chart

10. Click the 3-D Column Chart sheet tab.

11. Choose Chart→Location and select Sales from the As Object In drop-down list.

12. Click OK to embed the chart into the Sales worksheet.

13. Now drag the chart down to position it below the worksheet data.

14. Press the $\boxed{\text{Shift}}$ key while dragging the bottom-right corner-sizing handle to resize the chart to the same width of the worksheet data.

Add Data Labels

15. Click the Chart Wizard button.

16. Click Next twice then click the Data Labels tab.
    Notice that the same screens appear as when you created a new chart.

17. Choose the Value option and click the Finish button.
    Excel displays data labels at the top of each column. The data labels display the actual values from the worksheet. Notice, however, that the data labels are too crowded. Data labels aren't really appropriate here because they crowd the chart.

18. With the chart still selected, choose Chart→Chart Options from the menu bar.
    This is the same screen that appears in Step 3 of the Chart Wizard.

19. Remove the checkmark from the Value box and click OK to remove the data labels.

20. Feel free to experiment with the Chart menu and the Chart Wizard then continue with the next topic.

Chart Objects

Charts are composed of various objects. For example, the legends, titles, and columns are all types of objects. You must select an object before you can perform an action on it. You can select an object by clicking it with the mouse. Once selected, you can delete, move, size, and format the object. You delete a selected object by tapping the $\boxed{\text{Delete}}$ key, move a selected object by dragging it with the mouse, and change the size by dragging a sizing handle.

Formatting Chart Objects

Use buttons on the Formatting toolbar to format titles and other objects containing text, including changing fill and font colors.

Use these buttons on the Formatting toolbar to format text objects and add fill colors to objects.

In this exercise, you will format titles and add background color to the column chart.

Change Text in the Titles

1. Click the chart title in the column chart to select it.

2. Click the mouse pointer Ⅰ just in front of the word Performance in the title.
   The flashing insertion point should be just in front of the word Performance.

3. Type the word **Rep** and tap the [Spacebar] to make the title **2003 Sales Rep Performance**.

4. Click the Revenue title (on the left side of the chart) to select it.

5. Now select the word Revenue within the title box by double-clicking the word.

6. Type the replacement word **Sales**.

Format the Titles

7. Click the Chart title 2003 Sales Rep Performance.

8. Click the Font Color drop-down [A▾] button on the Formatting toolbar and choose a blue color.

9. Format the Sales and Quarter titles with the same blue color.

Apply a Fill Color to the Chart Area

10. Click the chart area to select the entire chart.

11. Click the Fill Color drop-down [◇▾] button on the Formatting toolbar and choose a light fill color.
    The entire chart area should be filled.

12. Feel free to experiment with the formatting techniques discussed in this exercise.

The Chart Toolbar

The Chart toolbar appears when a chart sheet is active and when an embedded chart is selected. The Chart toolbar is used primarily for formatting chart objects. You can use the View→Toolbars→Chart command to display the Chart toolbar if it does not automatically appear.

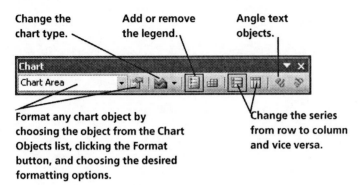

Change the chart type.

Add or remove the legend.

Angle text objects.

Format any chart object by choosing the object from the Chart Objects list, clicking the Format button, and choosing the desired formatting options.

Change the series from row to column and vice versa.

 Hands-On 6.9   Use the Chart Toolbar

In this exercise, you will change the axis title alignment to vertical. You will also experiment with the Chart Type and Legend buttons on the Chart toolbar.

Change the Orientation of the Sales Title

1. Choose View→Toolbars from the menu bar.

2. If the Chart option is already checked, close the menu by clicking the worksheet. Otherwise, choose Chart and the Chart toolbar will appear.
   The Chart toolbar will be anchored above the worksheet or float in the worksheet area.

3. Click the Sales title on the left side of the chart.
   All buttons on the Chart toolbar should now be available.

4. Follow these steps to display a formatting box for the title:

   A Notice that Value Axis Title is displayed in the Chart Objects box. The Chart Objects box always displays the name of the selected object. You can also choose the object you wish to format from the drop-down list.

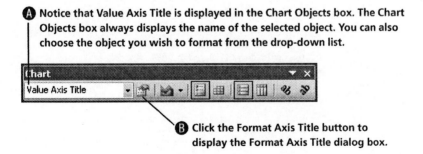

   B Click the Format Axis Title button to display the Format Axis Title dialog box.

 TIP! *You can right-click any chart object and choose Format… from the context menu to open the dialog box for that object.*

5. Click the various dialog box tabs and notice that you can format the title text, apply a font color, and set other formatting options.

6. Click the Alignment tab.

7. Follow these steps to change the orientation:

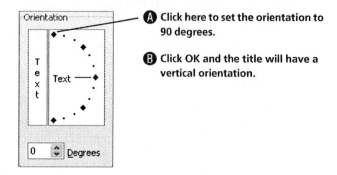

Ⓐ Click here to set the orientation to 90 degrees.

Ⓑ Click OK and the title will have a vertical orientation.

Experiment with the Chart Toolbar

8. Click the chart area to select the entire chart.

9. Follow these steps to explore the Chart toolbar:

Ⓐ Click the Chart Type drop-down button and choose a chart type such as 3-D Cylinder from the bottom row of the list.

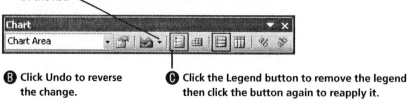

Ⓑ Click Undo to reverse the change.

Ⓒ Click the Legend button to remove the legend then click the button again to reapply it.

10. Feel free to experiment with the options on the Chart toolbar.

Exploding Pie Slices

When creating a pie chart with the Chart Wizard, you can choose an exploded pie chart sub-type, which breaks the pie into individual pieces. You can make just one piece stand out by dragging it farther away from the pie. If you don't choose the exploded option, you can still explode all pieces using the dragging method outlined in the following Quick Reference table.

QUICK REFERENCE: EXPLODING PIE CHARTS

Task	Procedure
Explode one slice	■ Click once to select the entire pie.
	■ Click the slice you wish to explode.
	■ Drag the slice out from the pie.
Explode all slices	■ Click once to select the pie.
	■ Drag any slice (without clicking first) and all slices will separate.
Restore an exploded slice	Select the entire pie and drag any exploded slice back into the pie.

Hands-On 6.10   **Explode Pie Slices**

In this exercise, you will explode pieces away from the pie chart.

Explode the Smith Slice

1. Click the Pie Chart worksheet tab to activate the sheet.

2. Click the chart area to make sure the pie is not selected.

3. Click anywhere on the pie to select it.

4. Now click once on the Smith slice to select just that slice.

5. Follow these steps to explode a pie piece:

Ⓐ Position the mouse pointer on the Smith slice.

Ⓑ Drag the slide to the left and away from the rest of the pie.

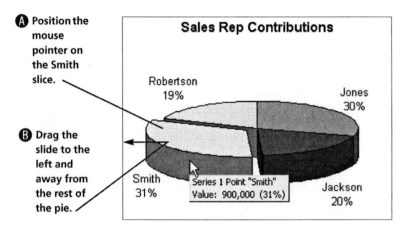

Explode All Slices

6. Drag the Smith slice back so the pie is whole again.

7. Click outside of the pie to deselect it.

8. Click anywhere on the pie to select it.

9. Drag any slice out of the pie to explode all of the slices.

10. Reverse the explosion by dragging any slice back to the center of the pie.

11. Now explode just the Smith slice again.

Changing the Rotation and Elevation of Pie Charts

You can rotate a pie chart to bring an important slice into view. Likewise, you can change the elevation to make an important slice more noticeable. You change the rotation and elevation using options on the 3-D View dialog box. The 3-D View dialog box is displayed with the Chart→3-D View command. Rotation and elevation can also be changed for a 3-D column or a bar chart.

In this exercise, you will rotate the pie chart and change its elevation.

1. Click outside of the pie then click the pie to make sure the entire pie is selected.

2. Choose Chart→3-D View from the menu bar.

3. Follow these steps to adjust the rotation and elevation:

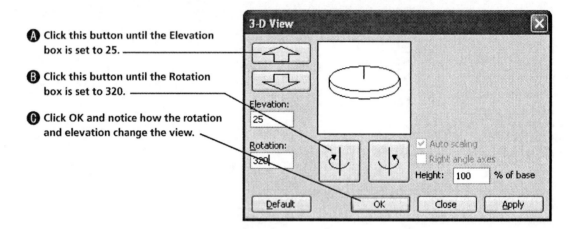

A Click this button until the Elevation box is set to 25.

B Click this button until the Rotation box is set to 320.

C Click OK and notice how the rotation and elevation change the view.

4. Feel free to experiment with any of the topics you have learned in this lesson so far.

5. Save your workbook when you have finished and continue with the next topic.

Modifying Data in the Plot Area

When charts are embedded in a worksheet, you can simply drag new data directly onto the chart and the chart will be updated automatically. For charts located on a separate sheet, you must use Copy and Paste to plot new data onto the chart. To remove data, use the Chart→ Source Data command and change the data range. You can also use this command to change the data range.

Hands-On 6.12   Modify Data in the Plot Area

In this exercise, you will change the data range in the column chart. You will also drag data onto the plot area to add it to the chart.

Change the Source Data

1. Click the Sales sheet tab then click the chart area of the column chart.

2. Choose Chart→Source Data from the menu bar.

3. Follow these steps to change the data range so only the first and second quarter data are plotted on the chart:

Ⓐ Click between the dollar sign and the letter E in the Data range box, tap ⌊Delete⌋, and type C.

Ⓑ Click OK.

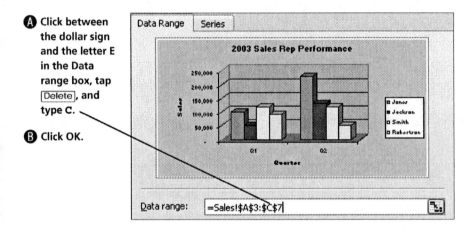

The new data range is plotted now with only the first and second quarter data. Your chart should resemble the following illustration.

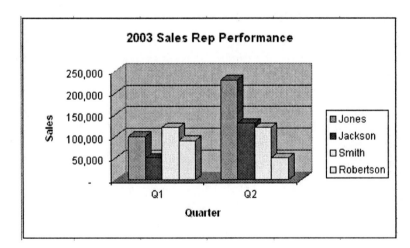

Drag Data onto a Chart

4. Follow these steps to drag the third quarter data onto the chart:

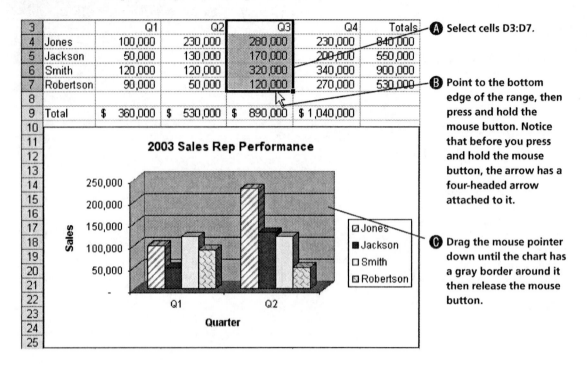

A Select cells D3:D7.

B Point to the bottom edge of the range, then press and hold the mouse button. Notice that before you press and hold the mouse button, the arrow has a four-headed arrow attached to it.

C Drag the mouse pointer down until the chart has a gray border around it then release the mouse button.

5. Select cells E3:E7 then drag that range down onto the chart.
The chart is now plotted with data from all four quarters.

Formatting Data Series

Each data series in the chart has its own color. For example, in the column chart you have been working with, Jones' data is the blue bar in each quarter. Thus, all the blue bars equal the data series for Jones. The data series can be changed to a new color or have a pattern effect. Patterns are especially helpful when printing a chart on a black and white printer; deciphering patterns on the bars is easier than deciphering varying shades of gray. The legend indicator matches the color or pattern of the data series.

Hands-On 6.13 Format Data Series

In this exercise, you will change the color and pattern of data series in the column chart.

1. Follow these steps to format the data series for Jones with a diagonal pattern:

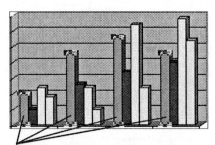

Ⓐ Click on any of the blue data bars and notice that all of the blue bars are selected. Then, choose Format→Selected Data Series from the menu bar.

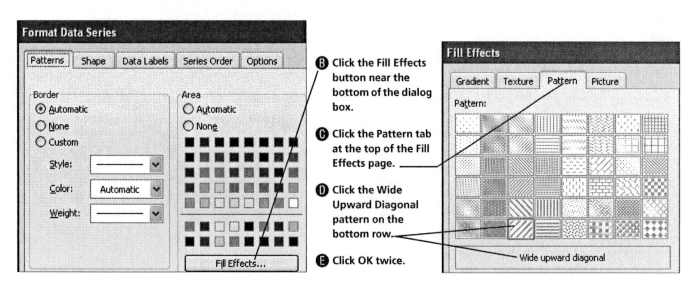

Ⓑ Click the Fill Effects button near the bottom of the dialog box.

Ⓒ Click the Pattern tab at the top of the Fill Effects page.

Ⓓ Click the Wide Upward Diagonal pattern on the bottom row.

Ⓔ Click OK twice.

Notice that all the bars for Jones appear with the diagonal pattern. Notice also that the legend indicator for Jones has the same pattern.

2. Select another data series and format it with your choice of patterns.

3. When finished, save the changes and continue with the next topic.

Creating Diagrams

Diagrams are used to illustrate concepts. Unlike charts, diagrams are not based on the numeric data in the worksheet. Excel has six types of diagrams: Cycle, Target, Radial, Venn, Pyramid, and Organization charts. The following table describes each type of diagram.

Type	Description
Cycle	Shows a process with a continuous cycle
Target	Shows steps toward a goal
Radial	Shows relationships of elements to a core element
Venn	Shows areas of overlap between elements
Pyramid	Shows a foundation based relationship
Organization Chart	Shows hierarchical relationships

 Hands-On 6.14   Create an Organization Chart

In this exercise, you will create an organization chart that shows the hierarchy of the sales team.

1. Click the Sheet2 tab and rename it **Org Chart**.

2. Choose Insert→Diagram from the menu bar.

3. Click the Organization Chart diagram type then click OK.

4. Follow these steps to create the diagram:

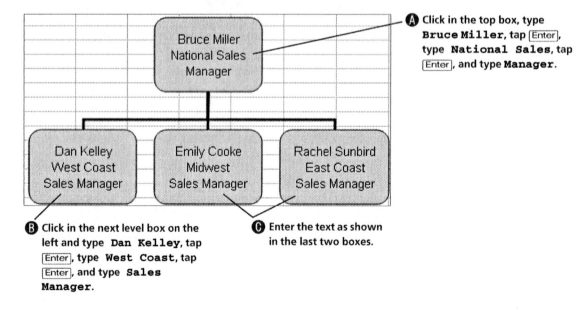

Ⓐ Click in the top box, type **Bruce Miller**, tap [Enter], type **National Sales**, tap [Enter], and type **Manager**.

Ⓑ Click in the next level box on the left and type **Dan Kelley**, tap [Enter], type **West Coast**, tap [Enter], and type **Sales Manager**.

Ⓒ Enter the text as shown in the last two boxes.

Add Subordinates

5. Follow these steps to add the sales reps to the chart as subordinates to the sales managers:

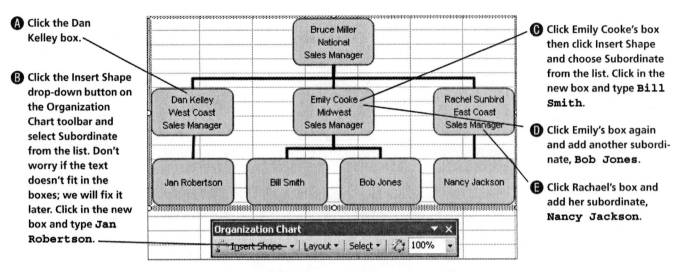

A Click the Dan Kelley box.

B Click the Insert Shape drop-down button on the Organization Chart toolbar and select Subordinate from the list. Don't worry if the text doesn't fit in the boxes; we will fix it later. Click in the new box and type **Jan Robertson.**

C Click Emily Cooke's box then click Insert Shape and choose Subordinate from the list. Click in the new box and type **Bill Smith.**

D Click Emily's box again and add another subordinate, **Bob Jones.**

E Click Rachael's box and add her subordinate, **Nancy Jackson.**

The organization chart should now match the preceding illustration. Notice that as you add boxes, the existing boxes get smaller. You will fix this in just a few minutes.

Formatting a Diagram

As your organization chart gets bigger, you may need to change the diagram's overall size, layout, or font size to accommodate all the names. You can choose from several layouts. You can also use the formatting toolbar to format text in any of the boxes.

 ## Hands-On 6.15   Format the Organization Chart

In this exercise, you will resize the diagram and change the layout to vertical boxes for the subordinates.

Resize the Diagram

1. Follow these steps to resize the diagram:

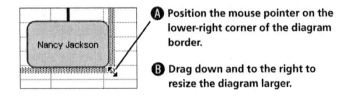

A Position the mouse pointer on the lower-right corner of the diagram border.

B Drag down and to the right to resize the diagram larger.

If some of the boxes still don't display all of the text, you can change the layout or use any of the formatting buttons on the Formatting toolbar to reformat the text in an organization chart.

Change the Layout

2. Follow these steps to change the layout for the subordinates:
   Feel free to resize the chart as you deem appropriate as you complete the following steps.

Ⓐ Click anywhere on the border surrounding the diagram, click the Layout drop-down arrow, and verify that the AutoLayout is turned on (the icon in front of the word will be highlighted). If it is not, choose Auto-Layout and close the menu.

Ⓑ Click Emily Cooke's box, then click the Layout drop-down arrow and select Right-hanging.

Ⓒ Using the same technique you used for Emily's box, change the other sales manager boxes to the right-hanging style.

Formatting Text

3. Click Bruce Miller's box and change the font to 10pt, Bold.

4. Click Dan Kelley's box then hold down the ⏻Shift⏻ key and click the two other manager boxes.
   The three manager boxes should be selected and display the sizing handles around them.

5. Change the font to 9pt, Bold on the three manager boxes.

6. Using the same technique as in step 4, select the four subordinate boxes and change their font to 9pt, Bold.

7. Feel free to experiment with any of the topics you have learned in this lesson.

8. When finished, save the changes and close the workbook.

Concepts Review

True/False Questions

1. You can rename a worksheet by double-clicking the sheet tab and typing the new name.   TRUE   FALSE

2. Embedded charts are updated when the worksheet data changes.   TRUE   FALSE

3. Charts on separate chart sheets are not updated when the worksheet data changes.   TRUE   FALSE

4. Column charts are most useful for comparing the parts of a whole.   TRUE   FALSE

5. Column charts have category and value axes.   TRUE   FALSE

6. The Chart Wizard can only be used to create embedded charts.   TRUE   FALSE

7. The Chart Wizard is used to explode pie slices.   TRUE   FALSE

8. You must select an embedded chart before you can move or resize it.   TRUE   FALSE

9. Diagrams are based on numeric data.   TRUE   FALSE

10. You can change the layout of an organization chart.   TRUE   FALSE

Multiple Choice Questions

1. Which procedure is used to change the position of a worksheet in the sheet order?
   a. Double-click the sheet tab and drag the tab to the desired location.
   b. Click the sheet tab and choose Edit→ Move or Copy Sheet from the menu bar.
   c. Drag the sheet tab to the desired location.
   d. Both b and c

2. Which command is used to move an embedded chart to a separate sheet?
   a. Edit→Move Chart
   b. Chart→Location
   c. Chart→Move
   d. This cannot be done

3. Which chart is best for showing a trend over a period of time?
   a. Line
   b. Bar
   c. Column
   d. Pie

4. Which technique is used to insert data labels after a chart has been created?
   a. Select the chart and click the Data Labels button on the Chart toolbar.
   b. Select the chart and choose Insert→ Data Labels.
   c. Select the chart, choose Chart→Chart Options, click the Data Labels tab, and choose the desired data labels format.
   d. Data labels cannot be inserted after a chart has been created.

Skill Builders

Skill Builder 6.1   Create a Column Chart

In this exercise, you will create a column chart to display student enrollment at a university.

Expand a Series

1. Open the Enrollments workbook.
   Notice that the enrollment data has been completed in column B but that the years have not been completed in column A. Notice that the first two years (1988 and 1989) form the beginning of the series 1988–2004. The best way to expand this series is with the fill handle.

2. Select cells A4 and A5.

3. Drag the fill handle down to row 20 to expand the series.

4. Click the Left Align ▤ button to move the years in column A to the left edge of the column.

Create the Chart

5. Select the range A3:B20.
   This range includes the enrollment data and the Year and Total Enrollment headings.

6. Click the Chart Wizard ▥ button.

7. Choose the column chart type and the first subtype.

8. Click Next to display the Step 2 of 4 box.
   Take a moment to study the Step 2 dialog box and notice the problem. Excel is interpreting the years 1988–2004 as numbers. The numbers appear as a data series in the chart. The years are the short columns to the left of the tall, thin enrollment data columns. The years should actually be displayed as labels on the horizontal category axis. You will correct this in the next few steps.

9. Click the Series tab on the dialog box.
   The Series tab lets you modify the data series plotted in the chart.

10. Follow these steps to remove the years from the series and to add the years as Category (x) axis labels:

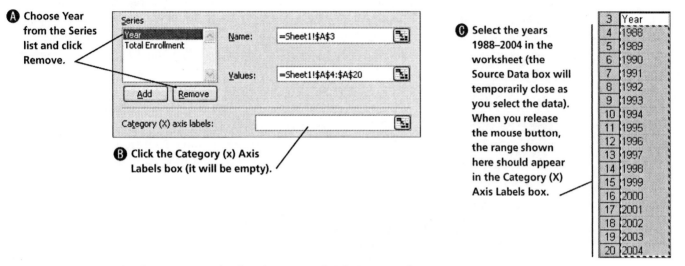

A Choose Year from the Series list and click Remove.

B Click the Category (x) Axis Labels box (it will be empty).

C Select the years 1988–2004 in the worksheet (the Source Data box will temporarily close as you select the data). When you release the mouse button, the range shown here should appear in the Category (X) Axis Labels box.

The dates are now displayed in an angled fashion on the Category axis.

11. Click Next to continue with Step 3 of 4.

12. Click the Titles tab and type the title **Student Enrollments** in the Chart Title box.

13. Click the Legend tab and remove the legend.

14. Click Finish to complete the chart.
Take a few moments to study your worksheet and chart. Be sure you understand the relationship between the worksheet data and the chart.

Convert the Chart to a Line Chart

Suppose you are interested in seeing only the trend in enrollments as opposed to the enrollments in individual years. You can easily convert this chart to a line chart.

15. Make sure the chart is selected.

16. Choose Chart→Chart Type from the menu bar.

17. Choose Line as the Chart type and choose the fourth subtype.

18. Click OK to convert the chart to a line chart with data markers.

Format the Chart Title

19. Click the Student Enrollments chart title.

20. Use the Font Color **A ▾** button to format the title with any color you like.

21. Feel free to format the chart and title in any other way you desire.

22. Save the changes and close the workbook.

Skill Builder 6.2   Create a Doughnut Chart

In this exercise, you will create a chart for Holy Doughnuts. The chart will show the contributions of various types of doughnuts to the total sales volume for two different years. What type of chart will you use? Why, a doughnut chart! Like pie charts, doughnut charts are useful for comparing parts of a whole. However, doughnut charts can contain more than one data series. Each ring in a doughnut chart represents a data series.

Set Up the Worksheet

1. If necessary, start a New Workbook ⬚ and create the following worksheet. Format the numbers in columns B and C as Comma Style with 0 decimals. In A1:C4, change the font to 12 pt and bold. Also, merge and center the Units Sold heading over cells B3 and C3 and AutoFit columns B and C.

	A	B	C	D	E
1	**Holy Doughnuts Volume Comparison**				
2					
3		**Units Sold**			
4	**Type of Doughnut**	**2003**	**2004**		
5	Creme Filled	12,000	14,500		
6	Frosted	10,500	9,000		
7	Nut Covered	2,300	2,500		
8	Glazed	7,000	8,200		
9	Old Fashioned	4,500	4,300		

Create the Chart

Doughnut charts function much like pie charts because they compare parts of a whole. Therefore, you select the data in a manner similar to the way you select data for pie charts.

2. Select the data in the range A5:C9.

3. Click the Chart Wizard 📊 button.

4. Choose Doughnut as the Chart type and choose the first subtype.

5. Click Next twice to display the Step 3 of 4 box.

6. Click the Titles tab and enter the Chart title **Doughnut Sales: 2003 vs. 2004**.

7. Click the Data Labels tab and check the Percentage box.

8. Click the Finish button to create an embedded chart.

Format the Percent Labels

9. Click any of the percent labels in the outer ring of the doughnut to select all percentages for the series.

10. Use the Font Color ![A] button on the Formatting toolbar to choose a high-contrast color such as red or white.
    This will differentiate the numbers in the outer ring from those in the inner ring. Notice that the doughnut chart does not provide a title or label to identify the rings as 2003 or 2004. This is a deficiency that can only be overcome by using a textbox and arrows or lines to label the rings.

11. Save the workbook as **Doughnut Chart** and close it.

Skill Builder 6.3   Create Pie Charts

In this exercise, you will create four pie charts to illustrate employee expenses for Hollywood Productions—a motion picture production company. The pie charts will show how employee costs are divided among departments and how each department's employee costs are allocated. You will create each chart on a separate chart sheet.

Create the Company Chart

1. Open the workbook named Expenses.

2. Follow these steps to select the required data:

3		Marketing	Production	Finance
4	Salaries	3,400,000	4,500,000	1,200,000
5	Benefits	1,292,000	1,980,000	336,000
6	Travel	1,700,000	1,500,000	120,000
7	Total	$ 6,392,000	$ 7,980,000	$ 1,656,000

Ⓐ Use the mouse to select the range B3:D3, as shown here.

Ⓑ Press and hold down Ctrl while you select the range B7:D7.

3. Click the Chart Wizard ![icon] button and create the pie chart shown to the right on a separate chart sheet.
   Make sure the chart type, title, and labels match the chart shown here. Also, notice that the chart does not include a legend.

4. Double-click the Chart1 sheet tab and change the sheet name to **Holly-wood Chart**.
   You can use long names when naming sheets.

5. Rename Sheet1 **Employee Expense Data**.

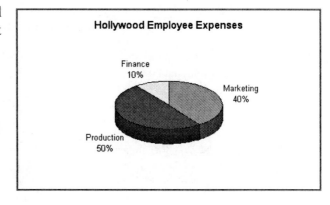

Create a Pie Chart for the Marketing Department

6. Select the following range:

3		Marketing	Production	Finance
4	Salaries	3,400,000	4,500,000	1,200,000
5	Benefits	1,292,000	1,980,000	336,000
6	Travel	1,700,000	1,500,000	120,000
7	Total	$ 6,392,000	$ 7,980,000	$ 1,656,000

7. Click the Chart Wizard button and create a pie chart on a separate chart sheet. Use the same chart type and labels as in the previous chart but use the title **Marketing Employee Costs**.

8. Rename the sheet **Marketing Chart**.

9. Click the Employee Expense Data sheet tab to return to that sheet.

Create Pie Charts for the Production and Finance Departments

10. Use the techniques described in this exercise to create the same style pie charts for the Production and Finance departments. Create each chart on a separate chart sheet. Use the chart titles and sheet names shown

3		Marketing	Production	Finance
4	Salaries	3,400,000	4,500,000	1,200,000
5	Benefits	1,292,000	1,980,000	336,000
6	Travel	1,700,000	1,500,000	120,000
7	Total	$ 6,392,000	$ 7,980,000	$ 1,656,000

in the following table. Select data for the Production department chart as shown. You will need to decide how to select the data for the Finance department (although that should be an easy decision to make).

Chart	Use This Title	Use This Sheet Name
Production	Production Employee Costs	Production Chart
Finance	Finance Employee Costs	Finance Chart

11. Follow these steps to move the Employee Expense Data sheet tab:

A If necessary, scroll to the right using the tab scrolling buttons until the Employee Expense Data tab is visible.

⏮ ◄► ⏭	Hollywood Chart	Marketing Chart	Production Chart	Finance Chart	**Employee Expense Data**

Ready

B Drag the Employee Expense Data tab to the left until it is in front of the Hollywood Chart tab. You may need to drag part way then use the left tab-scrolling button and continue dragging.

Explode Pie Slices and Increase Elevation

12. Click the Hollywood Chart tab to activate it.

13. Click once on the pie, pause, and then click the Production slice (the largest slice).

14. Drag the slice out slightly to explode it.

15. Choose Chart→3-D View from the menu bar.

16. Increase the Elevation ⬆ to 25 and click OK.

17. Click the Marketing Chart sheet tab.

18. Explode the Salaries slice (the largest slice) and increase the elevation to 25.

19. Explode the largest slice and increase the elevation to 25 for the Production and Finance charts.
Take a few moments to click the various sheet tabs and check out your charts. Feel free to format and enhance your charts in any way.

20. Save the changes and close the workbook.

Skill Builder 6.4   Create a Line Chart

In this exercise, you will create a worksheet and line chart to track the trends in a stock portfolio.

1. Start a new workbook.

2. Follow these guidelines to create the worksheet shown to the right:

■ Notice that the dates in cells A4 and A5 form the beginning of a series. You can enter these dates, select them, then drag the fill handle down to cell A11 to complete the series.

	A	B	C	D
1	Stock Portfolio Trends			
2				
3		Silicon Technology	Dakota Mining	Anderson Diesel
4	9/6/2003	58 1/2	32	45
5	9/13/2003	59	31	43
6	9/20/2003	56	28	45
7	9/27/2003	59	30 1/8	48
8	10/4/2003	63	33	49
9	10/11/2003	68	34	47
10	10/18/2003	70	34	42
11	10/25/2003	69	36 1/2	38

■ Columns B–D contain mixed numbers (whole numbers and fractions). Just type the numbers exactly as shown with a space between the whole numbers and fractions.

■ AutoFit columns B–D.

3. Select the range A3:D11.

4. Use the Chart Wizard 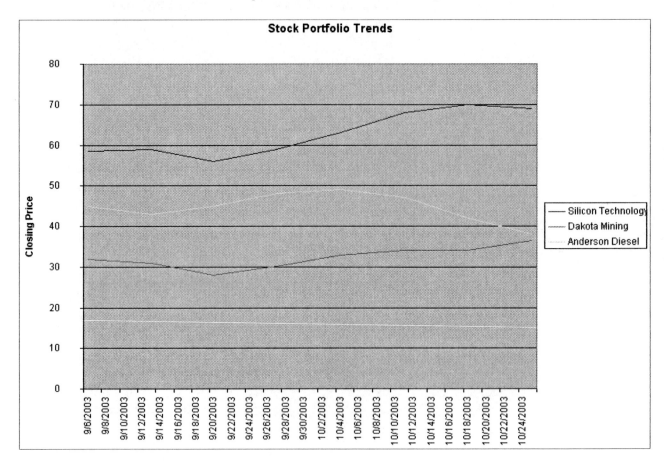 button to create the line chart shown in the following illustration. Use the first line chart subtype and place the chart on a separate chart sheet named **Line Chart**. Make sure you use the same titles and legend as shown.

Stock Portfolio Trends

Closing Price

Legend:
- Silicon Technology
- Dakota Mining
- Anderson Diesel

X-axis dates: 9/6/2003, 9/8/2003, 9/10/2003, 9/12/2003, 9/14/2003, 9/16/2003, 9/18/2003, 9/20/2003, 9/22/2003, 9/24/2003, 9/26/2003, 9/28/2003, 9/30/2003, 10/2/2003, 10/4/2003, 10/6/2003, 10/8/2003, 10/10/2003, 10/12/2003, 10/14/2003, 10/16/2003, 10/18/2003, 10/20/2003, 10/22/2003, 10/24/2003

5. Save the workbook as **Line Chart** then close it.

Assessments

Assessment 6.1   Create a Line Chart

In this exercise, you will create a line chart on a separate sheet, rename the sheet tabs, and print a chart.

1. Start a new workbook and create the following worksheet:

	A	B	C	D
1	SysTech Stock Performance			
2	March 2003 Through February 2004			
3				
4	Date	Stock Price		
5	3/1/2003	78		
6	4/1/2003	82.6		
7	5/1/2003	83		
8	6/1/2003	78.6		
9	7/1/2003	72		
10	8/1/2003	62		
11	9/1/2003	65.8		
12	10/1/2003	72.6		
13	11/1/2003	85		
14	12/1/2003	86		
15	1/1/2004	90		
16	2/1/2004	92		

2. Use the worksheet data to create the following chart on a separate chart sheet. Make sure to set up the data labels and title as shown.

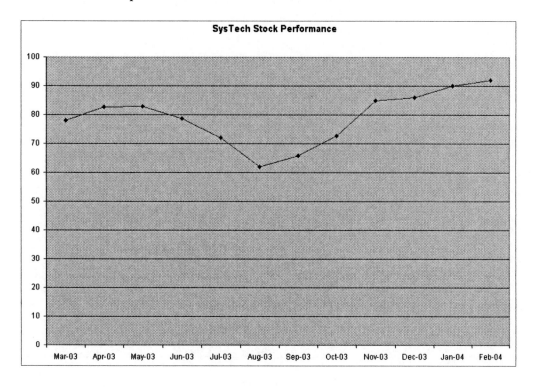

3. Rename the Chart1 sheet **Stock Performance**.

4. Rename the Sheet1 sheet **Supporting Data**.

5. Print both the worksheet and chart.

6. Save the workbook as **SysTech Performance** then close it.

Assessment 6.2   Create an Embedded Column Chart

In this exercise, you will create a column chart embedded in the worksheet then move, resize, and print the chart.

1. Create the worksheet and embedded column chart shown in the following illustration. Use the font size of your choice for the title in cell A1. Notice that the column chart is 2-D. The differences in row 6 are simply the budget numbers minus the spent numbers. Notice that the negative differences dip below the x-axis in the chart. Adjust the position and size of the embedded chart as shown.

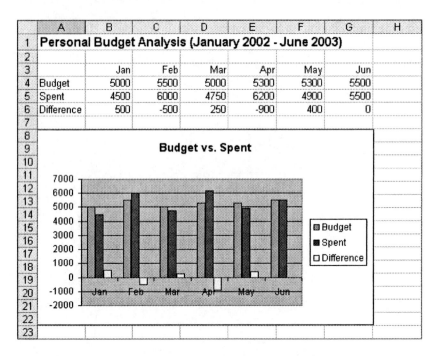

2. Print the worksheet and embedded chart on a single page.

3. Save the workbook as **Budget Analysis** then close it.

Assessment 6.3   Create a Worksheet and Pie Chart

In this exercise, you will create a worksheet and a pie chart based on the data in the worksheet. You will also apply an AutoFormat to the worksheet, insert formulas in the worksheet, and move, resize, and explode a piece of the pie chart.

1. Use these guidelines to create the worksheet and chart shown in the following illustration:

   ■ Type all numbers and text entries as shown, but use formulas to calculate the New Balance in column E and the Totals, Highest, and Lowest in rows 9–11. The formula for New Balance is New Balance = Beginning Balance + Purchases – Payments. Calculate the Totals in row 9 with AutoSum and use the MIN and MAX functions for the Highest and Lowest calculations in rows 10 and 11.

   ■ Use the font size of your choice for the title cell A1, and then format the remainder of the worksheet with the AutoFormat Classic 2 style.

   ■ Create the embedded 3-D pie chart shown in the illustration. The pie chart slices represent the new balance percentages of each customer. The pie chart does not represent any of the data in rows 9–11.

   ■ Adjust the position and size of the embedded chart as shown in the illustration.

   ■ Explode the Bishop slice and adjust the chart rotation and elevation.

   ■ Bold all pie slice labels and format the chart title with bold and italic.

2. Print the worksheet and embedded chart on a single page.

3. Save the workbook as **Accts Rec Rpt** then close it.

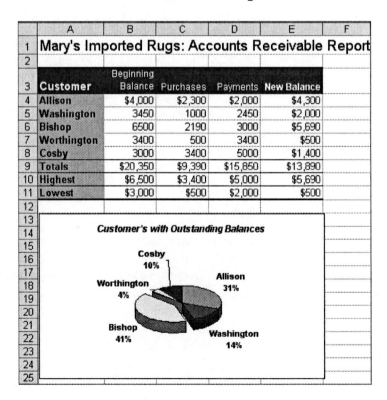

Critical Thinking

Critical Thinking 6.1   On Your Own

Open the workbook named Delivery Expenses. Create an embedded column chart that displays the miles driven by each driver. Use the chart title **Miles Driven**. The name of each driver should be displayed at the base of the columns. Use data labels to display the precise number of miles driven at the top of each column.

Create another embedded column chart that displays the total expenses for each driver. Use the chart title **Total Expenses**. The name of each driver should be displayed at the base of the columns. Use data labels to display the total expenses at the top of each column.

Adjust the size and position of the column charts so they are side by side and positioned below the worksheet data. Format the worksheet to print on a single page in landscape orientation. Save the changes and close the workbook.

Critical Thinking 6.2   On Your Own

Open the workbook named Test Results. Create a 3-D pie chart on a separate chart sheet that shows the percentage each Unit Type contributes to the total units produced. Include data labels that show the percentage and unit type label of each unit type. Do not display a legend. Use the chart title Percent of Unit Types Produced. Rotate the chart so the largest slice is in the front of the chart. Increase the elevation of the chart and explode the largest slice. Add a pattern of your choice to each individual slice of the pie. Change the sheet name to **Pie Chart**.

Insert a new column to the right of the Passed Test column. Use a formula in the new column to calculate the number of units that did not pass the test. Create a column chart on a separate chart sheet that compares the units produced to the units that did not pass the test. Use the Stacked Column chart subtype, which is simply a variation of the regular side-by-side columns. Display a chart legend but no data labels. Use the title **Total Produced vs. Did Not Pass**. Change the sheet name to **Stacked Column Chart**. Reorganize the sheets so Test Results is first in the sheet order, Pie Chart second, and Stacked column Chart third. Save the changes and close the workbook.

Critical Thinking 6.3   On Your Own

Open the workbook named Billings. Create an embedded pie chart that shows the contribution of each company type to the total billings. Include data labels that show only the company types. Do not display a legend. Use the chart title **Billing Breakdown**. Position the chart below the data. Save the changes and close the workbook.

Critical Thinking 6.4   Web Research

Use Internet Explorer and a search engine of your choice to locate a Website that offers free stock quotations and charts. Search for the symbols CSCO, IBM, and ORCL and display charts for each of the stocks. Set up an Excel workbook that includes a row for each stock and columns for each of the past 12 months. View the chart for one of the stocks and enter the approximate value of the stock into your worksheet for each of the past 12 months. Create a line chart on a separate chart sheet that includes all three stocks on the same chart. The chart should show the stock trends over the past 12 months. Use the chart title **12 Month Stock Trends**. Change the name of the chart sheet to **12-Month Trends Chart**. Save the workbook as **Stock Trends**.

Critical Thinking 6.5   Web Research

Use Internet Explorer and a search engine of your choice to find the Gross Domestic Product of the G7 industrial nations in any given year. The G7 nations include the United States, Germany, Japan, Great Britain, France, Italy, and Canada. Set up a worksheet that lists the nations in order by largest GDP. The GDP numbers will be measured in trillions of dollars. You can eliminate the 12 zeros from the numbers and just include the multiples. For example, if a nation has a GDP of 1.4 trillion dollars then use the number **1.4** in the worksheet. Create an embedded column chart to compare the various GDPs. Include data labels in the chart and a descriptive title. Save the workbook as **Comparative GDPs**.

Critical Thinking 6.6   On Your Own

Open the workbook named Stock Purchases. Create a column chart on a separate chart sheet. The column chart should include columns for the purchase price and current price of each stock. Identify each pair of columns by the appropriate stock symbol. Use the chart title **Gains and Losses**. Include a legend that identifies the columns as either Purchase Price or Current Price. Name the chart sheet **Gains and Losses Chart**. Save the changes and close the workbook.

Using File Storage Media

You may wish to use storage media besides the floppy disk referred to in most of the lessons. This appendix contains instructions for downloading and unzipping the exercise files used with this book, and an overview for using this book with various file storage media.

In This Appendix

The following topics are addressed in this appendix:

Downloading the Student Exercise Files

The files needed to complete certain Hands-On, Skill Builder, Assessment, and Critical Thinking exercises are available for download at the Labyrinth Website. Use the following instructions to copy the files to your computer and prepare them for use with this book.

Hands-On A.1   Download and Unzip Files

Follow these steps to download a copy of the student files necessary for this book:

1. Launch Internet Explorer.

2. Enter **labpub.com/students/fdbc2003.asp** in the browser's address bar and tap Enter.
   A list of books in the applicable series appears. If you don't see the title of your book in the list, use the links on the left side of the Web page to display the list of books for your series.

3. Click the link for your book title.
   A prompt to open or save a file containing the student exercise files appears.

4. Click the Save button.

5. Choose your file storage location and click Save.
   After a pause, the exercise files will begin downloading to your computer. Continue with the next step after the download is complete.

6. Click the Open button on the Download Complete dialog box. Or, open your file storage location and double-click the newly downloaded file if the dialog box closed automatically.

7. Click OK, and then follow the step for your file storage location:
   - **Floppy Disk:** Click the Browse button, choose the 3½ Floppy A: drive, click OK, and then click the Unzip button.
   - **USB Flash Drive:** Click the Browse button, navigate to your USB flash drive, click OK, and then click the Unzip button.
   - **My Documents Folder:** Click the Browse button, navigate to the My Documents folder, click OK, and then click the Unzip button.
   - **Network Drive Folder:** Click the Browse button, navigate to your assigned folder on the network drive, click OK, and then click the Unzip button.

8. Click the Close button after the files have unzipped.

Working with File Storage Locations

New technologies continue to expand the variety of available computer storage media. The 3½ inch floppy disk has been around since about 1983. That's incredibly ancient in the fast-moving field of computers. It's easy to use other storage media with this book. Potential alternative storage locations include:

- The My Documents folder

- A USB flash drive

- A folder on your local hard drive

- A folder on a network drive

Using Alternative File Storage Locations

Depending on the file storage media you select, some steps you perform in the exercises will differ from what you see illustrated. However, with a little practice you should find it easy to interpret the instructions for use with your file storage media.

Example: Using a USB Flash Drive

You are performing an exercise in which you create and save a new file. If you are using a USB flash drive, simply substitute the drive letter for your flash drive for the 3½ Floppy (A:) drive shown in the figure instruction.

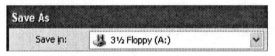

The storage location as it appears in the book

The storage location as you perform it on the screen

Using a Floppy Disk

If you use a floppy disk to store your exercise files, you should be aware of space limitations. This section explains how to keep track of the available space on a floppy diskette, and how to delete unnecessary files to conserve space.

Storage Limitations of Floppy Disks

As you work through the exercises in this book, you will create numerous files that are to be saved to a storage location. A floppy diskette may not have enough storage capacity to hold all files created during the course (particularly if you perform all of the Skill Builder and Critical Thinking exercises). Thus, you may want to use an alternate storage location for all files accessed and created during the course.

Checking Available Space on a Floppy Disk

If you choose to use a floppy disk as your storage location, you may reach a point at which the disk fills up and no additional files can be stored on it. However, if you regularly check the available space on your floppy disk, this problem should not arise.

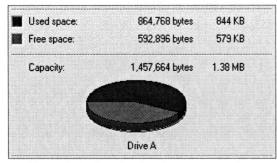

Windows can display a pie chart of the available space on your floppy disk.

Freeing Up Space on the Floppy Disk

If your floppy disk runs short of space, you will need to selectively delete files from it. You should delete files from lessons already completed, freeing up space for exercises in the current lesson.

 TIP! *Use the following procedure to check your available floppy disk space before you begin work on a new lesson. If you have less than 100 KB remaining on the disk, delete some files to free up space.*

Hands-On A.2   Check Free Space on a Floppy Disk

1. Open a My Computer window.

2. Right-click the 3½ Floppy (A:) drive and choose Properties from the context menu.
   Windows displays a pie chart with details on the used and available space on the floppy disk.

3. Examine the Free Space information and click OK.

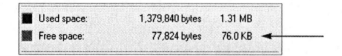

4. Follow the step for the amount of disk space remaining:
   - Close ⊠ the Properties window. Close the My Computer window if there is more than 100 KB of space remaining on the disk. Skip the remaining steps in this procedure. You are finished and ready to proceed with the next lesson.
   - Close ⊠ the Properties window. Continue with the remaining steps in this exercise if there is less than 100 KB of space remaining on your floppy disk.

Delete Unnecessary Files

5. Double-click to open the 3½ Floppy (A:) drive.

6. Choose View→List from the menu bar.
   The My Computer window displays your files as a compact list.

7. While holding down the [Ctrl] key, select files for lessons that preceded the one you are working on now and tap the [Delete] key on the keyboard. Choose Yes if you are asked to confirm the deletion of these files.
   Windows deletes the selected files.

8. Close ⊠ the My Computer window.
   You now have plenty of space for your work in the next lesson.

 TIP! *If you accidentally delete an exercise file needed for a later lesson, don't worry. You can repeat the procedure outlined in Hands-On A.1 to download and unzip the student exercise files as many times as necessary.*

Using a USB Flash Drive

A USB flash drive stores your data on a flash memory chip. You simply plug it into a USB port on any computer and Windows immediately recognizes it as an additional disk drive. USB flash drives typically are able store 32 megabytes (MB) or more of your data files. Large capacity USB flash drives can store 512 MB or more.

Most USB flash drives are about the size of your thumb and plug into any available USB port on your computer.

USB Flash Drive Letter

When you plug in a USB flash drive to a Windows computer, Windows automatically assigns it the next available drive letter. Windows uses drive letters to identify each drive connected to the computer. For example, the primary part of the hard drive is always identified as the C: drive. The CD/DVD drive is typically the D: or E: drive.

Devices with Removable Storage

3½ Floppy (A:)   DVD/CD-RW Drive (E:)   **This USB flash drive is the F: drive.**   Removable Disk (F:)

!TIP! *Your USB flash drive may receive a different drive letter on different computers. This does not affect any files stored on the drive.*

Hands-On A.3   Rename Your USB Flash Drive

You may find it convenient to rename your USB flash drive to make it easier to recognize when you save or open files.

 TIP! *Some Windows systems may not give you renaming privileges for drives.*

1. Plug the USB flash drive into an available USB port.

2. Open a My Computer window.

3. Right-click your USB flash drive and choose Rename from the context menu.

 NOTE! *In the next step, Windows may display a prompt that you cannot rename this flash drive. You have not done anything wrong! You can use the drive with its current name. You may also want to try renaming it later using a different login.*

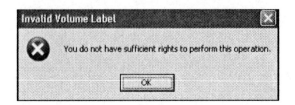

4. Type **FlashDrive** as the new drive name and tap ⌷Enter⌷. Click OK if you receive a prompt that you do not have sufficient rights to perform this operation.
If you were unable to rename the flash drive, don't worry. Renaming the flash drive is a convenience for recognition and has no other effect.

Using the My Documents Folder

Windows creates a unique My Documents folder for each login. This folder resides on the main system drive (usually the C: drive). The Office 2003 application programs provide a My Documents button in their Open and Save As dialog boxes to make navigation to this folder convenient.

The My Documents button in the Word 2003 Save As dialog box

Using a Network Drive Folder

You may use a system connected to a network. There may be a folder on a network server computer in another location that is dedicated to storing your work. Usually, you will find this folder within the My Network Places folder of your computer. The Office 2003 application programs provide a My Network Places button in their Open and Save As dialog boxes to make navigation to this folder convenient. You may have to navigate deeper into the folder to locate your personal network drive folder.

The My Network Places button in the Word 2003 Save As dialog box

Index

Numerics
3-D View dialog box, 193

A
absolute cell references, 73–78
accounting currency style, 103
alignment of objects/text, 105–106, 145
arithmetic operators, 68
AutoCalculate, 85
AutoComplete, 13–14
AutoCorrect, 43–44
AutoFill, 17–18
AutoFit, 148
AutoFormat, 116–117
AutoSum, 64–67, 81
AVERAGE function, 80, 81
axes, chart, 178

B
bar charts, 178
borders, 113–115
built-in charts, 178–185

C
calculations
 (*see also* formulas; functions)
 AutoCalculate, 85
 AutoSum, 64–67
 dates in, 138
Cancel button, 11
category axis, charts, 178
cells
 active, 6, 7
 alignment, 105–106, 145
 borders and colors, 108, 113–115, 190
 copying/pasting, 17, 117–125
 deleting, 11, 151–153
 editing, 40–42
 Format Cells dialog box, 102–105
 indenting of text in, 108
 line breaks in, 142–144
 merging/splitting, 106–107
 reference designations, 20, 68, 72–78

replacing formats, 155–158
 selecting, 20–22
character formatting, 108–112, 200
Chart menu, 188
charts
 diagrams, 198–200
 formatting, 187–199
 moving and sizing, 185–186
 printing, 186–187
 types, 178–185
Chart toolbar, 191
Chart Wizard
 creating charts, 178–183
 modifying charts, 187
clearing cells, 42
Clipboard, Office, 118
closing workbooks, 24–25
colors
 fills and patterns, 113–115, 190
 sheet tabs, 176
 text, 108
column charts, 178, 179–182
columns and rows
 copying heading rows, 119
 modifying, 147–155
 resizing, 106
 selecting, 21
 totaling numbers in, 64–67
comma number format, 100, 102
comments for cells, 42
constant values vs. formulas, 11
copying and moving
 cell contents, 17, 117–125
 charts, 185–186, 194–196
 worksheets, 176
COUNT function, 80
currency number format, 100, 101–102
Cut/Copy/Paste commands, 117–119, 124–125
Cycle diagram type, 198

K

keyboard shortcut commands
  absolute cell references, 73
  adding lines within cells, 142
  AutoSum, 64
  displaying formulas, 79
  editing entries, 40–41
  entering data, 11
  entering formulas, 69
  entering functions, 81
  finding/replacing, 155
  Format Cells dialog box, 102
  inserting dates, 140
  navigating in worksheets, 6
  number formatting, 101
  opening workbooks, 25
  printing, 46
  selecting cells, 22
  text character formats, 108

L

legends, chart, 179
line breaks inside cells, 142–144
line charts, 182–184

M

MAX function, 80, 83
menu bar, 5
Merge and Center button, 106–107
merging/splitting cells, 106–107
MIN function, 80, 84
mixed cell references, 73
moving and copying
  cell contents, 17, 117–125
  charts, 185–186, 194–196
  worksheets, 176
multiple workbooks/worksheets, 176–177
My Documents folder, 221
My Network Places, 221

N

name box, 8
negative numbers, 103, 104
network drive folder, 221
Normal.dot template, 109
NOW( ) function, 140
numbers
  entering, 15–16
  formatting, 15–16, 100

O

objects, chart, 189–190
Office Clipboard, 118
online Help, 49–51
opening workbooks, 25
operations, mathematical, 68
order of operations, 68
Organizational chart, 198–200

P

Paste command, 117–119
Paste Options command, 117, 124–125
percent number format, 100, 102
pie charts, 184–185, 192–193
point mode in formulas, 69–71
Print Area, 48–49
printing
  charts, 186–187
  data, 46–49
Print Preview, 46, 186
Pyramid diagram type, 198

R

Radial diagram type, 198
ranges of cells, 68, 119
Redo and Undo buttons, 41
references for cells
  formulas, 72–78
  overview, 20, 68
relative cell references, 72
removing text/objects (*see* deleting)
renaming worksheets, 176, 177
repeating number sets, 17
Replace feature
  data, 11, 155–158
  formatting, 155–158
right-dragging technique, 120, 121–123
rotating
  chart objects, 191–192
  pie charts, 193–194
  text, 145–146
rows and columns (*see* columns and rows)

S

saving worksheets/workbooks, 22–24
scrolling through worksheets, 6
searching for data, 155–158

ISBN 1-59136-036-6